A *Los Angeles Times*
A FINALIST FOR THE BOOKS FOR A BETTER LIFE AWARD
ONE OF *NEWSDAY*'S FAVORITE BOOKS OF THE YEAR
A *KANSAS CITY STAR* BEST BOOK OF THE YEAR

"Lerner, a literary agent who was most recently executive editor at Doubleday, assumes the posture of a writer's sympathetic friend, coach, and psychotherapist all rolled into one. . . . Lerner candidly draws on her experience working both sides of the fence, as poet and teacher of writing workshops as well as editor and agent. She offers hard-nosed advice on topics overlooked, such as the dynamics of the author/editor and author/agent relations; struggles against the temptation of alcohol and drugs; the testing of book titles for marketability; acrimony over jacket art. . . . The book's real value, however, lies in compelling the ambivalent writer to confront his or her inner dreams, demons, and strengths."
—*Publishers Weekly*

"What writers want is good company and by writing this book, Lerner has given them just that. *The Forest for the Trees* provides excellent companionship for the long-distance race confronting every writer. . . . [Lerner's] prose is supple, witty, always informative, and frequently moving. . . . This elegant and funny and informative and passionate and moving book is not only a course in the great dance but a fine example of the dance itself. *The Forest for the Trees* will move many tortured writers that much closer to becoming well-published authors."
—*The Providence Sunday Journal*

"*The Forest for the Trees* is a delightful and very helpful read, a distillation of both editorial and writerly wisdom. You will enjoy it, and learn something from the book, whether you are an aspiring writer, editor, or professional already on the court."
—*The Seattle Times*

"Experienced book editor Lerner has done everything right in her desire to offer relevant guidance to writers. This combination memoir and handbook is reading for the soul."
—*Booklist*

"When Lerner writes about the relationship between publishers and writers, the reader feels privileged, as though forbidden secrets were being divulged on how to get published."
—*BookPage*

THE FOREST FOR THE TREES

AN EDITOR'S ADVICE TO WRITERS

BETSY LERNER

RIVERHEAD BOOKS

NEW YORK

RIVERHEAD BOOKS
Published by the Penguin Group
Penguin Group (USA) Inc.
375 Hudson Street, New York, New York 10014, USA
Penguin Group (Canada), 90 Eglinton Avenue East, Suite 700, Toronto, Ontario M4P 2Y3,
Canada (a division of Pearson Penguin Canada Inc.)
Penguin Books Ltd., 80 Strand, London WC2R 0RL, England
Penguin Group Ireland, 25 St. Stephen's Green, Dublin 2, Ireland
(a division of Penguin Books Ltd.)
Penguin Group (Australia), 250 Camberwell Road, Camberwell, Victoria 3124, Australia
(a division of Pearson Australia Group Pty. Ltd.)
Penguin Books India Pvt. Ltd., 11 Community Centre, Panchsheel Park, New Delhi—110 017,
India
Penguin Group (NZ), 67 Apollo Drive, Rosedale, North Shore 0632, New Zealand
(a division of Pearson New Zealand Ltd.)
Penguin Books (South Africa) (Pty.) Ltd., 24 Sturdee Avenue, Rosebank, Johannesburg 2196,
South Africa

Penguin Books Ltd., Registered Offices: 80 Strand, London WC2R 0RL, England

While the author has made every effort to provide accurate telephone numbers and Internet
addresses at the time of publication, neither the publisher nor the author assumes any responsibility for errors, or for changes that occur after publication. Further, the publisher does not
have any control over and does not assume any responsibility for author or third-party websites
or their content.

The passage from Maxwell E. Perkins's March 30, 1942, letter to Marcia Davenport is excerpted
with permission of Scribner, a Division of Simon & Schuster, from *Editor to Author: The Letters
of Maxwell E. Perkins*, edited by John Hall Wheelock. Copyright © 1950 by Charles Scribner's
Sons. Copyright renewed © 1978 by John Hall Wheelock.

An excerpt from the letter Susan Cheever wrote to the *New Yorker* in response to James Atlas's
article "The Fall of Fun" is used with Cheever's permission.

RIVERHEAD is a registered trademark of Penguin Group (USA) Inc.
The RIVERHEAD logo is a trademark of Penguin Group (USA) Inc.
First Riverhead hardcover edition: March 2000
First Riverhead trade paperback edition: April 2001
First Riverhead revised and updated trade paperback edition: October 2010
Riverhead trade paperback ISBN: 978-1-59448-483-4

The Library of Congress has cataloged the Riverhead hardcover edition as follows:

Lerner, Betsy.
   The forest for the trees : an editor's advice to writers / Betsy Lerner.
      p. cm.
   Includes bibliographical references.
   ISBN 1-57322-152-X
   1. Authorship. 2. Authors and publishers. I. Title.
   PN147.L44 2000   99-053355 CIP
   805'.02—dc21

PRINTED IN THE UNITED STATES OF AMERICA

10 9 8 7 6 5 4 3

FOR MY AUTHORS

CONTENTS

I really think that the great difficulty in bringing "The Valley of Decision" into final shape is the old one of not being able to see the forest for the trees. There are such a great number of trees. We must somehow bring the underlying scheme or pattern of the book into emphasis, so that the reader will be able to see the forest in spite of the many trees.

—*Maxwell Perkins, in a letter to Marcia Davenport*
(A. Scott Berg, in his biography Max Perkins: Editor of Genius, *recounts that author Davenport had turned in a completely disjointed manuscript of nearly eight hundred thousand words, which she revised over a five-month period, according to the editor's extensive notes. The book went on to sell six hundred thousand copies.)*

THE
FOREST
FOR THE
TREES

INTRODUCTION

I NEVER DREAMED OF BECOMING AN EDITOR. Like many English majors, I spent much of my time in college reading novels and poetry, never quite fixing my attention on how I might parlay those interests into a job. In the final months of college, I went to the Career Placement Office, only to discover that I should have signed up in my junior year for the ongoing programs and job fairs. When I visited the head of the English Department to explore the possibility of graduate school, he stared at me in disbelief: applications had been filled out in the fall.

During those frantic months of trying to secure employment, I met with the daughter of one of my mother's friends, an editor at Putnam. I put on my only dress for the interview, a cotton plaid A-line jumper with a rattan belt, and rode my bike to the publisher's offices on Madison Avenue. To calm my nerves before going in, I wolfed down a Häagen-Dazs ice cream cone. In the elevator, I realized the chocolate had stained my jumper.

The editor's office was lined with shelves of books, their

jackets face out. Most had huge type embossed in silver and gold. I didn't recognize a single title. Her desk was tidy, but the floor was piled high with manuscripts. I could tell that she was rushed, that her mother had put her up to this meeting, and I sat there somewhat lumpen and extremely ill prepared. After some pleasantries, she started the interview proper by asking whether I was interested in hardcover or paperback publishing. I looked nervously back and forth between her and her book-shelves, as if I were still in school and there was a chance that someone else might answer. *Hardcover or paperback?* Was there a difference? I asked.

Thirty résumés and a half-dozen interviews later, I had failed the typing test at every major publishing house in New York that would see me.

I wound up taking the only job I was offered, as a reception-ist in the library of a large financial institution. I probably don't have to point out that it paid twice as much as an entry-level publishing position. More important, it required no typing. In a few months' time, I was promoted to corporate file coordina-tor, which was every bit as Kafkaesque as it sounds. I spent most of my lunch hours endlessly browsing the dusty shelves a few blocks south at the Gotham Book Mart, a tiny shop wedged among the diamond dealers of Forty-seventh Street. I also picked up the monthly Poetry Calendar there, a broadsheet with tiny print that listed readings for the coming weeks, and scanned the bulletin board bursting with notices of all matters literary. It was there that I found a small advertisement for a poetry workshop. Enrollment was limited, and six poems had to be submitted for the leader's review by the following

Monday. I worked feverishly all weekend, selecting and revising my poems. When I learned, a few weeks later, that I had been accepted, I felt for the first time in a very long while that things just might work out for me.

That workshop, as it turned out, was a pivotal life experience. The teacher, Jorie Graham, then a young woman with only one book to her credit, changed the way I allowed myself to feel about writing. Until then, my writing had been a secret, almost shameful act. But during those Monday-night sessions among fellow poets I felt transformed, listening intently as Graham passionately critiqued our work and described her own fledgling efforts as a writer. I will never forget her exquisite recitation; she would hold the final syllable before a line break for a breath longer than anticipated or rush one line into the next to give it urgency and life. A year later, with a sheaf of twenty full-length poems, I applied to graduate school for an MFA in poetry.

To say that attending graduate school is the end of innocence is not an exaggeration. Once again I was wholly unprepared for what would befall me there or for the characters I would meet along the way. But for all the indignities suffered around the workshop table, one thing was very clear: I discovered that I was good at suggesting changes that could improve a fellow student's poem, whether it meant moving one stanza from the middle to the beginning, deleting a line altogether, or sometimes just changing a title. In my final year I became editor of the literary magazine, and I found that the pieces I liked best, believed had the most merit, were usually those that stirred debate or aroused strong feeling, whether or not we included them in our pages. I didn't know it then, but I was becoming an editor.

When I was granted an internship at Simon & Schuster in my final semester, my publishing career began in earnest. I remember my first day on the job. I had arrived early and was sitting in the reception area when a young woman came flying through, waving a sheet of paper and screaming, "Number six, number six!" The next thing I knew, she and an older woman were grabbing each other's elbows and jumping up and down, still screaming. I later learned that the older woman was the publisher and that one of their books had hit the bestseller list. I wondered if anything would ever make me that excited. One short year later, I caught a glimpse of myself running down that same corridor screaming with glee, an advance bestseller list in hand. A book my boss had been working on for many years, which I had helped in its final production stages, had hit the list. I had found my passion.

🌿

When I entered the business, I believed that writers were exalted beings. How else could they capture in a single phrase the emotional truth of a lifetime or render a scene that seemed more lifelike than life? How else could they risk their lives and livelihoods on a string of sentences, baring their souls in a world ever more hostile to artists and art? I was in awe of all writers, even those with less than perfectly realized works. They had broken through, and somewhere books existed with their names on them. Of course, it didn't take long for those pedestals to crumble.

As an editor, I was both privy to and subjected to every aspect of my authors' lives. And the more I worked with writers, the more I found myself thinking about the characteristics that contributed to any given writer's success or failure. I saw mediocre writers who were brilliant at networking and superb writers who couldn't part with their pages. Some seemed blessed with the confidence of entitlement, others cursed with paralyzing insecurities. I saw their defenses and fears, their hopes and ambitions. Very soon I was able to recognize which writers would hunker down for the long haul, revising their texts over and over, and which felt that simply producing a manuscript should be enough to secure a publishing contract. I also began to understand the cyclical nature of the publishing business, the brutality of the media, and the vagaries of the marketplace. But more than anything else, I grew close to my authors and saw firsthand how they soldiered on in their lonely work.

Before I entered publishing, I believed, like most people, that the life of a writer was to be envied. It wasn't until I began working with writers that I understood Truman Capote's brilliant assessment of the writer's dilemma: "When God hands you a gift, he also hands you a whip." Most writers are a breed apart, their gifts and their whips inextricably linked. And the writer's psychology, by its very nature, is one of extreme duality. The writer labors in isolation, yet all that intensive, lonely work is in the service of communicating, is an attempt to reach another person. It isn't surprising, then, that many writers are ambivalent, if not altogether neurotic, about bringing their work forward. For in so doing, a writer must face down that which he most fears: rejection. There is no stage of the writing process that doesn't challenge every aspect of a writer's personality. How well writers deal with those challenges can be critical to their survival.

Editors, like shrinks, have a privileged and exclusive view into a writer's psyche, from the ecstasy of acquisition to the agony of the remainder table. Some editors limit their concern to the challenges on the page, but in my experience the challenges on the page and the challenges in the person go hand in hand. While editors are most certainly concerned with matters of style, structure, voice, and flow, they are often faced with extratextual problems—keeping the writer motivated, seeing the bigger picture, finding the patterns and rhythms, subtexts and operating metaphors that may elude an author drowning in research or blocked midstream. In the most productive author-editor relationship, the editor, like a good dance partner who neither leads nor follows but anticipates and trusts, can help the writer find her way back into the work, can cajole another revision, contemplate the deeper themes, or supply the seamless transition, the telling detail.

This is not a book about how to write. There are dozens of excellent books about writing, be it fiction or nonfiction, from the most technical to the most esoteric. Rather, I hope to help you if you can't start or finish a project, or can't figure out what you should be writing. I offer advice to writers whose neuroses seem to get in their way, those who sabotage their efforts, those who have met with some success but are stalled between projects. I promise not to repeat the most common piece of writing advice: Write what you know. As far as I'm concerned, writers have very little choice in what they write (though I do have some advice for those who can't figure out their form). Nor will I Strunk you over the head with rules about style. Instead, I present ideas about how a writer's styles on and off the page work in tandem. Is your neurotic behavior part of your creative process or just . . . neurotic behavior? Do you expose too much in your writing? Or are you protecting yourself or someone else with silence? Are you an effective self-promoter or a self-saboteur? Have you bought into certain myths about the writing life that aren't helping your career?

The second half of the book describes the publishing process from an editor's point of view. I have tried to share my insights into the world of publishing from my days as a naive editorial assistant through my later years as an editor and finally as an agent and writer to show what really goes on there. I have some words of advice about the most commonly asked questions: Do I need an agent? Should I multiply submit my book? How long must I wait for an agent or editor to respond? What can I expect of my agent or editor? What happens once the book is accepted for publication? How do writers come up with titles? What if I hate the jacket? Should I hire my own publicist? Do I need a web presence, a website, a blog? Should I join Facebook or other social networking sites? Should I tweet? But more important, I try to give a feeling of what it's like to sit behind an editor's desk and read hundreds of manuscripts, of how an editor feels when she is either supported or thwarted in her efforts to acquire a project, or when a favorite author's book is universally panned or, worse, ignored. I've tried to provide a picture of the particular pressures editors and authors feel in today's publishing climate, and of what allows them to carry on in the face of so much industry instability.

In the ten years since this book was first published enormous changes have shocked the publishing industry. The biggest publishers in the land have merged into six major conglomerates; Amazon is no longer a feisty start-up. Sales have grown from $15.7 million in 1996 to $25 billion as of this writing. That's right. *Billion.* Of course, that is for all consumer goods, including the Kindle, the first handheld electronic device that finally took hold in the marketplace after many failed attempts. Ten years ago, consumers were wary of purchasing online. Amazon was a pioneer. Now, we buy everything from airline tickets to vintage sconces on eBay. During this time, and not coincidentally, independent booksellers' ranks were thinned by more than half; independents now represent 10 percent of store sales. Downloading books, whether on your reader, iPad, or mobile phone, is no longer in the realm of science fiction or a high-end gadgeteer's wet dream. While e-books account for an estimated 3 to 5 percent of the market, sales increased 177 percent in 2009 and are projected to eventually capture 25 to 50 percent of the book market, according to Ken Auletta's *New Yorker* article "Publish or Perish." Barnes & Noble, through an agreement with Google, has launched its own proprietary reader, the Nook, with hundreds of thousands of out-of-print books for free. Which reminds me: Google. Not around when I first wrote this book. I have the fat accordion file stuffed with photocopies and microfiched articles to prove it. Perhaps the greatest shift involves trust; we now rely on our computers for consumption, social interaction, information, and entertainment. Think about it: you can research, write, publish, promote, and sell your book without ever leaving your laptop. You can even win a Moby for best book trailer. Book trailer! Twenty years ago when I started in publishing, writers banged on typewriters, assistants sent Telexes, and editors enjoyed a few cocktails at lunch. Now, people are reading on devices, authors are tweeting, and editors carry yoga mats around town.

While I've never been accused of being trendy, I also changed careers in a move that has now been identified as a trend: editors becoming agents. While for me there perhaps could be no greater career than that of book editor, I crossed the line for a combination of reasons, personal and professional, including becoming a mother and wanting more freedom to work closely with a wide variety of authors. Though we are sometimes in adversarial positions, editors and agents essentially want the same thing: to see their authors well published and productive. Both experience that particular rush that comes from discovering a manuscript and helping it find its way in the world.

It is my deepest hope that this book will offer helpful advice to beginning writers, but even more that it will inspire the late bloomers, those who have worked in fits and starts over the years but have never just quit or given up the dream completely. This is also a book for people who sometimes believe the worst about themselves when it comes to their writing, who imagine themselves impostors, poseurs, dilettantes, and manqués. It is for people who torture themselves over their writing.

Whenever I attend writers' conferences, I am struck with the overwhelming sense of alienation that many aspiring writers seem to feel with regard to publishing. Many even believe there is a conspiracy of silence inside publishing houses about the way decisions are made, from acquisitions to the allocation of funds. I think it is nearly impossible for an unpublished writer not to suffer from battle fatigue; the disenfranchised are rarely comfortable. But even the most successful writers suffer from bouts of failure of confidence. In an interview in the *Hungry Mind Review*, Don DeLillo best described the predicament: "The writer has lost a great deal of influence, and he is situated now, if anywhere, on the margins of culture. But isn't this where he belongs? How could it be any other way? And in my personal view this is a perfect place to observe what's happening at the dead center of things. . . . The more marginal, perhaps ultimately the more trenchant and observant and finally necessary he'll become."

This book is about what I've seen and what I know. I wrote it to help writers achieve or get closer to their goals. At the very least, I hope that in contemplating your life as a writer you may get some perspective on your work, and in gaining that perspective, see the forest for the trees.

PART I.
WRITING

1.

THE
AMBIVALENT
WRITER

DO YOU HAVE A NEW IDEA ALMOST EVERY DAY for a writing project? Do you either start them all and don't see them to fruition or think about starting but never actually get going? Are you a short-story writer one day and a novelist the next? A memoirist on Monday and a screenwriter by the weekend? Do you begin sentences in your head while walking to work or picking up the dry cleaning, sentences so crisp and suggestive that they make perfect story or novel openers, only you never manage to write them down? Do you blab about your project to loved ones, coworkers, or strangers before the idea is fully formed, let alone partially executed? Have you ever accidentally left your notes or diary behind on a train or plane and bemoaned the loss of what certainly had been your best work? Have you ever been diagnosed with any combination of bipolar disorder, alcoholism, or skin diseases such as eczema or psoriasis? Do you snap at people who ask how your writing is going? *What's it to them?*

Do you fear that you will someday wonder where the years

went? How it is that some no-talent you went to high school with is being published everywhere you look? Or how some suck-up from graduate school is racking up prizes and being interviewed in the Arts section of the *New York Times*? Now you can't read the paper at all without thinking back to your class-mate and the fawning way he used to schmooze the professors. *God, he was so transparent.*

If you can relate to the above, you certainly have the obses-sive qualities—along with the self-aggrandizement and concur-rent feelings of worthlessness—that are part of the writer's basic makeup. However, you also have so many conflicting thoughts and feelings about writing and about yourself as a writer you are unable to choose one idea and see it through. You cannot focus. Just as you settle on one idea, another voice pops into your head. Or just as you sit down to write, you suddenly and inexplicably fall asleep. You are what I call the ambivalent writer. You have something to say, something you may feel des-perate to express, but you have no idea how to go about it. As a result, you are highly impressionable; everything strikes you but nothing sticks. You are volatile and vulnerable, but the energy it takes to quiet the voices leaves you depressed and listless. Every time you hear an author exchange barbs with Jon Stewart on *The Daily Show,* or browse at your local bookstore, you think: I could do that. You are both omnipotent and impotent.

For most writers, writing is a love-hate affair. But for the ambivalent writer who cannot attempt, sustain, or complete a piece of writing, the ambivalence usually shifts back and forth from the writing to the self. The inner monologue drums: *I am great. I am shit. I am great. I am shit.* But the writer with publication credits, good reviews, and literary prizes is not immune to this mantra either; in fact, the only real difference that I have been able to quantify between those who ultimately make their way as writers and those who quit is that the former were able to contain their ambivalence long enough to commit to a single idea and see it through.

I often encounter writers at conferences who tell me that they have a number of ideas they'd like to get working on but can't figure out which is best. They want some advice about which idea they should pursue, and often have some vague notion about what's selling these days. Asking for advice about what you should write is a little like asking for help getting dressed. I can tell you what I think looks good, but you have to wear it. And as every fashion victim knows, very few people look good in everything. Chances are that you have been writing or trying to write in one particular form all your life. There are very few writers who, by switching genres, say from novels to plays, suddenly achieve great results and conclude that they have been working in the wrong mode all along. But in my experience, a writer gravitates toward a certain form or genre because, like a well-made jacket, it suits him.

It is true that some people can write well in more than one genre. I am thinking of poet-critics, such as Czeslaw Milosz and Joseph Brodsky; poet-novelists, such as Denis Johnson and Margaret Atwood; novelist-critics, such as John Updike and Cynthia Ozick; and novelist-essayists, such as Susan Sontag and Joan Didion. But we are more likely to be suspicious of someone who attempts to write in more than one genre—who cross-dresses, generically speaking. When I was getting my

MFA, it was considered anathema, if not altogether taboo, for someone from the poetry side of the program to write a short story or for someone from the fiction side to write a poem. We suspect those who attempt creative work in more than one genre or field of being dilettantes or dabblers. Gone is the idea of the Renaissance man. In a *Paris Review* interview, Gore Vidal addressed the problem of literary ambidexterity: "Writers are the only people who are reviewed by people of their own kind. And their own kind can often be reasonably generous—*if* you stay in your category. I don't. I do many different things rather better than most people do one thing. And envy is the central fact of writing life."

Finding your form is like finding a mate. You really have to search, and you can't compromise—unless you *can* compromise, in which case your misery will be of a different variety. But just as there are probably only one or two people to whom you could commit yourself, there are probably only a few things you can write about, and only one genre, or maybe two, in which you might excel. It's no coincidence that most authors' bodies of work hover over two or three basic themes or take a single basic shape. Think of the novels of Trollope, Austen, Dickens, or Hardy; think of Hemingway, Faulkner, Fitzgerald. They each revisited the same themes, settings, and conflicts over the course of their writing lives. The James Joyces of the world, those who can move from short story to novel to epic, are rare, but then again, few writers master each form the first time out of the gate.

Even though most writers return to the same mine for inspiration, readers find infinite pleasure in watching their work change and deepen over time as they grapple with their obsessions. Think of Roth's Zuckerman, Updike's Rabbit, Ford's Bascombe. But if you aren't yet sure what your themes are or what category you should be writing in, you need to take a full accounting of all the reading and all the writing you have ever done or wanted to do. If you are one of the many people who dream of writing but have never successfully finished or, perhaps, even started a piece, I suggest you compile a list of everything you've read over the past six months or year and try to determine if there is a pattern or common denominator. If you read only literary novels, that should tell you something. If you've always kept a diary noting the natural world in all its variety, you might want to try writing nature essays.

It never fails to surprise me, in conversations with writers who seek my advice as to what they should write, how many fail to see before their very eyes the hay that might be gold. Instead of honoring the subjects and forms that invade their dreams and diaries, they concoct some ideas about what's selling or what agents and editors are looking for as they try to fit their odd-shaped pegs into someone else's hole. There is nothing more refreshing for an editor than to meet a writer or read a query letter that takes him completely by surprise, that brings him into a world he didn't know existed or awakens him to a notion that had been there all along but that he had never much noticed.

Some of the most striking and successful books are clearly born of a writer's obsession and complete disregard for what, supposedly, sells. Few editors would have gone for a book about a little-known murder in Savannah that took its sweet time describing every other quirk of the city and its inhabitants before addressing the crime. Whatever John Berendt was thinking when he set out to write *Midnight in the Garden of Good and Evil*, it couldn't have been the bestseller list, because almost anyone in the publishing industry would have told him that nobody would care about the story of a gay antiques dealer who languished in jail after shooting a cheap hustler. Clearly, Berendt was born to write this book. His strengths as a reporter, as a travel writer, and as a Southerner with a gothic sensibility for the macabre produced an original and unforgettable book that would stay on the *New York Times* bestseller list for a record-breaking 216 weeks.

The same could be said for the brilliant essay collections by David Sedaris. Publishing wisdom 101: Essays don't sell. Humor is tough. Good thing Sedaris didn't get the memo. Nothing would have predicted the massive success of Sedaris's eccentric and hilarious pieces, which makes their success that much sweeter. It is true that Sedaris began to attract a book-buying audience when NPR launched his essay "Santaland Diaries," which recounted his stint at Macy's as an elf at Christmas. Still, lots of writers are featured on NPR; his success defies the publishing industry's received wisdom. After the publication of his first book, most of his essays have appeared in the *New Yorker* and every single title has gone on to become a *New York Times* bestseller, the last two in the number one slot. That's not a fluke. A fluke would be the runaway success of *The Guernsey Literary and Potato Peel Pie Society*, since epistolary novels don't sell—that is, until one comes along and plants itself on the bestseller list for more than a year. And in this crazy, youth-driven culture,

Olive Kittredge, a book about a woman in her sixties—an unsympathetic character, I might add—wins the Pulitzer Prize and becomes a national bestseller.

It is true that most books that sit on the bestseller list fit a certain genre (crime, science fiction, romance, and so forth), and they are prized in part for how well they work within a certain formula. Their authors are successful for having created characters and stories so compelling that they engender intense loyalty among their readers, a following. On more than one occasion, I've heard a "literary" writer (usually one who is stalled or struggling) announce that he's thinking of writing something commercial; implicit is the idea that this project would be beneath his skills. I've always found this arrogance mind-boggling. If any writer could toss off a "commercial" novel and cash in, why haven't they? The reason may be obvious: it's not as easy as it looks. On the contrary, these writers deploy the tools of their craft, a craft they have honed and studied and labored at for years, if not decades. I don't believe that writers can choose a topic or genre the way you can choose a country you'd like to visit by spinning a globe.

Most writers have very little choice in what they write about. What is in evidence over and over is a certain set of obsessions, a certain vocabulary, a way of approaching the page. The person who can't focus is not without his own obsessions, vocabulary, and approach. However, either he can't find his form or he can't apply the necessary discipline that ultimately separates the published from the unpublished.

I believe that the writer who can't figure out what form to write in or what to write is stalling for a reason. Perhaps he is dancing around a subject because he is not ready to handle it, psychologically or emotionally. Perhaps he is unable to pursue a project because doing so would upset his world too much, or the people in it. Maybe not writing, maybe being driven crazy by the desire to write and the inability to follow through, is serving some greater goal, keeping some greater fear at bay. Fear of failure is the reason most often cited to explain why so many aspiring writers never realize their dreams. But I think it's that same fear of failure that absolutely invigorates those who do push through—that is, the fear of not being heard.

Certainly, the desire for success and the fear of failure run along a continuum. And the extent to which either motivates or paralyzes a given artist is dependent on a great many factors, including ability, ego, desire, and drive. But it's important to remember that success and failure are only part of the equation. The making of art and the selling of it are two entirely distinct enterprises. Any number of great writers have not received the appreciation all artists crave. In his lifetime, Charles Dickens, who published his novels serially, was considered a hack. Emily Dickinson saw only seven of her hundreds of poems published. Jane Austen published under a pseudonym for her entire life. Artists such as Virginia Woolf, Hart Crane, Sylvia Plath, and John Berryman, who tragically took their lives in midcareer, would never know the prizes, cultdom, and canonization their work would later receive.

Today too little is made of all the writing that doesn't seek publication, all the letter writing, email sending, recipe copying, and diary keeping—all the writing that minds our lives. Now there is a great emphasis on turning one's diary or blog into

THE AMBIVALENT WRITER ✦ 21

a published memoir or novel, and any number of books will advise you how to do so. Don't get me wrong. I love websites, blogging, and blogs (BetsyLerner.com, ahem), but I believe that, like diaries, they need to be shaped to be successful as books. Or as Ellen Wernecke put it in her 2008 article published by the A.V. Club, "Why buy the cow?" The article listed twenty-seven popular websites or blogs that became books, most notably Tucker Max's "fratire" *I Hope They Serve Beer in Hell*, basically a compendium of frat-boy rants, digs, and other spurtings by Max, a self-proclaimed "raging dickhead." Max's blog attracts a million visitors per month, the book has been on and off the bestseller list for three years, there's a film based on the book, and a sequel called *Assholes Finish First*. (Gotta admit, the dude has a knack for titles.) Some online material, like Max's, clearly translates to a book audience. Before him, any number of stand-up comics such as George Carlin, Jerry Seinfeld, and Chris Rock translated their routines into hugely popular books. In other words, I'm all for writers mining any and every aspect of their lives for their writing. But I also believe there is enormous value in the piece of writing that goes no further than the one person for whom it was intended, that no combination of written words is more eloquent than those exchanged in letters between lovers or friends, or along the pale blue lines of private diaries, where people take communion with themselves.

It's the writer who seeks publication but who cannot finish even one project who must ask himself whether his stalling is also a form of self-protection. I can assure you that you will never finish any piece of writing if you don't understand what motivates you to write in the first place and if you don't honor that impulse, whether it's exile or assimilation, redemption or destruction, revenge or love. "Getting even is one great reason for writing," said William Gass in a *Paris Review* interview. "I write because I hate. A lot. Hard. And if someone asks me the inevitable next dumb question, 'Why do you write the way you do?' I must answer that I wish to make my hatred acceptable because my hatred is much of me, if not the best part. Writing is a way of making the writer acceptable to the world—every cheap, dumb, nasty thought, every despicable desire, every noble sentiment, every expensive taste."

If Gass is extreme, I assure you he is not alone. Many of the best books are born of anger or pain, of the struggle for self-definition, freedom, and revolution. The best books, like newborns, come into the world screaming their arrival and gasping for breath—will they survive in the harsh light, in the communal air? If you are writing to prove yourself to the world, to quiet the naysayers at last, to make your cold and distant father take notice, I say go for it. If you are writing because no one has faith in you, or because no one sees you for who you are, or because you feel like an impostor, better yet. How else could Dostoyevsky have conjured the unnamed protagonist of his novel *Notes from Underground*, whose opening lines have stayed with me from the moment I first encountered them: *I am a sick man. . . . I am an angry man. I am an unattractive man. . . . I'm sensitive and quick to take offense, like a hunchback or dwarf.*

Chances are you want to write because you are a haunted individual, or a bothered individual, because the world does not sit right with you, or you in it. Chances are you have a deep connection to books because at some point you discovered that they were the one truly safe place to discover and explore feelings that are banished from the dinner table, the cocktail party, the golf foursome, the bridge game. Because the writers who mattered to you have dared to say *I am a sick man.* And because within the world of books there is no censure. In discovering books, you became free to explore the full range of human motives, desires, secrets, and lies. All my life, people have scolded me for having an excess of feeling, saying that I was too sensitive—as if one could be in danger from feeling too much instead of too little. But my outsize emotions were well represented in books, even in those that exercised enormous restraint in the telling: in the hearts of my favorite nineteenth-century novelists' highly repressed heroes and heroines there simmered all the feelings no one ever admits to. In the slyly dark and chilling lines of one of my favorite British poets, Philip Larkin, I found images that cracked the world open. I am not suggesting a writer let it bleed so much as I am suggesting that he harness whatever drives him.

I suggest you stalk your demons. The more popular culture and the media fail to present the real pathos of our human struggle, the more opportunity there is for writers. If you have been unable to make your work count or stick, you must grab them by the neck and face them down. And whatever you do, don't censor yourself. There's always time and editors for that.

Inasmuch as writing is a creative process, a certain amount of experimentation is essential. As in the discovery process in a trial, you must devote some time to following leads and interrogating suspects before a clear picture is revealed, before your case is as strong as possible. When I studied with Jorie Graham, I learned how to find these connections. At that time I was composing six- to eight-line poems, and I handed in a dozen or so for my private conference. When I arrived, she asked me to sit down and listen to her read a poem. She proceeded to recite a longish poem of around forty lines that sounded extremely familiar, though I couldn't place it. I actually thought it might be T. S. Eliot. As it turned out, and as you have probably guessed, the lines were mine. Jorie had put the fragments together in a way that created an actual narrative. She supplied a few transitional words, such as "before" and "now" and "later," at the beginning of stanzas. It was a miracle to me, this transformation of my acorns into an oak. I raced home after the conference and combed through my hundreds of fragment poems and put them into thematic if predictable piles: father, mother, body, and so on. I transformed the scraps into full-length works and produced my first poems that would be accepted by literary magazines and that would also gain me admission into graduate school.

If you are struggling with what you should be writing, look at your scraps. Encoded there are the themes and subjects that you should be grappling with as a writer. If you still can't figure it out, whatever you do, I beg you not to look at the bestseller lists. Do not set out to write the next *Eat, Pray, Love* or *Marley and Me*. A third of the projects publishers see these days make such claims. People who try to figure out what's hot and re-create it are as close to delusional as you can get. In the first place, once a trend is actually identified it is usually too late; your work will be regarded as opportunistic, as jumping on the bandwagon. It is true that when a trend or phenomenon is identified, a handful of books or more in the same genre enter the fray, and sometimes a writer will cash in on a real or imaginary perception about a certain category of book. But I assure you that you will be better served both professionally and personally if you find your inspiration and models within yourself, not on the bestseller list. Many of the unlikely books that made it there, that took the world by surprise, did so because they were original, inspired, and new.

A professor in graduate school used to annoy people terribly when she wondered aloud why we were all so competitive with one another. After all, she said, it wasn't as if we were all trying to write the same poem. She got that wrong. We all *were* trying to write the same poem. We were trying to write the one that would get into the *New Yorker*, and with rare exception every writer out there is in the same boat. There comes a time when you have to let go of the *New Yorker* fantasy in service of just getting on with it. If you are guilty of sending your first short story or poem off to the venerable magazine, as well as your second and third, in the vain hope of hitting the jackpot, you are not alone. The question is, where do you go from there? How do you stop trying to sound like Raymond Carver?

The ambivalent writer can't hear himself think, can't commit to a single vision, can't stop wondering if six other directions aren't the right ones to take. The ambivalent writer confuses procrastination with research. He can't hear through the static to find the one true voice. I know a lot of writers who beat themselves up on a regular basis, either for not writing or for not writing well enough. And when they are writing well they make themselves crazy over other things, and these things are not insignificant—how they're going to pay the rent, why they don't have health insurance, whether or not anyone out there will care. In Virginia Woolf's *A Room of One's Own*, she describes the great difficulty of producing a work of genius: "Generally material circumstances are against it. Dogs will bark; people will interrupt; money must be made; health will break down. Further, accentuating all these difficulties and making them harder to bear is the world's notorious indifference. It does not ask people to write poems and novels and histories; it does not need them. It does not care whether Flaubert finds the right word or whether Carlyle scrupulously verifies this or that fact. Naturally, it will not pay for what it does not want."

Writing demands that you quiet all the voices that would have you subscribe to Woolf's notion of the world and its "notorious indifference." Writing demands that you keep at bay the demons insisting that you are not worthy or that your ideas are ridiculous or that your command of the language is insufficient. But if you feel you need to seek advice as to what you should be writing, you are probably not ready to write. And this is my advice to you: Stop altogether and see how long you can go without writing. "Very young writers who don't know themselves obviously often don't know what they have to say," said Bernard Malamud. "Sometimes by staying with it they write themselves into a fairly rich vein. Some, by the time they find what they're capable of writing about, no longer want to write. Some go through psychoanalysis or a job in a paint factory and begin to write again. One hopes they then have something worth saying. Nothing is guaranteed. Some writers have problems with subject matter not in their first book, which may mine old childhood experience, or an obsession, or fantasy, or the story they've carried in their minds and imagination to this point, but after that—after this first yield—often they run into trouble with their next few books. Especially if the first book is unfortunately a bestseller."

❧

Writing is a calling, and if the call subsides, so be it. It may return in greater force the next time around. Some people say that you have to write all the time to get anywhere and that discipline will ultimately separate the men from the boys. But I assure you, you will never *make* yourself write. When writers say they have no choice, what they mean is: *Everything in the world conspired to make me quit but I kept going.* And most can't tell you why, as Lorrie Moore expressed in a *Publishers Weekly* interview: "I still think you should become a writer only if you have no choice. Writing has to be an obsession—it's only for those who say 'I'm not going to do anything else.'" Or as she began her brilliant story "How to Become a Writer," which by now should be required reading for anyone entering an MFA program, "First, try to be something, anything, else."

If the voices keep calling, if the itch remains, no matter how punishing the work or inhospitable the world, then you must persevere. Don't let publishers tell you that short stories don't sell if you're a short-story writer, don't give up on your memoir just because there seems to be a glut. Where would today's successful African American writers be if they believed the thinking that dominated publishing for a long time, that black writing doesn't sell? Thirty-three publishers rejected *Chicken Soup for the Soul*. "Seven million copies later," reported *Time* magazine, "the authors are living happily ever after."

I promise you, I am not offering the single most often repeated piece of writing advice: *Write what you know*. Writing what you know is a given. Writing what you know is unavoidable. All people write what they know, for God's sake. It's the air you breathe. The challenge is finding the structure that shows your stuff off to its best effect. In his book *On Writing and Publishing*, Mark Twain describes attempting to start the story of Joan of Arc six times over twelve years. "There are some books that refuse to be written. They stand their ground year after year and will not be persuaded. It isn't because the book is not there and worth being written—it is only because the right form for the story does not present itself. There is only one right form for a story, and if you fail to find that form the story will not tell itself. You may try a dozen wrong forms but in each case you will not get very far before you discover that you have not found the right one—and that the story will always stop and decline to go any further."

If the world of writing were music, would you be an opera, the blues, or rap? Is your best work lyric, dramatic, or interpretive? Can you be happy as part of the chorus, or, like an editor, doing the behind-the-scenes work? If the high wire is for you, if the spotlight is for you, if you believe that everyone should pay attention to you and to your work, then you must keep writing, and by that I mean you are compelled to write. Again: no choice. Ambivalence will never get you anywhere, unless, as Spalding Gray did, you mine every personal doubt for material and find a form, in his case the monologue, through which the very subject of ambivalence is rehearsed.

Try to remember that the time before you publish is the only time you will ever work in complete freedom. After you're published you will be forced to contend with the shockingly real voices of critics, agents, editors, family, friends, fans and detractors. You never get to be a virgin again, and more to the point, you never again have the luxury of writing in total obscurity. But like the married person who bemoans the loss of freedom from her single days, the published author who longingly recalls her past obscurity is a little hard to sympathize with. Though you may suffer from loneliness after you're married, it's bad form to complain about it to your single friends.

Writers take note: your struggle to produce a piece of writing of interest and value means nothing to the reader. The reader doesn't care what you went through to produce your work. He only cares if the piece succeeds, if it looks as if it arrived whole. If you aim to succeed with a book that's destined to last, one thing is certain: your work must bear your own stamp. You must be willing to hone your sentences until they are yours alone. You must have a belief in your vision and voice that is nothing short of fierce. In other words, you must turn your ambivalence into something unequivocal.

2.

THE
NATURAL

EVERY NOW AND THEN A WRITER COMES ALONG whom people call "the real thing." Like the character Robert Redford portrays in the movie *The Way We Were*, there is a romantic ideal of some beautiful creature who runs his onionskin paper through the Smith-Corona and produces breathtaking prose. People say he's a natural, a God-given talent. He's got the touch. I am fascinated by the question of whether this person exists or whether it's another great American myth. God knows, we romanticize the idea of the natural and love the thrill of discovering a fresh, new voice. At the same time, we are suspicious of those for whom success comes too easily, believing that people should suffer for their art. But perhaps the most deeply held belief about what is right and good is the notion that we are all created equal. I say take a look around the table at any writers' workshop, or around any playground for that matter, and you will quickly deduce one thing: equal we are not.

What does this really mean to the struggling writer? How

many writers were praised early on but were never able to sustain or fulfill their promise? And how many others, who seemed plodding and awkward in every way, continued to work without encouragement, determined to make themselves heard? I cannot tell you how many times I have been approached by aspiring writers at conferences who have asked me to tell them whether their pages show promise, whether they have any talent, or whether they should give up. They might as well ask me to evaluate a child's finger painting. The making of art is a mysterious process; the dictates of taste and judgments of others are often the least helpful to a developing artist. Because everyone can write, that is, type sentences, many believe that whatever they write should be publishable.

The serious writer understands that her craft may take years to develop. Not getting into an MFA program, not getting your work in a literary magazine, not getting an agent can be interpreted in a number of ways depending on the writer's ego. For some, it's a referendum on their entire career and future. In response, they rail against those who have slammed the door in their face; others, believing themselves unworthy, take their marbles and go home. It takes a certain kind of person to understand and cope with rejection as an appraisal instead of a judgment. Being able to tolerate the many disappointments and rejections is critical to a writer's survival, and I imagine that tolerance is formed early on. Jodie Foster, in an acceptance speech for one of her Academy Awards, thanked her mother, who, she said, acted as if every drawing she brought home from school were a Picasso. In an ideal world, everyone should be thus encouraged for any creative effort.

I know a writing instructor who is beloved among her students because she is deeply supportive of their work no matter what stage they're at. "It's not as if they're building bombs or hurting people," she says in defense of her approach. "They're just trying to do creative work." It's not that she doesn't know whose work actually shows promise and which students are likely never to write an interesting sentence as long as they live. It's just that she never fails to be astonished by at least one person per semester who seems at the beginning of the class as hopeless as they come and ends the course with a powerful piece of writing. Then, of course, there's Flannery O'Connor's opinion to consider. When asked whether she thought writing programs in universities actually discouraged young writers, she replied, "Not enough of them."

I won't say there is no such thing as a natural talent, but after working with many authors over the years, I can offer a few observations: having "natural ability" doesn't seem to make writing any easier (and sometimes makes it more difficult); having all the feeling in the world will not ensure the effective communication of feeling on the page; and finally, the degree of one's perseverance is the best predictor of success. It is some combination of ability and ego, desire and discipline, that produces good work. And a writer's success or faltering can usually be traced to some abundance or deficit of those elements. Some of the most gifted writers I've worked with were also the most self-sabotaging. Lack of discipline, desire for fame, and depression often thwart those whose talents appear most fertile, while some of those who struggle with every line persevere regardless.

I once had the privilege of editing the work of a professor whose writing had influenced me enormously in college. I was thrilled to have the opportunity to work with her and was more than a little perplexed when the editorial process didn't flow as easily as I had hoped. With every successive draft, with each step forward, we took the proverbial two back. Finally, we decided to work face-to-face to see if we could address the problem. Toward the end of a very long workweek, as we sat side by side for the first time, I noticed something peculiar. The writer inverted her letters as she made notes and sometimes wrote the second or third letter of a word before the first.

I sat up in my seat, regarded my hero, and, before thinking how my words might sound, blurted out almost accusatorially, "You're dyslexic, aren't you?"

She nodded slowly, as if to say yes, now my secret is out.

"How can you be?" I continued in disbelief. "How can you possibly write?"

Now it was dawning on me why we had struggled so much with the text, and I reeled to think of how arduous this work was for her. Yet her desire to communicate through writing far surpassed her impediment. As I sat shaking my head, she resumed her somewhat aristocratic bearing and said, with more than a hint of pride, "I've written five books, haven't I?"

While it may seem disingenuous to encourage a writer who seems to have no native ability, it is also arrogant to think we know how any given career will develop, or what combination of desire and will may result in a work that will have a profound effect on people even if it is never praised for its beautiful prose. The most popular books are often savaged by critics for their writing style, yet these writers are clearly connecting with readers. At the same time, a natural facility with language does not necessarily mean a natural ability to communicate ideas that find currency in the culture.

When I was getting my MFA, it became eminently clear to me that my fellow students and I were being indoctrinated with very specific ideas about taste. The people who were highly praised and encouraged were those who worked in a particular vein, whose voices most closely approximated those of the writers who were held up as masters. One woman working on a novel based on her own experiences as an undercover cop was told by a professor that solely because of the subject matter he could not possibly read or respond to her book. There was absolutely no room in the program for any kind of genre writing and absolutely no humor. I'll never forget the humiliation I felt when I thought I had finally made a breakthrough in my own writing by allowing my sense of humor into my work. A professor whom I worshipped sniffed at a few of these new poems before he cocked his eyebrow and said, "Well, if you want to be the poetic equivalent of Fran Lebowitz that's fine, but I can't possibly help you."

Asking whether you've got it, whether you should stick with writing or quit, is a little like asking if you should continue living. It's beside the point. No one can give you a reason to live. For most writers, being unable to write is tantamount to suicide anyway. "For me, writing is like breathing," Pablo Neruda said in a *Paris Review* interview. "I could not live without breathing and I could not live without writing." The world doesn't fully make sense until the writer has secured his version of it on the page. And the act of writing is strangely more lifelike than life. Even when a writer doesn't have a pen in hand or a keyboard beneath his fingers, the sentences are forming, the observations are being gathered, refined, retained, or rejected. The argument with the spouse, daughter, or checkout girl is being calculated and reduced for a later scene. Everything is fodder.

The natural writer is the one who is always writing, if only in his head—sizing up a situation for material, collecting impressions. James Thurber confessed, "I never quite know when I'm not writing. Sometimes my wife comes up to me at a party and says, 'Dammit, Thurber, stop writing.' She usually catches me in the middle of a paragraph." Martin Amis describes the same sensation, saying, "You develop an extra sense that partly excludes you from experience. When writers experience things, they're not really experiencing them anything like 100 percent. They're always holding back and wondering what the significance is, or wondering how they'd do it on the page."

For most writers, reading is also a very intense experience; they don't read so much as compete. The writer measures himself against every text he encounters, imagining he could do it better or wishing he had thought of it first. The natural writer would almost always rather be reading, writing, or alone, except of course when he needs something from one of the three basic food groups: sex, love, and attention. He may be a selfish son of a bitch, he may seem to care more about his work than about the people in his life, he may be a social misfit, a freak, or a smooth operator, but every person who does serious time with a keyboard is attempting to translate his version of the world into words so that he might be understood. Indeed, the great paradox of the writer's life is how much time he spends alone trying to connect with other people.

✦

When I meet a new writer, at some point I usually ask if he or she wrote as a child. I have found that the impulse to write, to record one's private feelings, often appears at a very early age; with few exceptions most authors started writing in childhood. If as a child you gravitated toward books and kept diaries or made up stories, it speaks to an inherent aptitude for language. In an essay entitled "Why Write," John Updike recalls, "When I was thirteen, a magazine came into the house, the *New Yorker* by name, and I loved that magazine so much I concentrated all my wishing into an effort to make myself small and inky and intense enough to be received into its pages. Once there, I imagined, some transfigured mode of being, called a 'writer's life,' would begin for me."

The child writer is an interesting creature. He tends to identify himself as an outsider and to be aware of an inner life at a young age. He usually has an overly developed sense of privacy and at eight or nine years old may already feel that he has something to hide or something to say. Truman Capote said he was nine or ten when it hit him. "I was walking along the road, kicking stones, and I realized that I wanted to be a writer, an artist. How did it happen? That's what I ask myself. My relatives were nothin', dirt-poor farmers. I don't believe in possession, but something took over inside me, some little demon that made me a writer."

John Cheever started telling stories to reward his classmates for completing their math assignments. "The teacher would promise that I would tell a story. I told serials. This was very shrewd of me, because I knew if I didn't finish the story by the end of the period, which was an hour, then everyone would ask to hear the end during the next period." Cheever was seventeen when he sold his first short story to the *New Republic*, twenty-two when the *New Yorker* started to publish his work regularly.

"I wrote stories from the time I was a little girl," recalled Joan Didion, "but I didn't want to be a writer. I wanted to be an actress. I didn't realize then that it's the same impulse. It's make-believe. It's performance." Bernard Malamud explained that "at eight or nine I was writing little stories in school and feeling the glow. To any one of my friends who'd listen I'd recapitulate at tedious length the story of the last movie I'd seen. . . . As a writer I learned from Charlie Chaplin." Woody Allen said that he had only comic books as a kid, but "was always the class writer. I remember very distinctly, I'd buy those little black-and-white notebooks and say, 'Today I'll write a mystery story.' I'd go home and write, and invariably they'd come out funny. I certainly couldn't care less if I ever performed again, and don't care much if I ever direct another film, but I would not like to be in a position not to write."

In the essay "Why I Write," George Orwell said, "From a very early age, perhaps the age of five or six, I knew that when I grew up I should be a writer. . . . I was the middle child of three, but there was a gap of five years on either side, and I barely saw my father before I was eight. For this and other reasons I was somewhat lonely, and I soon developed

disagreeable mannerisms which made me unpopular throughout my schooldays. I had the lonely child's habit of making up
stories and holding conversations with imaginary persons, and I
think from the very start my literary ambitions were mixed up
with the feeling of being isolated and undervalued. I knew that
I had a facility with words and a power of facing unpleasant
facts, and I felt that this created a sort of private world in which
I could get my own back for my failure in everyday life."

The child writer may be intensely verbal or intensely with-
drawn. One thing is certain: his urge to write things down is
predicated by the need to validate his experience. The child
who makes sense of his world, escapes or remakes it through
reading and writing, may never find another home as welcoming. "I felt trapped within my home and trapped within school,"
said Gloria Naylor, "and it was through the pages of books that
I was released into other worlds. I literally read my way from
the A's to the Z's in the children's section of the library. . . . I
don't believe this would have been enough to have created a
writer, although most writers first begin as avid readers. But a
writer needs something else—a conscious connection between
the validity of their personal experience and the page. . . . From
the age of twelve I made the vital connection between inarticulate feeling and the written word."

Often the child writer is accused of having an overly active
imagination, of being hyperactive or, the converse, of being
too reflective. By age six, Gore Vidal claims, he was reading
tales from Livy, by seven or eight he was attempting to write
novels, and between the ages of fourteen and nineteen he had
started five novels. The fifth, his first to be published, when he

was twenty-one, was *Williwaw.* "I never wanted to be a writer. I mean, that was the last thing I wanted; I expected to be a politician," wrote Vidal in an anthology called *Conversations with American Writers.* "Unfortunately—or fortunately, as the case may be—I was a writer. I simply could not *not* write. A writer is someone who writes, that's all. You can't stop it; you can't make yourself do anything else but that."

Some writers elicit encouragement from teachers or find acclaim as students. Robert Stone benefited from an early experience: "I had won a contest when I was in high school. Because my upbringing was in what you'd call a working-class context, I had the impression that being a writer was insubstantial and not altogether respectable. But it was basically what I wanted to do, even though I didn't realize it when I was younger. I always wrote. I always had a kind of narrative impulse to try to make sense out of things by telling stories about them, and I guess I also always had a certain facility with language and was also kind of in love with language."

Whether or not they work on the school paper or literary magazine, win prizes, and have intense relationships with their high school English teacher, teenage writers generally begin to develop some sense of themselves as writers. Some find role models in published authors. Updike says he revered Thurber from the age of eleven. "I wrote him a fan letter and when I was twelve he sent me a drawing, which I've carried with me, framed, everywhere I've gone since." Some remain in the closet throughout school, while others flaunt their talents, making a display of their aspirations.

College is the usual place where young writers experiment

with writerly personas. I fondly recall my college English Department's cast of characters: a handful of poseurs after the fashion of Kerouac and Cassady, one self-styled Gertrude Stein who ran a workshop out of her West Village apartment, which had black floors and a hot-pink fridge, a couple of macho-Hemingways, an effete Oscar Wilde, and of course the moody girl poets, myself among them. Later, in graduate school, two particular poets stood out. One, fancying himself a young T. S. Eliot, promptly dispensed with his first name in favor of initials, always wore a blazer, and carried a walking stick. The other seemed the absolute physical reincarnation of Delmore Schwartz. He never turned in a single piece of writing, as far as I can recall, but I believe he slept with most of the women in the program, and got into fights with most of the men.

⚘

Those writers who fulfill their early promise, who achieve wide and early acclaim, whose prose seems as effortless as the easy smiles captured in their glossy author photos, these young naturals face the double-edged sword of fame and its discontents. There is nothing we love more than young writers with their fresh, unimpeachable voices—and every year there is a new crop. At the beginning of a career a writer is all promise, all future, all horizon. There are no disappointing sales tracks, no mixed reviews, no piles of remainders. Though it is impossible not to envy their highly publicized book deals, their gorgeous dust jackets, and their newfound acclaim, I sometimes regard young novelists as sacrificial lambs lined up for the slaughter. Our appetite for novelty is insatiable, and these days a writer's career, which should take a lifetime to develop and mature, can flicker and burn out as fast as any starlet's. "It's a lot easier to launch a first novel than it is a writer in midcareer," said agent Lynn Nesbit in a *New York* magazine article called "How to Make a Bestseller." "Everyone likes to discover someone new. Especially when it's a girl."

Though the twenty-three-year-old wunderkind who gets a story in the *New Yorker* or a publishing contract while finishing her MFA is the envy of all her classmates and this season's publishing flavor, it is as likely as not that she will never be heard from again. I sometimes think a wall should be erected at every university writing program with the names of the missing etched into it. Nowhere is the Darwinian struggle for survival more keen than at our nation's creative writing programs, where the whiff of early success can establish or ruin a person for good. Michael Cunningham recalled his experience at the Iowa Writers' Workshop in an interview for *Publishers Weekly*: "I had a streak of luck at Iowa: a story in *Atlantic Monthly* and another in the *Paris Review*, which led me to the entirely false conclusion that if writing wasn't exactly easy, well, it was going to be easy for me. I would just write things and publish them. Boy, was I mistaken."

As it turns out, ten years elapsed between Cunningham's largely forgotten first novel and publication of the book that would establish his career, *A Home at the End of the World*. "I'm fast on my way to being a fifty-year-old who once had a story in the *Paris Review*," he recalled. "I was working either as a waiter, a bartender, moving around a lot, falling in love a lot and going wherever it took me." In one of publishing's more gratifying stories, Cunningham would receive the Pulitzer Prize ten years after *A Home at the End of the World* was published, for *The Hours*, which beautifully captured among many things the essence of time. But for every Michael Cunningham who struggles over the years, who persists and sacrifices in the face of constant rejection, and who finally receives well-earned recognition, there are countless others who, after early acceptance or success, either fail to continue producing or find their work met with stony silence.

Describing his journey in a *Poets & Writers* profile, Cunningham said, "Marilyn Monroe once said, 'I wasn't the prettiest, I wasn't the most talented. I simply wanted it more than anyone else.' And I sometimes think that I'm just one of the people who comes here every day and does it, even though I don't feel like it, even though it's difficult and I feel stupid and brain-dead and unequal to the task. . . . I have known writers over the years, enormously talented, who are so self-conscious about it, who are so terrified of ever writing a bad sentence, that they can't write anything at all. I think a certain fearlessness in the face of your own ineptitude is a useful tool." It is impossible, perhaps even for Cunningham himself, to know how he persisted during the long dry spells of his career, how he tolerated the feelings of inadequacy. But once a writer is recognized, once he or she is deemed a success, either early or later in a career, we tend to mythologize that success. To call him a natural.

A collective sigh of relief was heard among the more mature writers of America when the *New York Times Book Review* put on its cover three novelists who first published when they were over forty, under the headline "New Guys on the Block." One of the writers highlighted was Dennis McFarland, who had enrolled in the creative writing program at Goddard College after giving up a music career. There he was mentored by Frank Conroy. "I wrote a story that [he] liked, so I submitted it to the *New Yorker*. And what proceeded from that was the odd experience of having my first published story in the *New Yorker* and then not having them take anything again for the next eight years." What's worse, to have loved and lost or never to have loved at all? But without the encouragement of a mentor, or some other meaningful encouragement, the older a writer gets without seeing his work in print the less likely it is that he will pursue it.

The eighties was a particularly tough time for most writers, with the Brat Pack getting all the press, sharing headlines with actors, frequenting the hot clubs. I always thought that one of the few advantages of being a writer was that you didn't have to go out and dance in front of people or act as if you enjoyed being in the world. But now you were supposed to score coke and get your picture in the Style sections. Plus book advances seemed to follow an inverse formula: the younger you were, the more money you got.

Take heart, late bloomers. Early success can also mean early obsolescence. It can engender a whole host of problems, perhaps most disastrously when the ego becomes so inflated that the writer can never quite find her voice again. When an older writer becomes the hot new thing, his success is an example to all those who deferred or denied their dream. The best example is the story of a New York City teacher who, at sixty-six, finally found his voice. Frank McCourt, according to the *New*

York Times, "made fitful stabs at writing. He contributed articles on Ireland to the *Village Voice*, kept notebooks. But at the Lion's Head in Greenwich Village, where he became friends with Pete Hamill and Jimmy Breslin, he felt like an interloper, he said. They were writers. He was just a teacher." As a younger man, McCourt went to NYU, but that effort proved fruitless. Three decades later, as McCourt explained, "he had worked through his awkward self-conscious James Joyce phase and had gotten beyond the crippling anger that darkened his memories." And then, in a note to himself, McCourt found the voice of *Angela's Ashes*. "That was it. It carried me through to the end of the book." Four million hardcover copies, a Pulitzer Prize, and the National Book Critics Circle. Well, not too shabby for an old geezer.

✺

How much or how little "natural" ability anyone has is nearly impossible to gauge. When Emily Dickinson composed the lines that filled the pages she kept in her solitary desk, she could not know that her pure apprehension of the language, her immutable style, and her breathtaking line breaks would forever change the landscape of American poetry. She would never know that her unpublished meditations, with their bone-chilling observations about the human heart, would touch readers a century later.

I would like to believe that there are brilliant poems and novels tucked away in drawers and closets across the country. I would like to believe that correspondences exist as rich and revelatory as those between Vincent van Gogh and his brother

Theo, or between Rilke and his wife about Cézanne's powerful influence, or Flannery O'Connor and the woman identified
only as "A" in O'Connor's collected letters, *The Habit of Being*,
which provides some of the most astute thoughts on morality
and truth that one is likely to find. I would like to believe that
there is writing, which may or may not see the light of day,
that possesses genius and that the solitary figure behind its
manufacture composed her prose because writing is what came
naturally. This is what editors live in the hope of—that one day
they will somehow uncover and bring to the world a piece of
writing that will change the way we understand or perceive
the world.

❧

I am dismayed when I visit freshmen and sophomores in college,
and the first question they ask when I finish my spiel is whether
they need an agent and how they should go about getting one.
I am dismayed when they ask me about advances and whether
they should get an MFA, when they talk about the various
writing programs as if they were clubs or restaurants, hot for a
limited time only. Though I was a largely closeted writer during
college, and identified myself as an aspiring poet only to a few
friends who also wrote, I do not remember our conversations
tending toward deals and dollars. We had no idea what an
agent was for or that they even existed. Mostly we wanted to
know about writers—how they lived, how they wrote, whom
they loved. We took the subway up from Washington Square
to Books & Co. on Madison Avenue to hear our favorite poets
read from their new books. We haunted the Strand and other

bookstores looking for early Lowell or O'Hara. We nursed a single cappuccino for hours at Caffè Dante, scribbling in our diaries about how much everything hurt. We wished that the best minds of our generation had been destroyed by madness instead of packing it in and going to law school.

Perhaps it was naiveté that kept us from asking about agents and deals. (This, of course, would change in graduate school.) In college we were still looking for ways of being in the world, of being on the page. I believe that a certain amount of innocence is critical to the creative development of an artist. There is a necessary gestation period during which a writer should protect his work, because the minute he sends it out, or joins a writing group, or enrolls in an MFA program, he engages the part of himself that is focused on the result more than the work. For some people it's a quickening experience that can heighten their ambition and potentially improve their work. For others it's disastrous.

Most people, even those who wrote as children or showed promise as teens, usually give up shortly after college. Writing, like drugs and recreational sex, becomes an activity associated with youth. Others who persist get graduate writing degrees or live the life of the temp or bartender as they try to support a writing career, only to eventually quit as a career opportunity with benefits presents itself. Many try to write screenplays in the hopes of striking gold; many pursue careers in publishing; some enter the teaching or legal professions. The writing life is torturous, especially if you hope to make a livelihood from it. No matter how glamorous it may appear, even the most successful authors will say that their lives are fraught with peril and insecurity, both financial and emotional.

Some let the dream go gracefully. Others do not go gently, attempting to write over the years, beginning journals only to let them lapse, showing up for a writing workshop only to disappear after the first session. If this describes you, it does not mean that you lack ability, though it may mean that you lack ego. But if you can't give it up, if hearing how impossible the odds are only makes you dig in deeper, it doesn't really matter if you've got natural talent. Your job is to marshal the talent you do have and find people who believe in your work. What's important, finally, is that you create, and that those creations define for you what matters most, that which cannot be extinguished even in the face of silence, solitude, and rejection.

3.
THE
WICKED
CHILD

THERE IS NO QUESTION THAT THE WRITER
most notable for negatively exposing his family, not to mention
his entire tribe, is Philip Roth. The twenty-six-year-old writer
from Newark, New Jersey, was robustly accused of both anti-
Semitism and Jewish self-hatred when his short story "Defender
of the Faith" was published in the *New Yorker* in April 1959.
Roth is quick to point out in his autobiographical account of his
life as a fiction writer, *The Facts*, that the controversy was largely
due to context rather than content. "The pulpit sermons, the
household arguments, the discussions within Jewish organizations gauging my danger . . . might never have reached trouble-
some proportions had 'Defender of the Faith' been certified as
permissible Jewish discourse by appearing in *Commentary*."

Roth is right, of course. How we accept, reject, dismiss,
and award our writers has everything to do with how, when,
where, and by whom their work is presented. Still, no one, Roth
least of all, was quite prepared for the public outcry. He claims
that he had no intention of becoming known as a controversial

writer. "[I] had no idea that my stories would prove repugnant to ordinary Jews. I had thought myself something of an authority on ordinary Jewish life, with its penchant for self-satire and hyperbolic comedy, and for a long time continued to be as bemused privately as I was unyielding publicly when confronted by Jewish challengers."

Somehow the exposition of Wasp foibles wasn't nearly as threatening to John Cheever's or John Updike's people; but then again their audiences weren't desperately trying to assimilate into the American mainstream. But Roth, being the genius that he is, went right for the Jewish jugular and followed his first short-story collection with *Portnoy's Complaint*, the quintessential Jewish novel of our time, which lifted the curtain on Semitic *mishegoss*: Jews masturbating, Jews wanting to screw shiksas, Jews being Jewy. It was enough to give a person a heart attack. But was it good for the Jews?

Let's face it, if in your writing you lift the veil on your family, your community, or even just yourself, someone will take offense. Call it fiction, call it poetry, call it creative nonfiction—if you are revealing thoughts, secrets, wishes, and fantasies that you (and we as readers) would never otherwise confess to. That is part of the power of a book: it is an unspoken invitation into someone else's world, someone else's psyche. Every time a writer takes us backstage and gives us a glimpse of life behind the curtain, he or she risks being rejected by the tribe—especially if the portrait is in any way critical. You can't help but wonder what Jhumpa Lahiri's family and the larger Bengali community think of her extraordinary portrait of Indian

American life, especially the particular vulnerabilities between immigrant parents and their first-generation American children expertly carved out in many of her stories and in her novel *The Namesake*. What does the Dominican American community think of Junot Díaz and *The Brief Wondrous Life of Oscar Wao*, his jazzlike rendering of the immigrant experience as seen by a horny, overweight teenager who lives under a family curse as he tries to come to terms with his ambitions and limitations? Are they, like Philip Roth's angry mobs, ashamed, disgusted? Has Díaz betrayed family secrets, aired dirty laundry? Winning the Pulitzer, as both authors did, must help legitimize perceived transgressions. But if you dream of having your work stay alive beyond your tenure on earth, if you hope to see it beside the unforgettable voices that are part of our literary diaspora, then you must be fearless in every aspect of your writing.

Renowned editor and author Gordon Lish, in his famous writing class (which combined equal parts psychotherapy, boot camp, Jerry Springer, and Socratic method), used to shock the assembled company by asking whether we were waiting for our parents to die before writing something worth reading. Some students were offended by this suggestion, but I felt it made a great deal of sense. Writers tend to censor themselves for fear of what other people think, especially those at home. Imagine writing a sex scene or describing the inner thoughts of a character who felt that his mother was controlling and suffocating. Now imagine your mother reading it.

Philip Roth has, over the course of his career, constructed an elaborate hall of mirrors through which he refracts the self as character and character as self. Yet the dialogue between the id and ego running through his books provides an uncensored picture of the inner workings of a post–World War II Jewish American male. Paradoxically, the more Roth seems to reveal, the greater an enigma he is. One thing, however, is clear: he never dreamed that his work would hurt or embarrass his parents. "My mother was unambiguously proud of my first published stories. She had no idea that there could be anything seriously offensive about them and, when she came upon articles in the Jewish press intimating that I was a traitor, couldn't understand what my detractors were talking about. When she was once in doubt—having been shaken by a derogatory remark she'd overheard at a Hadassah meeting—she asked me if it could possibly be true that I was anti-Semitic, and when I smiled and shook my head no, she was entirely satisfied." When your mother approves, who cares if the whole of Hadassah thinks you're the devil?

Not all writers need enemies, real or imagined, to fuel their imaginations, nor do they necessarily write to expose their loved ones. I have found in my work with writers that those who appear most confident on the page are often those most confident of their parents' belief in them. One author with whom I worked over many years always struck me as blessed in the area of maternal support. She was the youngest of a large and gifted literary family but she was the first to publish. Her mother had been a writer and reporter for a major newspaper who, in accordance with the dictates of her era, subverted her drive and talents and redirected her energies into raising her family. She dutifully named each child for a deceased member of the family until the birth of this youngest child, for whom she chose a name of her own liking. "I looked at her in the hospital and saw how beautiful she was," the mother told me at the publication of her daughter's third book. "And then I gave her the most beautiful name I knew." When I asked if she always knew her daughter would be a writer, she replied without hesitation, "Oh yes."

It may be that those who are most loved and adored are those buoyed enough to write in the face of the world's indifference. It may be that the bolstered ego is the one resilient enough to live the disquieting writer's life. Many were convinced that Roth had it in for his mother, given the character of Sophie Portnoy, but they didn't understand that he had permission to create her. Reading *The Facts*, one gets the impression that Roth is the ultimate mama's boy, a prince, and that he could only paint a portrait of an über-Jewish mother because he was supremely confident of his own mother's love.

✻

For many writers, though, parental approval remains thwarted but much desired, if only on an unconscious level. The stamp of approval that publication can represent may feel like that longed-for approbation from a distracted or depressed mother or a cold and distant father. There is no better record of such anguish than that described in Franz Kafka's *Letter to His Father*. This slim volume is the extended lament of a son whose failure to please his impossibly rigid and terrifying father describes the predicament of all writers who are caught between a child's need and a parent's rejection. "When I began to do something you did not like and you threatened me with the prospect of failure, my veneration for your opinion was so great that the failure became inevitable. . . . I lost confidence in my own actions. I was wavering, doubtful. The older I became, the more material there was for you to bring up against me as evidence of my worthlessness. . . . The aversion you naturally and immediately took to my writing was, for once, welcome to me." But Kafka's tone of sharp adolescent rebuke quickly changes direction. "Of course it was a delusion; I was not, or, to put it optimistically, was not yet, free. My writing was all about you; all I did there, after all, was to bemoan what I could not bemoan upon your breast. . . . My valuation of myself was much more dependent on you than on anything else, such as some external success." In other words, the creator of *The Metamorphosis*, one of the twentieth century's most enduring parables of alienation, was himself crushed like a bug.

Just as a patient may spend months if not years in therapy protecting his or her parents, explaining that they did the best they could, rather than facing the sharp pain of their rejection or abuse, the writer resists exposing the family. Indeed, the desire to protect one's family is innate. Yet at the same time, the impetus to write often emanates from the need to express painful or shattering experiences. At the age of twelve, Charles Dickens was sent away from his family to work for twelve hours a day at a blacking factory housed in a rat-infested warehouse. When his father was finally released from debtor's prison, he apparently made no attempt to retrieve Charles from the factory; instead, upon collecting a small inheritance, he moved the rest of the family into a house.

Dickens's sense of abandonment is palpable in all his fiction, much of it peopled with orphans. In his autobiography Dickens recalled, "The deep remembrance of the sense I had of being utterly neglected and hopeless, of the shame I felt in my position; of the misery it was to my young heart . . . cannot be written. My whole nature was so penetrated with grief and humiliation of such considerations, that even now, famous and caressed and happy, I often forget in my dreams that I have a dear wife and children; even that I am a man; and wander desolately back to that time in my life." In author and psychoanalyst Leonard Shengold's book on the effects of childhood abuse and deprivation, *Soul Murder*, he posits that "Dickens became determined never again to suffer such helplessness and misery; the trauma fed an intense ambition."

Writers are motivated by many things, but it is often some variation on the Dickens theme, some lethal combination of hurt and desire, that keeps a writer in the ring. How is it that some writers are able to transform the stuff of their lives—its people and circumstances—into their own creations while others tiptoe around their subjects? One determining factor is entitlement, the feeling that you have the right to say whatever you want about whomever you want and, what's more, that your notions about people and their actions are defensible. Some writers have no qualms about writing nasty portraits of either strangers or loved ones. That's part of the pleasure of reading someone like Paul Theroux, who on the surface appears to be an equal-opportunity misanthrope.

Theroux's much-maligned memoir, *Sir Vidia's Shadow*, tells the story of his thirty-year friendship with V. S. Naipaul. It was written, he explains, after the abrupt and somewhat brutal ending of the relationship by the older writer. Naipaul mysteriously stopped returning calls and faxes from his protégé, and when questioned by Theroux in a chance meeting on a London street, told him, "Take it on the chin and move on." Well, telling a writer to take anything on the chin and move on is a little like asking a boxer not to hit back. Indeed, Theroux's critics felt that the book was little more than a series of sucker punches at Naipaul, an unseemly airing of dirty linen, or as one reviewer wrote, "one long Oedipal screed."

Theroux was accused primarily of using his mentor in a manner unbecoming a writer. There is a clear bias in the culture against those who pull a *Mommie Dearest*. In a *New York Times Book Review* essay, Theroux rejected the critics' label of revisionist and betrayer. "Meditating upon the world and what is most familiar is the preoccupation of writers," he began. "Sometimes that includes re-creating our nearest and dearest, and our secrets. . . . The best writers are the most fanatical; so the truest portrait of a writer can never be a study in virtue." Virtue or vice, there is no writer who does not brush up against the moral predicament of what is fair game, no writer who doesn't consider whether to withhold a telling detail for reasons of taste or simple human kindness. "I think 'taste' is a social concept and not an artistic one," explained John Updike in an interview reprinted in his collection *Hugging the Shore*. "I'm willing to show good taste, if I can, in somebody else's living room, but our reading life is too short for a writer to be in any way polite. Since his words enter into another's brain in silence and intimacy, he should be as honest and explicit as we are with ourselves."

In many ways writers are equally scared by their ambitious hearts. Just as they are often accused of exposing others, they often fear being exposed themselves, especially to their families. To be a writer, to come out of that closet, is to announce that you are different in some way. Until a writer is established and thus somewhat protected by the veneer of success that publication brings, his life and his struggle to emerge can be fraught with humiliation. Having a mentor, as the young Theroux learned, can be a defining experience and may provide the necessary confidence to release one's ambition. "His friendship was different from anyone else's. . . . He knew more about my writing ambition than I had dared to tell my own family."

Calling attention to your literary ambition, especially within a family dynamic, may involve unwelcome scrutiny, or worse, derision. One writer told me that after she was published, her family came to consider her a jerk. Another told me that her siblings were so jealous, they didn't read the book, or if they did, didn't say anything. When I asked the readers of my blog if they remembered any hurtful things people had said to them about their writing, the comments poured in. Most poignant were those involving family members. One woman recounted the moment she proudly handed her mother her PhD thesis. The mother's response: "Did you type that all by yourself?" At a wedding, a writer warmly greeted a cousin he hadn't seen for a long time and began to catch up. She asked him how his novel was coming along. He explained that, eight years and counting, he still wasn't done. His cousin tapped her index finger to her temple, to indicate that the problem might be in his head. But my all-time favorite came from a man who, as a teenager, confided in his father that he wanted to be a writer. "Writers," his dad replied, "are a dime a dozen."

It is the mentor who understands the struggles and the indignities, the mentor who inhabits the life the young writer craves, and the mentor who, in loco parentis, sets the standard. "It gave me great confidence to have his approval," continued Theroux, "but his approval was anything but casual. I was also intensely aware of his intelligence, and did not write a word without wondering what he would say about it." *Sir Vidia's Shadow* strikes me as a welcome cautionary tale for all writers in search of approval, parental or otherwise. The results can be shattering. Though Theroux is a wonderful stylist, beneath the veneer of his highly polished prose is a child's firm belief in his own tantrum.

Most writers, like most children, need to tell. The only problem is that much of what they need to tell will provoke the ire of parent-critics, who are determined to tell writer-children what they can and cannot say. Unless you have sufficient ego and feel entitled to tell your story, you will be stymied in your effort to create. You think you can't write, but perhaps you can't tell. Writing is nothing if not breaking the silence. The problem is, no one likes a snitch. On top of this, contemporary critics would have us believe that we are in an age of unparalleled navel-gazing. On the contrary, there is far greater cultural censure in taking one's pain seriously. As Alice Miller notes in her book *Banished Knowledge*, "Not to take one's own suffering seriously, to make light of it or even laugh at it, is considered good manners in our culture. This attitude is even called a virtue, and many people are proud of their lack of sensitivity toward their own fate and above all their own childhood."

For all the familial anxiety attendant on the publication of a first book, I am always struck when I find that the dedication page is devoted to the author's parents. Indeed, some of the most damning books about childhood or family life are thus dedicated. Pat Conroy's unforgettable first novel, *The Great Santini*, about the abuse a young boy suffers at the hands of his brutal military father, "is dedicated with love and thanks to Frances 'Peggy' Conroy, the grandest of mothers and teachers, and to Colonel Donald Conroy, U.S.M.C. Ret., the grandest of fathers and Marine aviators." Dorothy Allison dedicated her first novel, *Bastard Out of Carolina*, a horrific story about the abuse of a young girl and her mother's failure to protect her, to her deceased mother: "For Mama. Ruth Gibson Allison 1935–1990." Even J. D. Salinger dedicated his masterpiece, *The Catcher in the Rye*, to his mother.

Of course, parental approval isn't the most important thing in the world. One hopes that by the time a person reaches maturity, peer approval, mate approval, and more important, self-approval pick up where your parents leave off. But you don't have to be a Freudian to recognize the impact of parental influence. Our house is our world, and within its walls we find safety and comfort or coldness and danger or, more likely, something in between. We are praised and scolded according to a great many criteria, and we piece together our own little fictions of how and why we are the way we are.

If stories took you far away when you were a child, if characters from books kept you company as you peered out a rainy window and tried to discern that great mystery of how other people live, then you believe that books are the most important things in life. If you were drawn to books and in turn to writing, chances are you found the world wanting. You knew that a record had to be kept, or the world or you would disappear. People are motivated to write for a variety of reasons, but it's the child writer who has figured out, early on, that writing is about saving your soul.

⚜

Where, after all, does the drama of the gifted child begin but at her own dinner table? The material we continue to grapple with all our lives has more to do with that kid than any grown writer wants to admit. That's where you were told in any number of spoken and unspoken ways that you were good enough, or not good enough, or too good to be true. That's where you got the message that you would either go very far or amount to nothing. That's where you first encountered acceptance, rejection, approbation, or opprobrium. The messages you received may have enabled you to raise your hand in class, read your story aloud; something told you that people cared about what you had to say. Or perhaps you went underground because you sensed your ideas were shameful or dangerous. Or that you were suspect.

Just as one child takes the message of his glorious future and goes very far, another is paralyzed by the expectation. Likewise, the child who is consistently disparaged may make something of himself, just to show the bastard who called him worthless. Or he may set out on a course of self-destruction, believing himself as unworthy as the adult who crippled his small soul. But more than any emotional Molotov cocktail of abuse and deprivation, or any showers of love and support, I sometimes think, what distinguishes the person who goes on to become a serious writer is his or her tolerance or love of solitude.

Nothing in our culture applauds the desire to be alone. Being alone, in fact, is the great crime. From the time we are little, parents tend to worry if we spend too much time by ourselves. In school, there is probably nothing worse than being branded as a loner. The culture is suspicious of people who want to be alone. It's okay if you turn out to be a famously reclusive and highly regarded writer such as Thomas Pynchon, but not so okay if you wind up on national news being led away from a small shack in the woods where six bodies are buried.

I can't think of a riskier business than writing. Not only because so few succeed in conventional terms, with publication and some payment, but because it almost certainly requires banishment. First, there is the literal act of removing oneself, of choosing solitude. Then there is the psychological separation, holding oneself apart. And finally, the potential rejection of friends and family, critics and publishers. You don't have to be Philip Roth to incite the tribe. Far less incendiary portraits will forever taint your relations with loved ones. But you cannot censor yourself; successful writing never comes about through half measures. For most people the first book is about the family, if only metaphorically, and it must be conquered as surely as the walls at Jericho.

I now think that I was drawn to poetry during my high school years because it must have seemed to my young mind that I could hide my feelings, if not the truth itself, behind the language of metaphor and simile. To me, poems were like great collages that could be assembled so as to keep some people out. Images were locks to which only extremely perceptive readers had the key. Finally, a teacher in graduate school called me out. My poems were a series of opaque images connected by bad grammar, she said during a private conference in one of the airless rooms at Columbia's Dodge Hall. Then she placed her thin blue pencil on the table, looked me directly in the eyes, and asked if I was intentionally trying to confuse people, or did my obfuscation have some aesthetic design? At that moment I wished for two things: an oxygen mask to eject from some invisible overhead compartment, and an adult to place it over my ashen face.

I wasn't at the point in my writing life where I believed I had control over my intention. If someone had asked why I wrote, I would have said, *I just write.* I also would have claimed, *I can't help what I write.* As hard as I worked at revising my poems, I was working equally hard to keep meaning at bay. I was terrified for anyone—most of all myself—to discover what I was trying to say. You see, I was the good child. And I was heavily invested in being a good, achieving daughter. So you can imagine how terrifying it was when I first took my teacher's advice and finally stopped writing incomprehensible poems and wrote some pieces that even my parents could understand.

It would be overly simplistic and false to blame fear of exposure as the single reason I quit writing and became an editor. I think I quit writing poems for a variety of reasons, some of which I still struggle with. I do know that when I began my life as an editorial assistant after graduate school I found it far easier to work on other people's writing and I liked my job; after all, it provided plenty of vicarious writing experiences. As I got promoted through the editorial ranks, I found a great deal of the work rewarding and validating, such as good reviews for my authors, and their appreciation of my contribution. My closeness to authors and their work satisfied much of my own creative drive. As a young editor I was drawn to writers who went out on an emotional ledge. As I worked with them, I was also aware of my nose pressed up to the glass, in awe of their gifts as well as their fearlessness.

Conversely, when I read a relatively well-written manuscript that made no particular impression (which would describe most of the manuscripts editors evaluate), I couldn't help thinking, *Good child*. Here is yet another well-behaved manuscript that will be seen but not heard. In order to tell the truth (and I don't mean what happened in "real life" in any conventional sense, but the emotional truth), to raise what is only hinted at, the writer would have had to risk his place at the table, which is often too threatening. Unless you are the family provocateur whose role in life is whistleblower, it's damn hard to blow the house down when it's the only one you've got. Whether out of hurt, jealousy, shame, or a sense of violation, most family members will not be happy with your work whether you've written them in or, as in a will, written them out.

        ✦

One of the most public and wholesale rejections of a writer occurred in 1975, when *Esquire* published "La Côte Basque," an early chapter from Truman Capote's novel-in-progress *Answered Prayers*. Capote's women friends from New York's café society were horrified by the exposure of their secrets and promptly banished him from their inner circle. According to his editor, Joe Fox, at Random House, "Virtually every friend he had in this world ostracized him for telling thinly disguised tales out of school, and many of them never spoke to him again." Their little writer friend, the elfin troublemaker, had taken things just a little too far. Capote crossed a line he claimed he hadn't known existed, though he confessed to a certain amount of delicious anticipation before the piece ran, and he agreed to be photographed for the magazine's cover with a fedora wickedly tilted atop his head while he pared his fingernails with a very long blade.

    In George Plimpton's oral history of Capote, John Barry Ryan was bemused by the reaction. "The people who after 'befriending' Truman, accepting this asp onto their bosoms, were surprised that the snake bit!" he recounted. "Snakes bite! Truman certainly signed no Official Secrets Act. Everybody who was exposed to him in the period I'm familiar with knew if you told Truman something, it was the equivalent of telling forty other people. You would no more ask Truman to treat something as if for his ears only than you would throw bread upon the water and expect it to come back!" But as Liz Smith pointed out in her *New York* magazine article, detailing the public outrage in response to the story, "It is one thing to tell the nastiest story to all your fifty best friends; it's another to set it down in cold Century Expanded type." Capote committed the literary equivalent of premeditated murder: in cold type.

The reaction of Capote's New York City peers wasn't entirely unlike the response of a group of Dubliners more than fifty years earlier when a chronicle of Irish life with a cast of hundreds was published in a novel that was beginning to make some waves. According to Richard Ellman's biography, James Joyce waited in vain for the commendation of his fellow Dubliners when he published his masterpiece, *Ulysses*. Instead, "a tremor went through quite of few of his countrymen, who feared the part he might have assigned to them. 'Are you in it?' or 'Am I in it?' they asked the few people known to have copies."

Every writer uses the people in his life—what other experience does he or she have? For every Dubliner who was scandalized by the publication of Joyce's *Ulysses* and every East Side socialite who was shocked by Capote's "La Côte Basque," there are probably as many people who felt hurt that they were not included. What's worse: to read something scathing about yourself, or to be deemed unworthy of comment? Then there are those who think they are the basis for a character, when nothing was farther from the writer's mind. Joan Didion explains that her first novel, *Run River*, wasn't autobiographical except that it took place in Sacramento. "A lot of people there seemed to think that I had somehow maligned them and their families, but it was just a made-up story. The central incident came from a little one-inch story in the *New York Times* about a trial in the Carolinas."

If you are going to be honest and write about all the untidy emotions, the outsize desires, the hideous envy, and the disturbing fantasies that make us human, how can you not offend your loved ones, your neighbors, and your community? If you are a mother and you write a book about a mother who kills her child, how will people look at you? *What will they think?* If you confess to something far less heinous, such as enjoying being spanked, as Daphne Merkin did in the *New Yorker*, your morals will still be scrutinized by those who think such behavior is unbecoming to a mother. Henry Miller can enjoy a good spanking; an Upper East Side mom has some explaining to do. How can a writer have his main character, say Rabbit in *Rabbit at Rest*, sleep with his daughter-in-law and not at least arouse the suspicions of his loved ones? I'm not suggesting that anyone in Updike's family thought he was guilty of such a transgression, but if I were his son or daughter-in-law I might have felt a little uncomfortable at the next Thanksgiving dinner. *Um, could you please pass the yams?*

Writers want to believe that their readers are sophisticated enough to understand that writing and life are two different things, especially when it comes to fiction. Once a writer creates a scene, a character, or a snippet of dialogue, describes a room, a scent, an inflection of voice, she leaves "reality" behind.

Edith Wharton describes this frustration in her autobiography, *A Backward Glance*. "All novelists who describe what is called 'society life' are pursued by the exasperating accusation of putting flesh-and-blood people into their books. Anyone gifted with the least creative faculty knows the absurdity of such a charge. 'Real people' transported into a work of the imagination would instantly cease to be real; only those born of the creator's brain can give the least illusion of reality. . . . Nothing can be more trying to the creative writer than to have a clumsy finger point at one of the beings born in that mysterious other-world of invention, with the playful accusation: 'Of course we all recognize your aunt Eliza!'"

Though the writer's aim is to convey truth, it certainly isn't to tell the truth per se. There is simply nothing worse than a novice writer who cries out in his own defense, when a scene is criticized for not seeming real, that "it really happened that way." No, no, no. Everything you put on the page is a deliberate manipulation of what happened, written to keep the reader entertained, moved, sympathetic, horrified, scared, whatever. You are never writing what *really* happened. Instead, you are choosing words, building images, creating a rhythm, sense, and structure through which to move your characters and unfold your story. You are making a thousand minuscule choices that you hope will add up in such a way that your readers believe what they're reading is real. And this is why, when the writer is successful, the best fiction reads like nonfiction and the best nonfiction like a novel.

It was Capote who first blatantly and brilliantly combined the two categories with his "nonfiction novel" *In Cold Blood*. The effect was dazzling, and the book forever changed the face of contemporary nonfiction. Perhaps the acclaim so emboldened him that when he set out to write *Answered Prayers*, which he planned as the American equivalent of Proust's *Remembrance of Things Past*, he couldn't imagine that his efforts would be spurned. Like Edith Wharton, he expected some sophistication on the part of his refined society friends and was astonished by their nearly universal abandonment. "What did they expect?" he was quoted as saying. "I'm a writer, I use everything. Did all those people think I was just there to entertain them?" The desperation of his question supplies its own answer.

Though more than a few theories exist about the balance of this uncompleted novel, Capote's editor postulates that he never committed another word to the page. Increasing alcoholism and addiction were partially responsible for his inability to continue as a writer. But it also seems painfully true that Capote's great talent, which opened every door of his life and secured the love of those whose attention he craved, had finally and irrevocably slammed shut. "The problem was," said John Knowles, "he had no stature socially speaking. He had no family. He was only an ornament. There was nothing for him to fall back on. You could drop Truman overnight because you weren't going to alienate anybody. Truman was just all by himself out there."

Which is how most writers feel at the end of the day— especially if they've gone out on a limb. Even if you have position or family or people depending on you, the truth is that everyone is provincial at heart. Everyone defends his or her cave and clan. If you attack with humor you'll be given

THE WICKED CHILD ❧ 69

more leeway, but not much. But writing isn't about attacking, defending, or proving once and for all that these people are bad, phony, corrupt, or evil. It isn't even about telling the "truth." Great writing is meant to crush us, entertain and move us, return us to ourselves with some greater understanding of the world and its workings.

❧

You must give yourself permission to tell. Most important, give up the vain hope that people will like your work. People like vanilla ice cream. Hope that they love your work or hate it. That they find it exquisite or revolting. I think Cocteau had the right idea when he said, "Listen carefully to first criticisms made of your work. Note just what it is about your work that the critics don't like and cultivate it. That's the only part of your work that's individual and worth keeping." Throw off the shackles of approval, of wanting to be liked. The minute you capitulate to changing even a single adjective to please someone else, or choose one adjective over another to protect a person's feelings, you pull the plug on your own respirator.

Philip Roth admits that the attacks on him and his work at the beginning of his career were absolutely decisive in his growth and success as a writer. As he tells it in *The Facts*, after a particularly ugly public ordeal during which he was attacked by nearly all sides at a symposium called "The Crisis of Conscience in Minority Writers of Fiction," held at Yeshiva University, Roth swore over a pastrami sandwich at the Stage Delicatessen never to "write about Jews again." "I couldn't see then," Roth writes, "fresh from the event, that the most bruising public exchange of my life constituted not the end of my imagination's involvement with the Jews, let alone an excommunication, but the real beginning of my thralldom. . . . The Yeshiva battle, instead of putting me off Jewish fictional subjects for good, demonstrated as nothing had before the full force of aggressive rage that made the issue of Jewish self-definitions inflammatory. . . . How could I conclude otherwise when I was told that every word I wrote was a disgrace, potentially endangering every Jew?"

Unlike Capote, who was deeply dependent on the love and positive attention of his friends, Roth was fueled by the disdain his work exacted. Or rather, realizing he had touched a live wire, he went for the socket with his future books. As painful as any negative attention might be—symposiums gone wrong, scathing reviews, rejection by your entire people, nasty remarks at your mother's Hadassah meeting, a tell-all memoir by your ex that exposes your cruelty—it is only temporal. As Roth figured out early on, if your book causes a commotion, even the negative kind, you will have made a platform for yourself, something very few writers attain, and from there you will have something to live up to or something to live down. "My humiliation before the Yeshiva belligerents—indeed, the angry Jewish resistance that I aroused virtually from the start—was the luckiest break I could have had," Roth writes. "I was branded."

Many aspiring writers have gathered their marbles and gone home for far less cause. It takes a supreme talent and fierce self-belief to write in the face of so much acrimony. If you are a good child, you must stop trying to please or protect others with your work or, worse, your silence. And if you are a wicked child, you must transform your ambition into something more universal than the particulars of your own circumstance. If you can do that, you will have the last word.

4.

THE
SELF-PROMOTER

IN AN AGE WHEN FAME IS TANTAMOUNT TO godliness, perhaps the only modesty left is false modesty. Bald ambition in other professions is far more acceptable than in the arts—we still like our poets starving and our novelists tucked away in garrets. Indeed, when Apple Computer first introduced the PowerBook, it was shocking to see Tama Janowitz in the first of a series of advertisements that showed what "real" people had stored on their laptops. What kind of writer would make herself the object of such blatant commercialism? One who wants to extend her fame—or perhaps one who simply needs a new computer. If it's okay for athletes to endorse sportswear, why shouldn't Katie Roiphe hoist a spanking-new Coach bag? Lillian Hellman draped herself in mink, the Blackglama ad copy above her head asking the question every writer contemplates, whether he admits it or not: What becomes a legend most?

The contemporary frenzy of literary self-promotion is not without historical precedent. The man considered America's most important poet took it upon himself, just weeks before his thirty-sixth birthday, to self-publish one of the most ecstatic works of literature in the American canon. Imagine how the young Whitman must have felt when, just two months after publication, he opened a letter welcoming him unequivocally into the fold. "I am not blind to the worth of the wonderful gift of *Leaves of Grass*. I find it the most extraordinary piece of wit & wisdom that America has yet contributed," wrote Emerson upon receiving a copy. "I greet you at the beginning of a great career."

The letter was the literary equivalent of the Red Sea parting, providing passage to the promised land. What writer doesn't dream of such a reception? But after the publication of a few less-welcoming notices in various newspapers, the letter mysteriously found its way into the *New York Tribune* without Emerson's permission or knowledge. According to Whitman biographer Justin Kaplan, the editor of the *Tribune* may have persuaded the poet to release the letter, but once the encomium was released, "he fell on it like a hawk." Whitman sent copies of the *Tribune* clipping to Longfellow and other celebrities, arranged to have the letter printed in *Life Illustrated*, and circulated it widely to editors and critics in the form of a small broadside that he had printed up. And then, as if that weren't enough, he had Emerson's words (or blurb, in today's parlance) stamped in gold on the spine of the second edition of his book. "Torn out of context, gaudily displayed, this Ali Baba formula appeared to be an endorsement of the new poems Emerson could not possibly have seen," reports Kaplan. "And further compounding what a Boston paper had called 'the grossest violation of literary comity and courtesy that ever passed under our notice.'"

When you gaze at pictures of Walt Whitman, with his long white beard and searing eyes, when you consider the exuberant life force coursing through his poems, it's a little unsettling to imagine him salivating over his endorsement, tirelessly printing broadsides to distribute, and sucking up to celebrity writers of the day. Poets are frequently scene stealers; their flair for drama and their outsized lives the stuff of legend. Poets, like their poems, are good at making strong impressions. In a *New Yorker* article entitled "Big Poetry," Stephen Schiff describes Pulitzer Prize–winning poet Jorie Graham as a queenlike figure parading through her fiefdom, "swathed in black from head to foot, with enough bracelets and necklaces and rings to herniate a belly dancer. . . . She wears [them] to plant tulips at dawn." Another Pulitzer Prize winner, Richard Howard, always donned a sequined tie and would delicately lift a monocle, hanging from a long gold chain, to his eye before reciting a poem to our class. I fondly remember sitting cross-legged at the back of a packed auditorium at New York University, unable to see Allen Ginsberg except when he leapt up from behind the lectern to emphasize his words, his bald head springing up like some insane jack-in-the-box. And everyone's favorite eccentric, Marianne Moore, was as famous for her cape and tricorn hat— like a Buñuel priest crossed with Miss Clavel—as for her line breaks.

In sharp contrast to the gold-stamped self-proclamation of Whitman's arrival, Emily Dickinson's first halting lines to

Thomas Wentworth Higginson reveal how one's approach to one's work influences its reception. "Mr. Higginson, Are you too deeply occupied to say if my Verse is alive?" begins her delicate gambit to the *Atlantic Monthly* editor whose "Letter to a Young Contributor" caught her attention. Scholars and readers alike still wonder how a writer of her genius could have been satisfied without the consummation of publication.

"The Mind is so near itself—it cannot see, distinctly—and I have none to ask—" she continued in that first missive to Higginson, acute with trepidation, confessing that particular vertigo all writers experience as they peer down at their own work and feel dizzyingly insecure. "I enclose my name—asking you, if you please—Sir—to tell me what is true. That you will not betray me—it is needless to ask—since Honor is its own pawn—" It is almost as if in that first letter Dickinson foretold Higginson's eventual betrayal; she died leaving more than two thousand unpublished poems.

When I was making my first, shy forays into the world of literary magazines with my sheaf of poems, I would regularly attend poetry readings. I was always amazed at the young poets who pressed their manuscripts into the hands of famous poets after their readings. *The chutzpah. The nerve.* My friends and I would remain in our seats, collectively outraged at the sheer audacity, not to mention the hubris. After all, how could an established writer, upon completing his reading, his own words still ringing in his ears, possibly be interested in having some young writer's manuscript foisted upon him? What was he expected to *do* with it? Long after my friends and I had stopped condemning those strident young writers, I still found myself bemused by their actions. I continued to wonder what combination of ingredients propelled a writer to seek an audience outside herself and what mixture relegated her work to the drawer. We will never know what enabled Walt Whitman to promote his work with the fervor of a Paris Hilton. Nor will we know what series of rejections, internal or external, kept Dickinson from pursuing publication beyond the censorious Higginson. Though most writers live somewhere between Whitman's narcissism and Dickinson's dysphoria, I suspect that most writers dream of their own fame—whether or not they act on it.

❧

Do the act of creating and the desire for fame run along the same continuum? Are there brilliant writers out there who never attempt to get their work published? How ironic or sad or tragic is it that one of the greatest American writers stopped publishing his work for most of his adult life, his silence broken only when he sued the foolhardy soul who dared tamper with his writing, or when he blocked a biography by refusing to grant permission to his work and letters. In Joyce Maynard's memoir of her ten-month-long relationship with J. D. Salinger, she tells us that she finally worked up the courage to ask the blaring question at the center of his silence: Was he still writing? "He responds that he writes every day. Always has. As our friendship develops, he speaks about his writing just in passing, as if that goes without saying, and occasionally he will speak of having had one of those weeks where most of the pages end up in the trash."

Eventually Maynard broaches the second half of the question, asking Salinger why he doesn't publish anymore. "'Publication is a messy business,' he tells me. 'You'll see what I mean one day. All those loutish cocktail party–going opinion-givers, so ready to pass judgment. Bad enough when they do that to a writer. But when they start in on your characters—and they do—it's murder.'" But of all the advice Salinger gives the teenager, his most poignant message has to do with freedom, the freedom of the artist to work with impunity. "Some day," he tells Maynard, "there will be a story you want to tell for no better reason than because it matters to you more than any other. You'll stop looking over your shoulder to make sure you're keeping everybody happy, and you'll simply write what's real and true. Honest writing always makes people nervous, and they'll think of all kinds of ways to make your life hell. One day a long time from now you'll cease to care anymore whom you please or what anybody has to say about you. That's when you'll finally produce the work you're capable of."

In publishing her memoir, it might be said, Maynard finally took Salinger's advice and threw off the shackles of approval, his most of all. But she was roundly criticized for *using* Salinger, for exposing the writer who most avidly protects his privacy for her own fame. Maynard was included in a list of writers whom John Updike labeled "Judas biographers" because she exploited an experience with a more famous writer. No stranger to this kind of attack, Maynard has withstood the enmity of her peers since she first gazed out from the cover of the *New York Times Magazine* at the age of nineteen with her enormous eyes and bemused smile and a man's watch slipping around her thin wrist. "Maynard is no longer as famous as she once was," reported a *New York Times* feature on the writer, "but ask anyone of roughly her age who grew up in this country, and he will not only know who she is—but chances are he will react to her name with startling venom. Perhaps to them it seems like only yesterday that, as teenagers, they picked up that issue of the *New York Times Magazine* with Maynard on the cover and wondered, *Why isn't that me?*"

It is my educated guess that every time a writer gets a big advance, a big feature story, or a big movie deal, or climbs onto the bestseller list, other writers wonder, *Why isn't that me?* And we often conclude that the person at the center of attention somehow manipulated circumstances. "Oh, you know, he's a total self-promoter," we sneer when an up-and-coming writer aligns himself with a powerful editor or agent. No matter how a person arrives, at some point he is seen as complicit in his admission to the inner circle. What we fail to remember is that being a writer includes the implicit hope of becoming known. How comfortable or uncomfortable a writer is with that exposure may be the decisive factor in whether or not he is heard from.

I once acquired a book by a young writer whose proposal, unbeknownst to me, had made the rounds of the major publishing houses, all of which had turned it down. The proposal was ragged and unorganized, but the emotion and humor came through in a way that struck me and that I thought would appeal to young women struggling with self-esteem and identity issues. The writer arrived for a meeting on a drizzly March day, her head and upper body wrapped in a monklike shawl, her long eyelashes darkened by the rain. We talked about her memoir and what she hoped to accomplish with it, and I knew even before she left the meeting that I wanted to work with her; she was warm and funny and smart. And I had the feeling she would write a book I wished I could have read when I was her age.

No sooner did I sign up the book for a modest advance than my phone started ringing off the hook. "Do you have any idea who you just signed?" one reporter friend beseeched. "You know what she's done, don't you?" I acted as if I knew perfectly well, not wanting to seem the dupe of the century, and called her agent posthaste. I discovered that allegations of professional misconduct had attached themselves to this writer like lint. "She's a nightmare, I just hope you know that, a total networker," one editor chimed in. If you were to believe the rumors, she had plagiarized, had sex on the desk where she worked at a major magazine, and had snorted coke off a toilet seat. But her worst sin, it seemed, was wanting attention, and in that pursuit she mined her life for material and used her pen as if it were a needle in her arm.

Just as we are suspicious of the gold digger's love for her ninety-year-old husband, we view the writer who courts fame with suspicion, as if being serious about your work and being determined to see it disseminated were at cross-purposes. After all, how could a ruthless self-promoter or blatant fame-seeker possibly produce a work of importance? The moment you find the spotlight, or it finds you, people will project motivation and intent that may or may not apply to you. "The degree of derision Maynard inspires is astonishing," said Jonathan Yardley of the *Washington Post*. Another writer, a Yale classmate of Maynard's, said, "She has hacked her way through three decades wrapped in a delusion torn from an Oliver Sacks casebook: The Woman Who Mistook Herself for Someone Interesting." It is unclear which sin is greater: writing about oneself or achieving early success. From the audacious act of publishing her first memoir, *Looking Back*, at nineteen, to dropping out of Yale and offering herself up to the great one, to writing about the details of her domestic life in a vastly popular column, working non-stop to keep her three children diapered, fed, and well cared for, Maynard excavated her life for material.

Does any writer do otherwise? It is easy to say that Joyce Maynard only wants attention, but I would venture to guess that she hopes people will actually like what she writes. It's also easy to attack Maynard because she is a woman, and domestic life and female concerns are considered negligible. You can call her a Judas writer because it is still taboo, or at least bad form, to expose the sins of the fathers. (We all prefer to imagine the solitary genius of J. D. Salinger rather than contemplate his undercooked lamb-burgers and propensity for young girls.) And as with Capote, it's easy to lambaste Maynard because she has no influence to speak of beyond headline fodder; she doesn't control any powerful institutions. But the real reason it is so easy to attack her is that she leaves herself wide open.

❧

Even after many years as an editor working with first-time authors, watching them emerge into the spotlight, and observing how that process affects their egos, I find that my feelings waffle between admiration and consternation for those who bask in the glow of their own glory and those who cannot come to terms with their desire for greatness. I've always believed that one has to want in order to get, but when the want becomes all-consuming, or at least more consuming than the work itself, the process is perverted. Editors and agents encounter on a daily basis the many faces of ambition and its guises—including humility. I used to believe that an inverse relationship existed between self-esteem and greatness, that the writers who thought they were really great usually fell quite short of their own high estimation. And those who had a healthy dose of insecurity about their work usually produced the most accomplished prose. But it isn't always so. Sometimes the most self-satisfied and arrogant are truly brilliant. Which is why we keep letting them back for another dizzyingly explosive round of their punches.

Norman Mailer, the writer best known for literally punching out critics and making headlines (though his body of work actually towers over his publicity stunts), collected and annotated all of his assorted writings at the ripe old age of thirty-six, producing a single volume unabashedly titled *Advertisements for Myself*. The jacket featured a head shot that more closely resembled an actor's, with the author sporting a sea captain's cap jauntily tilted toward the back of his head, a stray curl insouciantly jutting onto his forehead. His bedroom eyes are trained somewhere in the middle distance, and his pretty lips are just slightly ajar. The occasion for this collection, according to the author, was "that I am imprisoned with a perception which will settle for nothing less than making a revolution in the consciousness of our time. Whether rightly or wrongly, it is then obvious that I would go so far as to think it is my present and future work which will have the deepest influence of any work being done by an American novelist in these years. I could be wrong, and if I am, then I'm the fool who will pay the bill, but I think we can all agree that it would cheat this collection of its true interest to present myself as more modest than I am." All right then.

The whole question of ego and writers is extremely tricky, but there is simply nothing more suspect than the self-satisfied writer. We are put off when a writer bursts on the scene and proclaims his own greatness, as novelist Dale Peck did in a much-publicized change of publisher. "I do think I'm one of the best writers around, and I want to be recognized for that," he was quoted as saying in the *New York Observer*. On the one hand, I admire Peck. Good for him for being able to say "I'm the greatest." But his pronouncement also reeks of self-satisfaction, and we like to imagine that our writers are suffering on behalf of their art.

In 2005, Lionel Shriver won the Orange Prize for her controversial novel, *We Need to Talk About Kevin*, about a mother unable to love her son, who perpetrates a Columbine-style massacre. Shriver seemed to receive even more ink for a statement she made to the press upon receiving the prize than for the book itself: "I have been very ambitious from the start on this prize," she famously said. "I wanted it badly." She defended her comment, saying that men are encouraged to compete, whereas women are meant to tamp down their desire for success. She's not wrong, and any person up for any prize probably feels the same.

Still, we prefer to have greatness conferred by others. But in our highly conflicted fame- and success-loving culture, we are also meant to act grateful, humble, and demure when our name is called and we step up to the podium to accept our trophy. We also hate sore losers. Runners-up, beware; if you are not gracious, you will be deemed an asshole. We like at least a dollop of self-doubt with our greatness. "You wouldn't be an artist if you didn't feel somewhere in your heart that you're better than everybody else and you're going to blow them away. . . . It takes a fanaticism and a dedication and a single-mindedness," confesses T. Coraghessan Boyle. (Beware of all writers who substitute initials for their given names—big ambitions are hiding behind those little old initials.)

Behind every writer who looks his editor in the eye and says, "I'm happy just to see my book published," or "I don't expect it to be a bestseller," there lurks a megalomaniac in the making. There isn't a writer who gets an editor to consider his work, or, better yet, a real live publishing contract from a press, who doesn't fantasize that his work might take the world by storm. Let's face it, no one sits down to write something that will be a colossal failure. No one even sits down to write something that will be a modest success. The question is, how much do you let your fantasies circumscribe your work, and how much do they fuel your ambition?

❧

The writer's persona on and off the page are not necessarily identical, but often there is a resemblance. A writer's work emanates from his personality, ego, sensitivities, blind spots, projections, and unconscious wishes. All these contribute to what we eventually call style. Not everyone can arrive at a party like Oscar Wilde and command the room; most writers are more inwardly focused. But even for those whose personal style attracts attention, the proof is always, finally, on the page.

"I don't think that style is consciously arrived at," said Truman Capote, "any more than one arrives at the color of one's eyes. After all, your style *is* you. At the end the personality of a writer has so much to do with the work. The personality has to be humanly there. Personality is a debased word, I know, but it's what I mean," said this writer with personality in abundance. "The writer's individual humanity, his word or gesture toward the world, has to appear almost like a character that makes contact with the reader. If the personality is vague or confused or merely literary, *ça ne va pas.*"

On the opposite end of the spectrum are the writers who suffer from imposter complexes. Even the most celebrated writers are plagued by self-doubt and suffer enormous bouts of failure of confidence. Susan Sontag, in a *New York Times Magazine* feature, confessed to having felt deep insecurity when she began writing *The Volcano Lover.* "When I started the novel, it seemed like climbing Mount Everest," she wrote. "And I said to my psychiatrist, 'I'm afraid I'm not adequate.'" In an interview in *Conversations with American Writers* ten years earlier, she presaged those same insecurities: "I am profoundly uncertain about how to write. I know what I love or what I like, because it's a direct, passionate response. But when I write I'm very uncertain whether it's good enough. That is, of course, the writer's agony."

In an introduction to Natalie Goldberg's *Writing Down the Bones*, Judith Guest, author of *Ordinary People*, confessed the following feeling after the publication of her runaway bestseller: "Years later I was still telling myself that I wasn't really a writer, but a trickster—and a very lucky trickster at that. I had written a first novel and it had achieved phenomenal success. I had stumbled upon the secret path and uncovered the rules and had been rewarded with much praise. Unfortunately, all of this was proving to be of very little use to me in the writing of the next novel. How could I have forgotten everything so quickly?"

Pulitzer Prize–winner Carol Shields became confident about her calling only in middle age. "There was a time," she was quoted as saying, "when I shrugged off my writing in embarrassment." Often the best writers are mortified by their work and fear that it's only a matter of time before others see through them. For every Mailer or Whitman writing his own ad copy, there are countless writers who can barely look themselves in the eye.

Sometimes a writer reminds me of the straight-A student who annoys everyone by claiming she will surely fail the test. As with the student, this writer's pages are often superb. (Interesting, too, is the writer who boasts of his greatness and usually falls far from the mark.) Still, why is our A student crying wolf? In the fable, the boy who cries wolf sort of deserves what he gets because of all the false alarms. For writers, history seems to have nothing to do with it; no matter how well their previous work was received, with each new piece of writing the wolf is once more at the door.

I was taken aback when a novelist with five books to her credit confessed that between projects she always falls into a deep malaise, during which she is utterly convinced that she will never write again, that she is absolutely lost and has no confidence that she will be able to figure out how to write again. But surely, I suggested to her, the success of your previous books bolsters you to some extent. She was resolute in her answer; it was as if Rumpelstiltskin had produced her manuscripts as far as she was concerned. I could hear in her weary, watery voice that she was being truthful, though this image didn't wash—it contradicted the one I had concocted of her based on her press. She had been the envy of many of my classmates when her stories started appearing in the *New Yorker* and her book became a cause célèbre. When I asked what she did when she was between books, how she dealt with her fear, she matter-of-factly replied, "I cry to my mom."

❧

Wanting to be read, wanting the recognition, whether it's Jacqueline Susann–style, all glitz and limos, or sweeping the grand slam of literary events, is not a crime. Sometimes a book is catapulted into the limelight irrespective of the author's intentions, as when Simon & Schuster refused to publish Bret Easton Ellis's novel, thus turning *American Psycho* into a *cause terrible*. Or when Salman Rushdie received the Ayatollah's fatwa for *The Satanic Verses*, which drove the author into seclusion under

British protection for many years. These wag-the-dog scenarios were too outrageous to have been dreamed up by even the most cynical publicist. I don't think you can blame a writer for becoming famous as a result of coming under attack. All the same, consider to what extent the attack was invited. When a writer chops up hundreds of young women in the pages of his book, he can't pretend that he didn't lob the first grenade. Which is worse anyway: to write an incendiary book that sputters out like a wet match (as many do) or to watch your kerosene-doused pages start a forest fire?

All writers are like bomb-throwers, whether they attack with dense academic prose or jazzy riffs of stream-of-consciousness writing. Every writer wants his words to inflame, to reach across that great abyss, also known as the space between people, with his words. And whether it's Easton Ellis–style, by mutilating hundreds of unsuspecting yuppies, or by denouncing a world religion, or by doing something quieter, more domestic, the writer hopes to leave an indelible impression. Thus, when a "quiet" writer like Elizabeth Bishop, or a "domestic" writer like Alice Munro, or an intellectually sensuous poet like Jorie Graham takes home the Pulitzer, it celebrates the kind of flash that doesn't blind but, on the contrary, illuminates.

Whether you write the way Vermeer paints, or explode on the canvas like Jackson Pollock, you must make your own impression; whether you prance down the hall in a cape, run for mayor, pose nude for your book jacket, schmooze every influential writer in the land, hit every club and literary haunt, or just stay home. You will invite as much comment and attention over the long term as the material warrants and the world deigns to bestow. A world, I don't need to add, that is desperately vying for our entertainment dollars, which explains why some writers, especially young writers, in their desire to be heard try to make a big noise. You must dazzle your readers if you want to keep them, but they may be just as dazzled by a description of a lonely cloud as by a mushroom cloud.

When you venture forth with your work, remember that reputations are built on very little and are lost on even less. How does a writer negotiate a capricious world that would just as soon destroy him as praise him? Mailer powerfully addressed the high cost and anguish involved in continuing to produce: "If I am going to go on saying what my anger tells me it is true to say, I must get better at overriding the indifference which comes from the snobs, arbiters, managers and conforming maniacs who manipulate most of the world of letters. . . . There may have been too many fights for me . . . too much brain-blasting rage at the minuscule frustrations of a most loathsome literary world, necrophilic to the core—they murder their writers, and then decorate their graves."

Mailer's sentiments may seem exaggerated, but the sad truth is that all too often the world seizes on a writer's work in death as they never did in life. Jonathan Swift's epigraph in John Kennedy Toole's posthumously published novel, *A Confederacy of Dunces*, highlights the powerful myth surrounding the misunderstood artist: "When a true genius appears in the world, you may know him by this sign, that the dunces are in confederacy against him." Toole's tragic suicide at the age of thirty-two and his mother's valiant efforts to secure publication are part of the book's lore. Perhaps because *A Confederacy of Dunces* was published during my own somewhat tortured college years, the story of its posthumous success obsessed me and my small circle of friends. We endlessly debated whether the book would have garnered the same attention and won the Pulitzer Prize had the author been alive. The unspoken question loomed large: Did his suicide elevate his literary stature, confer some genius as Swift suggests, heighten public interest? I'm not implying that a writer kills himself to achieve literary fame, but rather that our culture has made a cult of the self-destructive writer and thereby confirms fame.

Then there is the sad case of the writer who outlives her fame. "There are writers who die to the world long before they are dead," wrote Brendan Gill in his introduction to *The Portable Dorothy Parker*. "And if this is sometimes by choice, more often it is a fate imposed on them by others and not easily dealt with. A writer enjoys a vogue, and, the vogue having passed, either he consents to endure the obscurity into which he has been thrust or he struggles against it in vain, with a bitterness that tends to increase as his powers diminish." Parker's acerbic wit and famous circle of friends are the stuff of legend. We always imagine her as poised with a bourbon, a cigarette snug in its lacquer holder, and a mordant quip. Surely she would go out in a blaze of glory or slip away under a sea of booze and pills. As Gill points out, "So large a portion of her verses was the seductiveness of a neat, brisk doing away with herself, many people were astonished to read of her death, in 1967, from natural causes, as an old lady of seventy-three. . . . She had indeed taken an unconscionably long time to leave a world of which she had always claimed to hold a low opinion."

A skirmish that involved some of our literary lions struck me as the last roars of a few good men attempting to secure their place among the immortals. When Tom Wolfe's *A Man in Full*, his first novel to appear in ten years, plopped its massive self down in the number one spot on the bestseller list, it seemed as if every major author over sixty lined up, like boys at a dunking booth, to knock him down. Norman Mailer, John Updike, and Harold Bloom felt it incumbent on them to take a shot at Wolfe in our most influential papers, claiming his work mere entertainment. Good, yes, but not *literature*. "Why are all these old men rising off their pallets to condemn my book?" asked Wolfe in a *Newsweek* interview. "Because my book has cast a very big shadow, and people like Mailer and Updike find themselves in the dark. And what do you do when you find yourself in the dark? You whistle. They're whistling in the dark." Naturally, this is Wolfe's tune, but the contretemps in and of itself attests to the need of writers, no matter their stature, to secure and promote their own literature.

In yet another category, there is the writer who professes to be completely uninterested in his fame. "I think like a genius, I write like a distinguished author, and I speak like a child," proclaimed Vladimir Nabokov in the opening gesture of his collected interviews and pieces, *Strong Opinions*. "I pride myself on being a person with no public appeal. . . . I have never belonged to any club or group. No creed or school has had any influence on me whatsoever. . . . I am not interested in groups, movements, schools of writing, and so forth. . . . I don't fish, cook, dance, endorse books, sign books, cosign declarations, eat oysters, get drunk, go to church, go to analysts, or take part in demonstrations." And when asked what he thought of contemporary novels, he responded with the supreme confidence of an artist working high above the din: "They seem to be all by one and the same writer—who is not even the shadow of my shadow."

Whether you throw a long shadow or hide within its dark fold, never leaving home but through the tapping out of your own Morse code, as Emily Dickinson did through the long winters of her life, or run for mayor, punch out people twice your size, and stab your wife, as Norman Mailer did while producing some of his generation's most influential prose, you will ultimately live or die by your line.

5.

THE
NEUROTIC

WRITERS LOVE TO WORRY. BY THEIR VERY nature they are neurotic. And they tend to exhibit the gamut of phobic behaviors from nervous tics and insomnia to full-fledged paranoia and delusional episodes. Some pick their skin, some pull out their hair or, in more extreme cases, cut, burn, or scar themselves. Many suffer from allergies, asthma, skin eruptions, rashes. John Updike wrote the equivalent of a love letter to his psoriasis, nearly crediting it as the impetus for his literary career: "What was my creativity, my relentless need to produce, but a parody of my skin's embarrassing overproduction? Was not my thick literary skin, which shrugged off rejection slips and patronizing reviews by the sheaf, a superior version of my poor vulnerable own, and my shamelessness on the page a distraction from my real shame, my skin. . . . Dualism, indeed, such as existed between my skin and myself, instinctively struck me as the very engine of the human."

Some writers are hypochondriacal in the extreme, a condition that may be an extension of their already vivid imaginations or a bid for help and attention. "I often get very tense work-ing," said novelist and critic William Gass. "So I often have to get up and wander around the house. It's very bad on my stomach. . . . My ulcer flourishes and I have to chew a lot of pills. When my work is going well, I am usually sort of sick." For others, writing is the only way to alleviate what ails them. "When I'm writing I find it's the only time that I feel completely self-possessed, even when the writing itself is not going too well," remarked William Styron. "It's fine therapy for people who are perpetually scared of nameless threats as I am most of the time—for jittery people. Besides, I've discovered that when I'm not writing I'm prone to developing certain nervous tics, and hypochondria."

In addition to physical symptoms, people who write tend to develop a set of ritualized behaviors with regard to their work. These habits dictate when, where, and under what cir-cumstances they feel able to produce. There are early birds and night owls. Some need a bright café to compose. Others must steal away to a secluded spot or the equivalent of a safe house where no one knows their identity. Most require solitude. "The person who writes books must always be enveloped by a sepa-ration from others," writes Marguerite Duras. "It is the solitude of the author, of writing. To begin with, one must ask oneself what the silence surrounding one is—with practically every step one takes in a house, at every moment of the day, in every kind of light, whether light from outside or from lamps lit in day-light. This real, corporeal solitude becomes the inviolable silence of writing." Many, such as Styron, require some combination of solitude and community. "I think it would be hard for me on a South Sea island or in the Maine woods. I like company and entertainment, people around. The actual process of writing, though, demands complete, noiseless privacy, without even music; a baby howling two blocks away will drive me nuts."

I have also found that many writers have a nearly demagogic worship of their writing accoutrements. "My schedule is flexible," replied Nabokov in response to a question regarding his work habits, "but I am rather particular about my instruments: lined Bristol cards and well-sharpened, not too hard, pencils capped with erasers." "I write my first version in longhand," explained Capote. "Then I do a complete revision, also in longhand. . . . Then I type a third draft on yellow paper, a very special certain kind of yellow paper." In his *New Yorker* article "Wasn't She Great?" Michael Korda described the habits of his diva author Jacqueline Susann. "Jackie wrote on pink paper, and she had apparently not yet discovered the 'Shift' key on her typewriter (a pink IBM Selectric): she wrote everything in capital letters, like a long telegram, and added revisions in a large, forceful circular hand, with what looked like a blunt eyebrow pencil." Hemingway was said to sharpen twenty pencils before he started work. For other writers, the drill is less involved: "First coffee," said Gore Vidal. "Then a bowel movement. Then the muse joins me."

If you become successful as a writer, these ritualistic behaviors will become known as your "process." The paper you write on, the time of day you compose—these details will actually seem interesting to some segment of your reading public as well as to a few graduate students as they labor to unravel the mystery of your genius. Then all the quirks of character become part of what makes you tick. Suddenly it seems significant that you can write your first draft only in a moving vehicle, or that you like to lie in an open coffin, as Dame Edith Sitwell reputedly did, before beginning your day's work.

Should you fail to achieve success, all these behaviors look only like excuses or sick behavior. Every time you put a provision on the conditions under which you can work—I have to write in the morning; I can write only when alone; I need a composition notebook of lined paper exactly like those I used when I studied in France; I can't possibly write if I have a girlfriend/boyfriend; or I can write only if I'm going out with someone—you fail to grasp the essential truth of all great writing: it brooks no provisions. "One must be pitiless about this matter of 'mood,'" said Joyce Carol Oates. "In a sense, the writing will create the mood. If art is, as I believe it to be, a genuinely transcendental function—a means by which we rise out of limited, parochial states of mind—then it should not matter very much what states of mind we are in."

If you are meant to write, if you are ready to write, if what you must do is write, then all you really need is paper and pencil. Once you fully contemplate the fact that Tolstoy revised *War and Peace* over five drafts without the aid of a typewriter, or that every other writer before the advent of computers managed to scratch his quill into parchment or hammer away at his typewriter without the benefit of this month's Microsoft upgrade, you have to admit that your project really does not require a new PowerBook, an Aeron chair, or a fellowship at Yaddo. Yet when the writing demon seizes a person who can't actually commit anything to paper, he will look to almost any voodoo to find the words. Writers everywhere have purchased expensive technology, rented rooms, left loved ones, exiled themselves to grass huts, or worse without bringing a single project to fruition.

A newer addition to the procrastination follies has emerged in the form of the "writing coach." This is a person with sketchy credentials and a nurturing and/or taskmaster style who will, either by phone, email, or in person, relieve you of your cash in exchange for proffering motivation, support, and deadline enforcement. I know some extremely gifted and decorated authors who have hired coaches to help them jump-start, get back on track, or complete a project. This boggles my mind. Personally, I think the money would be better spent on a massage, a housekeeper, or Prada shoes. I realize I should not be critical of anything that helps writers achieve their creative goals, but I am. I don't think a writer, or any artist for that matter, should need a whip other than the one inside that drives him to create. The more you indulge in any neurotic notions about a set of necessary conditions that will enable you to write, the colder the trail will get. The problem is, none of this is writing. It's stalling.

✦

The definition of phobia is a persistent, abnormal, or irrational fear of a specific thing that compels one to avoid the feared stimulus. The problem for many writers is that writing itself is the feared stimulus. I've heard good excuses in my day, as we all have, as to why a manuscript will be late. Just once I'd like to hear a writer tell the truth about why he can't deliver. Just once I'd like to hear someone say: no words. The reason no one says it is because when there are no words, nothing will save you: not a laptop with a gazillion gigabytes, not a sabbatical, not even a room of your own. When the words don't come, you could have all of Versailles to yourself and it wouldn't make a damn bit of difference. When the words don't come, the bell is striking midnight and you are Cinderella, or worse, Jack Nicholson in *The Shining*, typing the same line over and over again: *All work and no play makes Jack a dull boy.* (Interestingly, in a later role as a writer in *As Good As It Gets*, Nicholson's character is a bestselling author, rich and prolific, yet riddled with so many neurotic tics and ritualized behaviors that he can barely cross the street.) Writers lie about why their manuscripts are late, because the possibility of not producing is always one terrifying keystroke away.

Sometimes a writer is thrown off his game when he lands a book contract; after years of producing with no hope of publication on the horizon, the long-sought contract paralyzes him. If a writer has a success with his first book, sometimes a second never follows. And when a writer works out of a deeply autobiographical vein, we worry if the well will go dry. The challenge to continue producing in the face of both creative blocks and what can amount to paralyzing fear is a little-discussed fact of writing life. Most writers appear neurotic; the truth is, we don't know the half of it.

What's useful about neurotic behaviors is that they lend a shapeless day structure. If you must use yellow paper, if you must drink a double espresso before starting, if you can only write for three hours every morning, then at least you have parameters. Developing a successful formula for getting pages written can make a crucial difference. When I studied with the late playwright Charles Ludlam, who founded the Ridiculous Theatrical Company, he said, and I've heard others echo this strategy, that he always stopped writing in the middle of a scene, even when the work was going well. He couldn't understand those who bemoaned the terror of the blank page when they could arrange to face one with a few sentences. Plus, he added, if you quit while the going's good, you're more inclined to rush back the next day. If all else failed, the Master of Drag recommended we try slipping into an evening gown and wig to see if that would get the writing juices flowing.

Imagine the anxiety level of a job that requires you start from square one every day. This is the writer's predicament. Every day you start from scratch, even when you're in the middle of a project. Will the muse, as Milton beseeched her, bring your roots rain? Remember, too, that the writer's uncertainty about the quality of his work is another reason to develop an arsenal of neuroses. Unlike the mathematician, who knows when he's solved a problem, or the scientist with his burden of proof, or the lawyer who tries his case before a jury, the solitary writer works in a vacuum, where it's easy to lose all perspective. Judging one's own writing can be like looking in a mirror. What you tell yourself about what you see in the reflection has far more to do with how you feel about yourself that day than with how you actually look.

✒

Do writers develop phobias or are they phobics to begin with? I believe that writers develop phobias for protection, to create a wall between themselves and other people. Such a wall allows them to enter the supremely narcissistic world of the page— the place where they are the happy masters of the sandbox. Whether a writer never leaves home, like Jane Austen, or is as peripatetic as Mark Twain, antisocial behavior is essential. An absolute solipsism takes over as the writer becomes more alive inside his work than in the real world. For many, the work would never come into existence unless its primacy were indisputable. What looks like neurosis and eccentric behavior may provide the crucial barricade that enables the writer to work when everything in life conspires to distract him or co-opt his energies.

"When I was writing in the house, everything wrote," said Marguerite Duras. "Writing was everywhere. And sometimes when I saw friends, I hardly recognized them. Several years were spent like that, difficult ones for me, yes, this might have lasted for ten years. And even when close friends came to see me, that, too, was horrible. My friends knew nothing about me: they meant well and came out of kindness, believing they would do me good. And strangest of all is that I thought nothing of it. This is what makes writing wild. One returns to a savage state from before life itself."

Whoever you are, whatever your bizarre behaviors, I say cultivate them. Becoming a writer never won anybody any popularity contests. And most writers couldn't win one if they tried. Most have a lumpy writer's body and an uninspired wardrobe and talk too much. Many writers can't help but focus on their work, often steering the conversation to their most recent article or book. There's nothing worse than being cornered by a writer at a party and listening to him drone on, with every other sentence beginning *As I say in my book.*

I've come to look at neurotic behavior as a necessary component of a writer's arsenal, the necessary defenses to screen out the rest of the world so that the ballet inside his head can begin to take shape. Yet just as he needs to block out distraction in order to work, he also needs to let a certain amount of life filter through. The writer tries desperately to control this flow as he wrestles with sentences on the one hand and the requirements of family, work, and social life on the other. The writer struggles to satisfy himself and also meet the minimum requirements most spouses and families expect. He loves his cage and hates his cage. "I am in chains," cried Kafka to his beloved. "Don't touch my chains."

What are we to make of writers who claim that nothing makes them as miserable as writing, and then swear never to be happier than when they are in the throes of a book? "The professional writers who dread writing, as many do, are usually those whose critical sense is not only strong but unsleeping, so that it won't allow them to do even a first draft at top speed," explained Malcolm Cowley in his introduction to a volume of *Paris Review* interviews. "They are in most cases the 'bleeders' who write one sentence at a time and can't write it until the sentence before has been revised." When William Styron, one of the bleeders, according to Cowley, was asked if he enjoyed writing, he replied, "I certainly don't. I get a fine warm feeling when I'm doing well, but that pleasure is pretty much negated by the pain of getting started each day. Let's face it, writing is hell." For Hemingway, the pain and pleasure seemed erotically linked. "[I] suffer like a bastard when [I] don't write, or just before, and feel empty and fucked out afterwards. But [I] never feel as good as while writing." And in *A Moveable Feast*, Hemingway again draws a parallel between the act of writing and lovemaking. "After writing a story I was always empty and both sad and happy, as though I had made love."

But was it good for you?

It is impossible not to see the analogies between sex and writing. A writer seduces, enchants, titillates, beguiles, and befriends. One banters and charms, woos and whispers. You are nothing if not courting your reader. Are you selfish or generous, leisurely or hurried, overwhelming or tentative? When you are successful, the reader feels as if you are talking only to him. The intimate charge that we get from books is an extension of how much the author, like a good lover, gives (or masterfully withholds). But the neurotic writer, like the novice lover, spends less time concerned with mastering his craft and worries instead: *Am I doing it right?*

If there's anything writers are more neurotic about than writing, it's money. Only a fortunate few can actually make a living from writing, and the struggle to support a career that offers no guarantees, no benefits, and no security makes most writers intensely insecure. Always there is the hope of "hitting the jackpot," having one's work met with praise as well as an audience of some amplitude. When asked how he felt about becoming wealthy, Frank McCourt, in a 1998 *New York Times Magazine* feature on the "new gilded age," responded, "Because I profited from a book about poverty, irony is my constant companion." When asked if his financial success had a downside, McCourt was characteristically amusing. "There is no downside. Money allows you to whine to your heart's content, and to be as happy or miserable as you choose. If your friends don't want to listen to your complaints, cast them aside! There are plenty of people who, for a large fee, will listen to the whines of the wealthy."

Writer Matthew Klam, the author of the *Times* article, volubly complained that while his friends were Lear-jetting about, the most he'd ever made was $21,000 in a year when he sold some short stories and a book proposal he still hadn't finished. He complained that his lowly financial status was embarrassing, especially when he talked to a good friend who was about to purchase a yacht. "Some days, to ease the undercurrent of tension when we talk," writes Klam, "he pretends to envy me. 'You write because you have no choice, Klam,' he says. 'It's your calling, so stop complaining. Your whole day could be spent in a bathrobe.'"

Many people think that writers, successful or not, actually do spend their entire lives in pajamas. There is a disbelief in our culture that writing, or the creation of any art, is actually work. One of my writers was seeing a therapist with the stated goal of, among other things, taking herself more seriously as a writer, though she already had two critically acclaimed books to her credit. Still, on more than one occasion the therapist felt no compunction in asking the writer to change the time of her appointment. When the writer protested, the therapist explained that since the writer didn't have a "job," moving her

appointment shouldn't be a problem. On top of that, the therapist wanted her to come in during the morning (my author's
best writing hours) when, the therapist explained, most people
were at work; she saved the after-five sessions for the gainfully
employed.

The world does not owe writers a living. Still, some writers insist that writing for anything other than money is foolish.
Samuel Johnson famously declaimed, "No man but a blockhead
ever wrote, except for money." I wonder what Johnson would
have thought of today's bloggers. Never have more written for
less (usually nothing). Dorothy Parker, when asked the source of
her impetus to write, after roundly dismissing her childhood as
inspiration, replied with characteristic brevity, "Need of money,
dear." Capote, at the very beginning of his career, insisted on
the importance of getting paid. "I never write—indeed, I am
physically incapable of writing—anything that I don't think I
will be paid for." Few writers start earning money right out of
the gate, as Capote did, and most struggle for years before their
efforts receive any compensation. But if money is what a writer
is after, as opposed to, say, publication, why wouldn't he pursue
a career on Wall Street or in some other lucrative profession?
Show me a blockhead who says he writes for money and I'll
show you a big fat liar.

When Joyce Maynard was accused of writing her Salinger
memoir to make money, she voiced a fair opinion. "It troubles
me that people speak about writing for money as ugly and
distasteful. During the first flurry of criticism for this book, all
kinds of people said, 'Oh, she's doing it for the money.' And I
thought, Well of course I get paid! Imagine someone suggesting

that a doctor shouldn't get paid." But later, in what I think is a more deeply truthful reflection, Maynard also confessed that "no amount of money" could have persuaded her to write this story at any other stage of her life. "And it wouldn't be something I'd get into now if I didn't feel it was the right thing to do."

Maynard must have known that writing about Salinger would invite derision. Yet she clearly hoped that people would be interested in her story and empathize with her, no matter how naive that hope now seems. No amount of money can compensate for a writer's lifetime of sacrifices—sacrifices that no one has asked him to make and that few truly appreciate. As a culture we are interested only in success, and by that measure the successful artist's suffering is negated when he wins either monetary or critical acclaim. While the writer whose work fails to find any currency is utterly dismissed. It's a no-win situation. Working in the face of so little understanding must be debilitating, though I fondly recall some remarks Tracy Kidder shared at a sales conference. He described the difficulty of hanging out at an old-age home as he gathered the material for his book *Old Friends*. After describing how depressing the experience could be at times, and how it forced him to grapple with his own mortality, Kidder smirked and looked out at his devoted sales force with his characteristic twinkle. "I'm not gonna bullshit you guys," he said. "I also go fishing every day. How bad can it be?"

Still, it can be painful to acknowledge the personal cost and sacrifice of writing. In a letter to his patron during a crisis of faith, Chekhov confided, "There are moments when I positively lose heart. For whom and for what do I write? . . . Does the public need me or not? I cannot make it out. Write for money? But I never have money, and from the habit of it I am almost indifferent to it. For the sake of money I work poorly." You can't help but wonder if Chekhov wasn't trying a little reverse psychology on his patron, just as Hemingway, echoing the same idea a century later, confessed to Maxwell Perkins in a letter that he didn't "think there is any question about artistic integrities. It has always been much more exciting to write than to be paid for it and if I can keep on writing we may eventually all make some money."

I've heard more than a few writers, upon receiving their first book contract, exclaim that they would have done the work for free, so thrilled are they to finally land a publisher. Short-story writer Nathan Englander, in a *New York Times* interview, said he would have been just as happy to get a complete set of the Modern Library from his publisher than the highly publicized advance he received; he was just thrilled to be published by Knopf. Now he tells them! Though Englander might be a blockhead for saying so, I believe that most writers are motivated by the same desire to see their work published, to see it out in the world.

There is no way to ensure that doing good work or working hard guarantees financial return for a writer. Likewise, any publisher motivated solely by profit would do better to liquidate his assets and invest his money in real estate. Though most publishers are part of larger media conglomerates, they're still in a nickel-and-dime business, as one of my first mentors said when I stared in disbelief at my first profit-and-loss sheet and contemplated how little profit a given book actually generates.

If you want money, look elsewhere. It's that simple. For the working writer there are simply no reliable dividends. And in a world where self-worth is measured by one's portfolio, it's awfully hard to keep singing for your supper.

When writers hear about huge advances for first-time authors or see books they deem unworthy rise on the bestseller lists, they begin to wonder if there isn't some master plot that has been set in motion for the express purpose of driving them mad. A writer's self-worth is tied up in a great many things, but money has the distinction of being the most tangible item in a sea of intangibles. I was taken by a comment Stephen King made in a 1991 *Publishers Weekly* interview. Here was a writer whose body of work at that time included more than 89 million copies of his twenty-seven books in print saying, "I'd like to win the National Book Award, the Pulitzer Prize, the Nobel Prize, I'd like to have someone write a *New York Times Book Review* piece that says, 'Hey, wait a minute, guys, we made a mistake—this guy is one of the great writers of the twentieth century.' But it's not going to happen, for two reasons. One is I'm not the greatest writer of the twentieth century, and the other is that once you sell a certain number of books, the people who think about 'literature' stop thinking about you and assume that any writer who is popular across a wide spectrum has nothing to say. The unspoken postulate is that intelligence is rare. It's clear in the critical stance; I hear it in the voice of people from the literary journals where somebody will start by saying, 'I don't read Stephen King,' and they are really saying, 'I don't lower myself.' "

Ask a writer whether he'd rather sell a lot of copies or win

the National Book Award, and you will better understand his
particular motivations. A rational person wouldn't hesitate to
answer the question: understanding that more sales means a
wider readership and more money, he would pick copies sold.
But most writers want prestige as much as they want money. I
don't think that King would give up a single one of his readers
for any prize, though the exclusion of his genre by the literary establishment clearly chafes. Writers should want money;
writers deserve money. And I salute any writer who feels he
is fairly compensated. But I will never believe that writers are
motivated solely by money—at least not at the outset of their
careers. Writers want love, and they hope that through their
work, they will be recognized as gifted. And that is why most
writers are so crazy. When a writer gives his editor the pages of
his manuscript, or when his book is published, his entire sense
of himself is in limbo. Waiting for feedback is like waiting for
the results of a biopsy.

🌿

Every editor becomes a de facto therapist, whether or not he
engages in the therapeutic as well as the editorial process. His
author presents a set of symptoms as clearly as a patient visiting a doctor. Editors have to figure out how to get pages out
of those who can't let go. We have to reassure those who can't
stop revising (often making the book worse). We have to figure
out how to deal with authors who call or email every day, or
more than once a day, and those who never call. Then there
is the writer who constantly baits his editor for information
about her other authors, so that he can try to discern whether

he is the big fish in her small pond, or the small fish in her big one. There is no profit in this game, as any parent of rivalrous siblings will tell you; it's best not to engage. Most writers lie or exaggerate about how little of our time and attention they need. No one likes to be perceived as needy, and there is nothing like the risk and exposure of publishing a book to call forth tremendous insecurity.

Editors witness the innermost anxiety of their writers, vicariously living the author's life through the books they help bring into the world. I was always fascinated by the way my authors coped during the nerve-racking months approaching publication. Writers crave and fear exposure in different measures, and how well they deal with becoming public can be a predictor of future success. I was also emboldened by the strength of those whose convictions were tested when their work provoked strong negative reactions. I was never more proud than when one author held her ground during a heated debate about her book following a reading. At one point a belligerent man stood up with a raised fist and declared that not only was her book a disgrace but that she had wasted her Ivy League education to boot. She told him he didn't have to buy or read her book if he didn't want to, and as far as she was concerned, he could write his own damn book.

When an editor works with an author, she cannot help seeing into the medicine cabinet of his soul. All the terrible emotions, the desire for vindication, the paranoia, and the projection are bottled in there, along with all the excesses of envy, desire for revenge, all the hypochondriacal responses, rituals, defenses, and the twin obsessions with sex and money. In other words, the stuff of great books. Of course, without craft, no amount of personal eccentricity, no depth of human strangeness will make your work good. You must channel your neurosis in the service of prolonging and improving your writing life. Otherwise, just as surely as the phobic becomes paralyzed in the face of his terror, you will turn writing into your enemy; it, too, in a final paranoid twist, will seem to be out to get you.

Nothing is more vexing for an editor than trying to help a writer who has become too neurotic to write. Scared and defensive, riddled with rationales and justifications, provisions and excuses, he can no longer get back to that place where writing is like a balm. But when the writer faces it all down and delivers something of beauty, all is forgiven.

6.

TOUCHING
FIRE

THE ONLY PLACE YOU'RE LIKELY TO FIND more alcoholics than an AA meeting is a writing program. While I was in graduate school, a group of so-called cowboy poets were famous for going out every night and getting drunk, which invariably led to brawling or other crazy behavior, which they would then boast about in the writing lounge the next day, swigging down the tarlike coffee that must certainly be a staple of every writing department lounge. They would get tight and loosen a tooth or two. They would carouse and cheat on their girlfriends back home, wherever that was. They cavalierly rolled their spiral notebooks (no Moleskines for these cowboys) into the back pockets of their jeans as they swaggered into class, always late and always needing to borrow something: a pen, a lighter, an aspirin. They were young guys, getting off on their youth, their muscular poems, their own sense of reverie, as if they had personally discovered language. They took leaks wherever they liked, marking the city and their haunts like a pack of dogs. The booze helped them bond; it lit them up and fueled the nocturnal adventures they later wrote about. Everyone in the program naturally resented them: they were arrogant; they were good-looking. They played their parts so well it seemed as if central casting had sent us those big-drinking poets.

Central casting also sent our writing workshop a few garden-variety drunks, whose drinking led to melancholia rather than carousing and whose poems tended toward the self-pitying. We had one stone-cold junkie, one Valium zombie, a handful of students taking antidepressants (this was before Prozac, a medication that has undoubtedly changed the face of writing programs across the country), a manic-depressive or two, and one wreck who might as well have walked out of a Cindy Sherman photograph. Every time this woman needed a pencil or something else from her bag, she made an enormous show of emptying its contents onto the conference table, spilling vials of pills along with keys and combs and lipsticks. Then she would make a frantic show of collecting the contents, stretching her body across the table to retrieve the runaway vials. Of course, we resented her, too. *Such a display! Such carrying on!* I realize only now that in her own incoherent way she was asking for help. While we romanticize alcoholism and drug addiction in fiction and poetry, the reality is that we flee from those who can't hold their liquor, from those whose instability threatens to capsize our own wobbly ships.

I had been editing for enough years to know better than to acquire a project from a writer only a year in recovery from his crack addiction. But I loved his proposal and hoped that the contract would give him a cushion. He would disappear for months at a time, take weeks to return my call, and then promise more pages than even Rumpelstiltskin might have been able to spin from the raw material of his life. I'd beg him to set a realistic goal, such as twenty pages by the end of the month, but he would promise to churn out seventy-five pages in two weeks. We'd go back and forth on this, with him insisting that he needed the pressure to produce. "I'm not just a crack addict," he'd say with a laugh. "I'm a pressure junkie, too."

I'd assure him that I would be happy with any number of pages he could produce, but I needed some evidence of progress to keep granting extensions now that the contractual delivery date was long past. He'd always sympathize with my position, even joke about my rotten luck for getting him as an author. We'd end the call with some jokes and a mini–pep talk, and I'd hang up the phone all but certain that I'd never see a page. And sadly, I never did. Even after we had been through this drill more than a few times, I would grow frantic when my phone calls to him went unreturned. I would call his agent, and we would both leave worried messages, hoping against hope that he wasn't using drugs again, spiraling into oblivion. Eventually he would call, apologies and guilty self-recriminations would ensue, an extension would be granted. Finally I realized that I had become part of a new addictive cycle through which this writer replayed his life's central drama: the story of the boy who was worse than everyone else, the story of a boy beyond the reach of help. After three years we finally canceled the contract. It was the only project I ever lost. I never heard from the writer again.

Some might argue that the addict renders those who would help him impotent, caught in the powerful grip of his addiction.

After the commercial failure of *The Great Gatsby*, F. Scott Fitzgerald's deterioration escalated and his hard drinking began to alienate those closest to him, including his lifelong agent, Harold Ober. After Ober refused to bail Fitzgerald out for the umpteenth time, Fitzgerald broke off business relations. His life from that point on reads like a catalog of binges, delusions of productive work and new ideas, periods of being on and off the wagon. The syndrome became so predictable, according to A. Scott Berg in his biography of Maxwell Perkins, that when Fitzgerald secluded himself in a North Carolina hotel to dry out, the loyal editor anticipated the eventual fallout. "He knew Fitzgerald would need the support of all the friends that he could get, but Scott was hard put to find them just then. That year, almost simultaneously, three of his friendships with Perkins's writers deteriorated."

Can you imagine Ernest Hemingway, Thomas Wolfe, and Ring Lardner doing an intervention for their old friend? The sad truth is that alcoholism and addiction have always wrecked lives, and nothing is more painful than watching a brilliant young writer turn into a pathetic drunk or addict, making excuses for months or even years to cover for a lack of productivity, showing up hours late for every appointment, eyes dilated into huge saucers, finally turning in pages so frantic or sloppy in their composition that an editor despairs of being able to make anything out of them.

Drinking or drugging is always a flight response, whether it's from fame, critical attack, rejection, or most commonly, being unable to write. When an excess of desire and ambition is met with frustration, when all the longing in the world doesn't materialize in a coherent sequence of pages, the vulnerable writer may reach for his favorite poison. I have watched writers lose years to alcohol abuse and then blame the drinking on their inability to write. Pearl Kazin Bell remarked that "Dylan Thomas knew when he was in his midthirties that he was never going to write the kind of poetry he had written during the war, that it would just be a bad imitation of things he had done before. I think that's one of the reasons he went on drinking—to be done with it."

✴

From de Quincey's opium eaters to John Cheever's dissolute diaries, history shows that writers and artists have more than their share of addictions. What is unclear is whether they or the culture is more responsible for exaggerating and elevating those excesses to dramatic and, in some cases, romantic-seeming proportions. Many of today's writers, mercifully, have sobered up. As Denis Johnson wrote in "Now," the most widely quoted poem from his first collection, *The Incognito Lounge*, which was circulated widely at AA meetings during the 1980s because it represented a new voice for the newly sober, "Darkness, my name is Denis Johnson / and I am almost ready to / confess." The lines fairly echoed the cadence of the standard AA greeting: *Hello, my name is X, and I am an alcoholic.* Finally, here was a writer chasing down his demons instead of the other way around.

A lot of ink has been spilled in an effort to describe and come to terms with the nature of alcoholism, including Caroline Knapp's *Drinking: A Love Story*; Pete Hamill's *A Drinking Life*;

Carrie Fisher's *Wishful Drinking*; Mary Karr's *Lit*; Augusten Burroughs's *Dry*; and Susan Cheever's plaintively titled memoir, *Note Found in a Bottle*. From William Burroughs's classic *Junky* to Linda Yablonsky's *Story of Junk*, a raft of addiction narratives has also washed up on our shores, including *The Night of the Gun* by David Carr, *Portrait of an Addict as a Young Man* by Bill Clegg, *Broken* by William Cope Moyers, and *More, Now, Again* about Ritalin addiction by Elizabeth Wurtzel. David Sheff's *New York Times* bestseller about his son Nic's addiction, *Beautiful Boy*, was published concurrently with Nic's own account, *Tweak*. Dr. Michael Stein describes a year in the treatment of a patient in *The Addict*. In *Pillhead*, Josh Lyons chronicles a generation's abuse of prescription drugs, and Nick Reding, in *Methland*, captures how crystal meth has taken hold of small-town America. Of course no other memoir has caused as much outrage as James Frey's *A Million Little Pieces*, which was lambasted in the press when it came to light that Frey had fabricated and exaggerated much of his story.

James Atlas wrote a piece lamenting the demise of the good old days of wine and roses: "The drunken dinner party, the makeout session in a bathroom at Nell's, the joint inhaled in a taxi full of revelers careering through SoHo at dawn—these are ancient history by now, exotica recorded in some yellowed Jay McInerney novel that's gathering dust on the shelf." While aware of his romanticizing, Atlas describes the cultural shift, both economic and political, that no longer celebrates the daring, outsider status of the artist. "Writers and artists wrecked their health, destroyed their marriages, and died young so that the rest of America could enjoy art from a safe distance.

The sacrifice had to be made. It was their job. Surely this was the lesson of Hemingway blowing his brains out, of Jackson Pollock wrapping his car around a tree. They died that art might live."

It's hard not to get wistful reading about the various debaucheries chronicled in Atlas's article, the hungover Robert Lowell chain-smoking in the basement of Quincy House, the young, drunken Mailer "brandishing a bottle of whisky" in Sanders Theatre, Hemingway downing daiquiris in Key West. It's easy to imagine that Pollock foretold his chrome-exploding death in every painting he detonated on canvas. But these are not the good old days. These are the days of twelve-step programs, when alcoholism is understood as a disease, not a side effect or an occupational hazard of being a tortured artist. James Atlas might also lament the days when the *New Yorker* didn't run letters to the editor, since he was roundly scolded by Susan Cheever the week after his article ran. "I was amazed to read James Atlas's romantic evocation of the fun we used to have in the New York Literary World. As someone who was a child at those parties where Literary Greats stumbled around lecherously in an opaque cloud of cigarette smoke, I can testify that for those involved—certainly for many wives and most children—that scene was anything but fun. A tragedy of the generation that came before ours was that many of this country's wonderful writers were also alcoholics. Every drunk—whether or not he can write—leaves a trail of destruction, desolation, confusion, and sadness which goes on for generations. It's certainly true that my father's novels and stories are redolent with romantic images of the perfect martini and the ideal adultery, but those stories are *fiction*—images created by a man who never found either." Cheever herself would mine all this and more in three memoirs about her own addictions.

Nothing, however, can compare to John Cheever's own journals, which mark each tortured juncture along the way of his alcoholic dissolution. From the earliest entries to the last, one sees a man struggling with a drinking problem in all its Sisyphean heartbreak. In a 1952 entry Cheever describes the cycle in a moment of total clarity: "When the beginnings of self-destruction enter the heart it seems no bigger than a grain of sand. . . . But when you try to trace back the way you came into this abyss all you find is a grain of sand." By the end of the decade, he is completely resigned, though still somewhat cavalier about his problem. "I am a solitary drunkard. . . . At four or half past four or sometimes five I stir up a Martini, thinking that a great many men who can't write as well as I can already have set themselves down at bar stools." Just a year later Cheever confesses to the toll drinking is taking on his life. "In the morning I am deeply depressed, my insides barely function, my kidney is painful, my hands shake, and walking down Madison Avenue I am in fear of death. . . . I would very easily destroy myself. It is ten o'clock now and I am thinking of a noontime snort."

In charting the ever-diminishing hour from which he is able to successfully abstain from drinking, Cheever remains painfully aware of his losing battle. "Now Thursday morning," he writes in 1967. "Twenty minutes to eleven. I am in the throes of a grueling booze fight. . . . There is really nothing to do but sit

here and sweat it out. I can write myself a letter. Dear Myself,
I am having a terrible time with booze. Ride it out."

By 1972, Cheever confesses that the "cruel addiction" has
accelerated to the point where it starts sometimes before day-
break. "On waking, I want a drink. . . . Now I can think of
nothing but the taste of whiskey. . . . At about half past nine
my hands begin to shake so that I can't hold a paper or type
correctly." Later that same year Cheever finally, mercifully, takes
his first faltering steps toward getting help. "After planning to
visit A.A. for twenty years," he writes, "I finally make it."

ᴥ

As we learn more about addiction, genetics, and brain chemis-
try, it seems likely that those who are prone to self-medication
may also have a physiological component that contributes to
the increased craving. It may be merely a genetic glitch that
makes one person more susceptible to the addictive powers
of drink than another. Whether an artistic temperament is a
feature of that same genetic complexity remains to be seen. But
even if the link proves dubious, the writers who most publicly
drowned their sorrows—Cheever, Bukowski, Williams, Capote,
Fitzgerald, and so on—provide enough lore to keep alive the
notion that the artistic temperament is inextricably linked to
self-medicating behaviors.

Being a writer or wanting to write is to live in a perpetual
state of anxiety, where the chances of failing far outweigh the
rate of success. It's a constant free fall, especially between projects, for the celebrated and the unknown alike. "Everything

is will and the great obstacle is fear," said Gordon Lish in an interview about writing. "It comes down in every instance to this dualism between what one wants and what one may be afraid to have." When the fear becomes overwhelming, when the anxiety nearly takes you out, it may seem that only a gin and tonic can take the terrible edge off. Hard-drinking poets, misunderstood artists, and junkie novelists will go to any length to quell the panic that builds inside them as they contemplate actually writing something or mounting a stage. According to Diane Wood Middlebrook, Anne Sexton needed to drink before every public appearance and had developed a "set of rituals" to get her through her reading tours. "Arriving in any hotel room, she followed an inviolable procedure, going directly to the bathroom to turn on the shower full blast and hang her performance clothes in the steam, then to the ice machine for supplies to chill the first of many glasses of vodka tipped from the stash in her suitcase. Juiced, she was manic, an absolute necessity for performing."

Writers have always used drugs and drink to disinhibit themselves. In the beginning, the intoxicating effects of alcohol and drugs can prove prodigious. But once the tail is wagging the dog, the effects are generally deleterious. "God is your type-writer," a priest once told Sexton, during what appeared to be a spiritual crisis when she could no longer connect the words to her vision, but as her biographer wrote: "Alcohol was now Sexton's chief, self-prescribed medication, taken morning, noon, and night." When a writer crosses the line, when the addiction is all-consuming, even the redemptive powers of art are rendered mute. The typewriter is mute. "Alcohol helped generate the curves of feeling on which her poetry lifted its wings," continues Middlebrook, "but it dropped her too, into depression, remorse, sleeplessness, paranoia—the normal host of furies that pursue alcoholics. . . . She had the drunk's fluency but not the artist's cunning."

✳

The only literary affliction more romanticized than addiction is mental illness. The connection between artistic temperament and manic-depressive illness has been extensively described in Kay Redfield Jamison's book *Touched with Fire*. In reviewing the most recent research available, Jamison concludes that compared with the general public, writers and artists exhibit a vastly disproportionate rate of manic-depressive or depressive illness. However, and this is the part that is all too often overlooked, "not all (not even most) writers and artists suffer from major mood disorders." It's just that manic bursts of artistic creation make for better copy. Mania is nothing if not intoxicating. And when it is joined with creative energy and vision and inspiration, the results can be dazzling. More often than not, however, the mania is attached to darker forces, and at the very height of an artist's performance there may come the killing hand.

We confer greatness only posthumously upon those who suffer from mental illness. In life, unless you have your disease under control, it will be a source of gossip and speculation for most people, if not of downright derision. No matter what you do or what you produce, rumors about your so-called condition will follow you, and your behavior, opinions, and work will be scrutinized for signs of your illness. I will never forget an editorial meeting I attended in London a number of years ago. A famous older editor began the meeting by announcing that he wanted to publish the British edition of William Styron's book *Darkness Visible*, about the writer's nervous breakdown. He became increasingly voluble during the meeting, insisting on the importance of the book. The newly installed and rather arrogant young editor-in-chief shot down the acquisition with the predictable refrain "too American." At this, the older editor started pounding the table with his fists, searching our stunned faces for commiseration. Then he turned to me, waved the slim volume in my face, and said, "You're American; tell him why it's a bestseller." I was stunned into silence, though I knew the publishing history of the book quite well. First serialized in Tina Brown's *Vanity Fair*, it had been the talk of New York. The older editor gave me a look I will never forget, the look of a betrayed man. Then he sent the book flying down the center of the conference table in a gesture of surrender and disgust and marched out of the meeting. The editor sitting next to me leaned over and conspiratorially whispered, "He's mad, you know." I later learned that in fact he did suffer from manic-depressive illness.

If you suffer from manic depression, your work and behavior will be judged accordingly. Is your excessive output the result of your mania? Are you brilliant or just theatrical? Are you truly suffering or self-indulgent? No one will say, if your book is years late in coming, Give him as much time as he needs, he's a mad genius. People don't tolerate the erratic behavior that usu-ally accompanies mood swings—at least not for long. Had you known Virginia Woolf in her lifetime, you might have been put off by her moodiness, her depression. Snap out of it, you might have thought. Likely you'd have grown weary of bipolar poets Lord Byron, Delmore Schwartz, John Berryman, and Robert Lowell. *God, are they full of themselves.* People who suffer from depression or bipolar illness are draining, demanding, and sometimes deluded. They may also be charismatic, electrifying, and exciting, but that high wattage comes with a cost that can often mean the alienation of friends and family, and compromised work, or the inability to work at all. In life, these writers often try people beyond reason, especially if they are unwilling to seek treatment. In death, it is easier to romanticize mental illness in writers, to call it genius. And thus we continue to fuel a steadfast mythology about artists and the mysterious artistic process (which I prefer to call hard work).

We have similarly romanticized suicide, especially among our poets. No poet has gained more acclaim in the aftermath of taking her own life than Sylvia Plath. Even the briefest sampling of the poet's diary is dizzying for its wild mood swings and self-dramatizing:

Tuesday, February 10: How clear and cleansed and happy I feel.

Thursday, February 20: I myself am the vessel of tragic experience.

Tuesday afternoon, March 11: Oh how my own life shines, beckons . . .

Thursday morning, April 17: I feel as I were rising from a grave, gathering my moldy, worm-riddled limbs in a final effort.

It's not surprising when a writer, in the youthful desire to create an artistic persona, gravitates toward the seductive edge described in Plath's work and that of other artists. But as Kay Redfield Jamison rightly points out, "Most of the controversy surrounding the 'mad genius' debate versus 'healthy artist' debate, however, arises from confusion about what is actually meant by 'madness,' as well as from a fundamental lack of understanding about the nature of manic depressive illness." It's one thing to have intense feelings and indulge one's moods; it's quite another to be catatonic or delusional. I don't think anyone has better summed up the terrible waste that results from manic depression than Robert Lowell in a conversation with his publisher, Robert Giroux, after starting the then newly available drug lithium carbonate, which apparently was extremely effective for the poet. "It's terrible, Bob," he said, "to think that all I've suffered, and all the suffering I've caused, might have arisen from the lack of a little salt in my brain."

The person bouncing between the poles of mania and depression and/or obsessed with destroying himself is noxious, and most people are worn thin by the constant dependency and the broken promises of a brighter future. The person aloft in manic flight is so utterly self-involved that his accelerated state precludes any real communion. He is Icarus-like in his quest, which is certain to end in flames. Thirty-five years after Sylvia Plath took her life—and after thirty-five years of silence about her death—her husband, Ted Hughes, published the poems he'd written about their life together. *Birthday Letters* would become a bestseller (Hughes's only) and further fuel our ongoing fascination with Plath and her tragic end. The collection was touted as an intimate account of Plath's struggle as she produced the greatest poems of her career. More heartbreaking, to my mind, was the unfolding narrative of Hughes's struggle to love her as her illness worsened.

One reason we romanticize these artists is that on some level they make us feel safe. The person touched with fire becomes the container for all of our own suicidal tendencies, the excess emotions that frighten and weaken us. The person who crosses the line stands in for our collective self-destructive impulses and maybe, for just a little while, sates the savage god.

Depression, on the other hand, with none of the high-octane creative output, the hypersexuality, the brain computing faster than a superconductor, is a pure drag. The wool-blanketed brain of the depressive fights for a clarity that is just beyond reach. For a person whose emotional oxygen supply grows weaker by the day, there is nothing worse than morning, than springtime, than signs of life. Someone in the throes of clinical depression slowly but surely stops functioning. Very few artists manage to create anything at all during depressive episodes. Mania only makes you think you are great; it does not ensure greatness. And depression only makes you feel worthless; it does not confer worthlessness. It's difficult enough to know if your writing is any good on an average day, let alone when seen through the distorted valuations produced by mood swings.

In September of 2008, David Foster Wallace—many would argue, the best writer of his generation—took his life. The usual romantic cant surrounding an artist's death was absent, perhaps a sign of greater understanding of the severity of depression. A piece by D. T. Max in the *New Yorker* was as much a case history

of the tragic consequences of mental illness as it was an account
of how the writer had arrived at his peerless position in the literary landscape. It chronicled the course of Wallace's depression
from his undergraduate days at Amherst College until the end
of his life, citing every medication he had taken and their effect
on the writer. As Wallace's depression deepened, he lost the
ability to work. In an email to his friend Jonathan Franzen, he
wrote, "The whole thing is a tornado that won't hold still long
enough for me to see what's useful and what isn't. I've brooded
and brooded about all this till my brooder is sore." Later he
would write his friend again, "I go back and forth between (a)
working to assemble a big enough sample to take an advance,
and (b) recoiling in despair, thinking . . . I'd pitch everything
and start over." A *New York Times* obituary cited James Donald
Wallace as saying that David "had been taking medication for
depression for twenty years and that it had allowed his son to
be productive." He talked about the last year of Wallace's life,
when side effects from the medication drove him to abandon
it, only to see the depression return. "He'd been in the hospital a couple of times over the summer and had undergone
electro-convulsive therapy. Everything had been tried, and he
just couldn't stand it anymore."

No one, including his father, romanticized Wallace's illness
as the source of his artistic genius. His death was tragic, and the
final word on a lifetime struggle with depression. His abundant
gift shined through despite his illness, not because of it.

For all we know about mental illness, it is still stigmatized
and stigmatizing. Whether you live out your days undiagnosed

and untreated or struggle to find adequate therapy and medications, the path to treatment is rocky and hellish. Medications,
when they are useful at all, tend to become less effective over
time, as was the case with Wallace, and no one really knows
anything about long-term use. You are never home free.

✤

I can usually tell within seconds whether one of my writers
is flying high or sinking into depression. The voice gives it
all away: the breathlessness and giddiness of the manic; the
monotone or quavering delivery of the depressed. When writers disappear and fail to deliver pages, depression is usually the
reason, and there is very little an editor can do or say to convince them that it will lift, that they will write again. Likewise,
when writers work at a fever pitch, driven by mania or massive
quantities of stimulants, they tend to think they've produced
their best work ever and can become belligerent or hostile when
informed otherwise.

While more than a few of my authors have been in treatment at one time or another, only once did I receive a call from
an author's psychiatrist. The doctor told me that my publisher
and I were putting undue pressure on this writer, that she
needed more time to finish her book, and that touring would
probably kill her. I had begged the writer dozens of times
over the months during which we were supposed to get the
book into production to call it quits and take a much-needed
rest. I cited other great writers who suffered breakdowns along
the way and to whom we gave extensions in light of health

concerns. Long before her shrink came on the scene, I had made my own diagnosis.

But the writer begged and pleaded to keep the publication date. She swore she would get it all done. She said not getting the book done would kill her, and I went along with her. She began working around the clock, then took up residence in our offices, where I'd find her collapsed most mornings, a new sheaf of pages spun out on my chair, sometimes brilliant, sometimes incomprehensible. The office she inhabited began to look like an art installation at the Whitney, every surface covered with books, pages, articles, empty cartons of Chinese food, soda cans, brown bags leaking sugar packets from the endless cups of tea she consumed. The room resembled the inside of her head. And when she occasionally dozed off, my coworkers would peer in and whisper. No one knew what to do with her, and I was losing perspective on the book as well. Certainly what kept me going was my belief in her brilliance and her high-octane prose, which had an energizing effect on me that few other writers could approximate. But I had never been between such a rock and a hard place professionally, and I no longer knew what course of action would prove helpful or harmful. Near collapse myself, I confessed to our deputy publisher that I feared she would never stop revising. He offered to talk with her and impose a final deadline. Then he invoked those two words we all remember well from high school as we raced to finish a test we felt certain we'd fail: *Pencils down.*

In the end she forged ahead and we went forward with the book's publication. I still sometimes wonder if we made the right decision. My author was hardly the first to fall apart while producing some of the best writing of her career. In retrospect, I can't help feeling that the frenzy and drama were as much a part of the method as the madness. She convinced me that going forward saved her. Had she been wrong, I would never have forgiven myself.

A number of years later, one of my most treasured authors, Lucy Grealy, died of an accidental overdose. Her memoir, *Autobiography of a Face*, was a chronicle of her rare childhood cancer that left her face disfigured. It only became clear over time that Lucy was using heroin—first "recreationally," before turning deadly, her habit much more serious than she had let on. She called me a few months before she died, sounding manic and desperate at the same time, her remarkable bravery now bravado. We spoke at length about her difficulty writing her novel. It was unclear to me whether her struggle was because she wasn't experienced in writing fiction or because she hadn't figured out what she needed to say—it hadn't occurred to me that the reason was depression and that she was self-medicating, to use a clinical term for what in fact was self-destruction. In *Truth and Beauty*, her extraordinary memoir of her friendship with Lucy, Ann Patchett lets her frustration and desperation with Lucy's drug use rise to the surface along with her fierce belief in her friend. "'Lucy's not going to die,' I said. Suddenly I was angry. 'These are candy-ass suicide attempts. She may wind up homeless. She may alienate everyone she knows, but she isn't going to die. Lucy will be the last one of us left standing.' Life had been conspiring to kill Lucy since she was ten years old, and life had failed. At every turn she wrestled with death. She always won."

I reread *Autobiography of a Face* after Lucy died. I still saw the brave girl, the magnificent ways in which language and poetry opened inside her. "Language itself, words and images, could be wrought and shaped into vessels for the truth and beauty I had so long hungered for." But there, too, was the insurmountable loneliness and suffering. "I read various philosophers and imagined my soul, separate and clear of heart and mind. At times I was so lonely I was amazed I didn't expire right there on the spot, as if loneliness that strong were a divine thunderbolt that could strike me down at any moment."

I understood that while Lucy immensely enjoyed the fame and attention the publication of her book brought her, it failed to provide any catharsis. And I wondered how much any artist experiences catharsis per se. It struck me that the creating of art serves a need but doesn't necessarily fill it. And for those afflicted with depression, addiction, or bipolar disorder, illness exacerbates and thwarts the ability to create. Untreated, it destroys art and then life.

❧

"Many artists and writers believe that turmoil, suffering, and extremes in emotional experience are integral not only to the condition of human suffering but to their abilities as artists," writes Jamison. "They fear that psychiatric treatment will transform them into normal, well adjusted, dampened, and bloodless souls—unable, or unmotivated to write, paint or compose." It may be hard to envision William Blake on the couch describing his visions, or Hemingway droning on to a small bearded man about his cat fetish, but if you can't get your work done because you are suffering from some form of depression or worse, avail yourself of help. Writers live inside their heads more than most people. As Jamison baldly and correctly states, "No one is creative when paralytically depressed, psychotic, institutionalized, in restraints, or dead because of suicide." Having someone to help you grapple with problems is a good thing. Medication may be beneficial. Remember, creativity is inalienable. No shrink can take it away from you.

To the extent that we are still fascinated by altered states, creative genius, mental illness, and suicide, it is because we all, just once, would like to touch fire. We, too, want to feel our wings spread as we soar toward the sun. As Anne Sexton writes in her poem "Live," "I say *Live, Live* because of the sun / the dream, the excitable gift." Who knew better than she how, in playing with fire, one always gets burned.

PART II.
PUBLISHING

7.

MAKING CONTACT: SEEKING AGENTS AND PUBLICATION

WHILE I WAS IN GRADUATE SCHOOL, I REPLIED to a classified ad in the *Village Voice*: "Sm Lit Agcy Sks P/T Asst Gram Pk Loc." I took the Number 1 train from Columbia University's 116th Street station down to 23rd Street and wound my way east to Gramercy Park. Though I knew the city well, the block took me by surprise, so pristine were the brownstones, their long, graceful windows with heavy glazing obscuring the scenes within. Lacquer-black wrought-iron banisters with curlicues and ornate detail garnished the elegant stairs that led up to the brightly painted doors. I approached with awe and trepidation; could the smeared address on the newsprint in my now sweaty palm match up with one of these beautiful buildings?

After college I had taken a job at an investment bank, whose offices were housed in a monolithic Midtown tower. For two years I worked in their corporate library fetching financial documents for the then Masters of the Universe. These were the Gordon Gekko days. But now, as I wandered down this tree-lined street, I was transported to a nineteenth-century New

York in a Jamesian swirl of excited anticipation. I was greeted at the door by a highly energetic and extremely skinny young woman, who told me to watch my step as we descended into what I would later learn was dubbed the Dungeon, the base-ment offices of the agency. The husband-and-wife team who owned the agency had their large loftlike offices in the aerie above.

The Dungeon consisted of two rooms connected by a long hall lined with bookcases, where the young woman worked with a senior agent. Every available surface was nearly toppling over with books. In the front office, a wall of manuscripts, file cabinets, and a Xerox machine held court. In the back were two desk areas, one long abandoned, piled high with old files. The other desk belonged to the senior agent, a beautiful woman with an extraordinary sense of stillness and grace, whose bulle-tin board was decorated with exquisite scraps, postcards, pieces of art, book jackets, and a variety of trinkets that I was eager to examine but tried to act nonchalant about. In comparison with the investment bank, where the only pieces of "art" allowed on the walls were framed tombstones from completed mergers, this office teemed with the life of the mind and creativity I had always craved.

The senior agent asked me why I wanted the job, and I explained that I hoped to acquire some worthwhile experience by the time I finished graduate school and that I had always imagined myself in either teaching or publishing. As she would later tell it, she tried everything she could to talk me out of publishing, but I only grew more smitten as she explained my various clerical responsibilities. Finally I felt bold enough to ask

about one of the book jackets on her wall. I can still see the
small, hand-tinted photograph of a young boy leaping a preci-
pice, and I admired it.

"Oh, do you like it?" she asked, removing the dust jacket
from the wall. "It's one of mine."

Confused, I asked if she was a writer, too.

"No, no. One of my writers," she laughed. "The jacket is for
one of my authors, one of my *clients*."

I didn't completely understand what she meant, and feeling
a bit foolish for not understanding, I didn't pursue it. What I
did know was that I was falling in love with the atmosphere,
as I dared to look around the small room, where every inch
of available space was also crowded with books. Finally, I was
shown through a back door that led to a gorgeous garden,
where I imagined lovely literary teas being served in the late
afternoon. After I assured the senior agent that neither the low
pay nor the long haul from Columbia would present any problem, she offered me the job.

A lot of people would have balked at the sheer amount
of paperwork, the stacks of files that needed to be weeded
out and sorted through, but I was a sponge soaking up every
piece of information I could. It was all fascinating to me, especially the rejection letters from the publishers: some so kind and
apologetic, some deeply involving and full of interesting ideas
about how the author might improve the material, others terse,
and still others were extraordinarily arrogant and unnecessar-
ily hurtful. (One of my jobs was to send the rejection letters
to the writers, culling those that might entice the razor blades
out of the medicine cabinets.) This, of course, was before email,

and the agents kept carbons of all their correspondence. It was my job to file the carbon copies, but before I shoved them into the overflowing file cabinets, I devoured them. I loved the letters the agents dashed off to clients, urging them on: *Great new chapter, keep up the good work.* Or the longer editorial letters offering structural advice, ideas about character development, or in one case, the suggestion to rewrite the novel from an entirely different point of view. Publishing, and especially editorial, has always functioned as an apprenticeship. In part, the nomenclature serves to keep salaries low for as long as possible. But it is also true that editing is art when done well, and it takes time and experience to master. Reading those letters on that thin, frosted paper was probably the best training of my career. And I worry to think what is lost as editors and agents type and electronically file their letters, their assistants completely out of the loop and none the wiser.

I marveled at the telexes we would receive from the UK and Spain, Japan and France. The foreign editions of books that arrived in their travel-weary cartons always looked a little hilarious with their incomprehensible titles and bad graphic art. Sometimes an author would drop by in the flesh, which always thrilled yet slightly embarrassed me. Somehow the real people behind the books, behind the files and letters and royalty statements, always seemed a little less glamorous than they had in my imagination. And then there was the retinue of foreign publishers and movie scouts and foreign agents who paraded through the office in search of projects for their own purposes. I'd often listen in on these meetings while I pretended to be otherwise engaged, filing royalty reports and mailing checks.

I did every kind of office work imaginable, but the most exciting and heady responsibility by far was reading. The first time the owner of the agency asked me if I read, I was confused. *Did I read?* What he meant was did I want to read manuscripts from the unsolicited pile, a Pisa-like tower threatening to crash down at any time. When I replied in the affirmative, he handed over a manuscript box from the top of the pile and told me to bring it back with a reader's report. I so clearly remember reading those pages. It was over a long weekend in the fall and I had gone home to visit my family. I sequestered myself with a blanket in a hammock off the side of the house. I read all four hundred pages and took elaborate plot notes. Then I worked on a reader's report for most of the next day, describing the plot, the tone, the setting, the quality of the writing. On some level I knew that the book was terrible, obvious and clichéd in every way, but I felt in awe of the task and the attendant responsibility. Who was I, after all, to judge this writer? Who was I to pass judgment on this Joe Shmoe who couldn't draw a convincing character or punctuate to save his life but who had, after all, written an entire novel? It was more than I had ever managed.

When I proudly handed in my four-page single-spaced report the following week, the owner took one look at it and said, "Do you really expect me to read this?"

Naturally, I was taken aback.

"Look," he said, "just tell me one thing. Did you like it?"

Did I like it? What did my liking it or disliking it have to do with anything? I had written a four-page critical report, a plot summary, an analysis of the author's intentions, and an assessment of the writing quality. *Did I like it?*

"No." I shrugged. "Not really."

"Then get rid of it," he said. "Write a rejection and I'll sign it."

I went back to my desk in the rear office and told the senior agent what had happened. I was more than a little agitated. I had spent the entire holiday working on the report, and on top of that I had the awful feeling that this guy's future was in my hands. *Who was I?*

"He didn't even want to read the report," I told her. "He just wants me to get rid of it."

"Well, kiddo," she said, "welcome to the real world."

I lost my publishing virginity that day. And I would lose it again and again at the hands of agents when I started my own eventual climb up the editorial ladder. One of my first mentors in the business referred to literary agents as necessary evils. When I crossed over to become an agent myself, many fellow agents called to wish me well, and a few said, "Welcome to the side of the angels." This amused me to no end since, in my mind, I had just made a deal with the devil. While some publishers do not like to work with agents, most of the larger trade houses prefer it. And some will recommend agents to writers who come to them unrepresented. It was none other than legendary editor Maxwell Perkins who suggested that a young Putnam editor named Diarmuid Russell, who had been fired for taking the author's part in a dispute over a contract, join up with Henry Volkening and start a literary agency. Perkins felt there was a shortage of good agents who could not only help clients sell their work to publishers but advise them in literary matters as well.

If there was a shortage back then, Perkins would no doubt be alarmed today at the glut. We now have all manner of agents: the mega-agent, the power agent, the boutique agent. We have West Coast agents, rugged northwestern agents, right-wing agents, old lefty agents, gay and lesbian agents, thriller and horror agents, pop culture agents, celebrity agents, romance agents, blogger agents, and good old-fashioned plain literary agents.

Agents come in all stripes and colors, and it is impossible to generalize about the work they do or the services they provide. But the first question all aspiring writers ask is whether or not they need one. And the answer, quite plainly, is yes. Once in a great while a writer is fortunate enough to be discovered, but most are in the unenviable position of relying on others to provide what they most desire: dissemination of their work. Eudora Welty was one of the rare exceptions. The very first two short stories she sent out, "Death of a Traveling Salesman" and "Magic," were published in a small husband-and-wife-run magazine called *Manuscript*. The couple wrote to her saying that "'Death of a Salesman' [*sic*] is one of the best stories that has ever come to our attention—and one of the best stories we have ever read. It is superbly done. And 'Magic' is only slightly short of it in quality."

Welty was ecstatic. "Is this the way it happens?" she wrote. "You just put something in the mail and they say okay. If they paid me a million dollars, it wouldn't have made any difference. I wanted acceptance and publication." She then had the continued good fortune of being contacted by Diarmuid Russell, the Putnam-editor-turned-agent. He'd been tipped off by a Doubleday editor who had recently made a trip through the

South in search of new talent. According to biographer Ann Waldron, Welty had never heard of literary agents before Russell contacted her, and she was unclear about their role, but she signed on nonetheless. It was more than a year before Russell was able to sell her first collection (even in the 1940s publishers were loath to take on short-story collections without the promise of a novel to follow). Still, he was convinced of the quality of her stories and sent them out repeatedly. "At times he feared his new client would lose confidence in him, as he seemed to be unable to convince editors how good her stories were," Waldron writes. "Eudora reassured him that she would not be 'bitter' if he never sold the stories, just impressed if he did."

❦

If you're just starting out, I can tell you that agents and editors do respond to well-written cover letters and to opening sentences that bring a manuscript to life. In fact, a cover letter usually announces the writer's facility with words or lack thereof. Some letters are so stiff and stilted they are almost painful to read. Others use the language to keen and clever effect, within the lines a promise of what is to come.

When I give writing workshops, I use two exercises to make the point of how important that first impression is. I distribute two handouts, the first a packet of query letters and the second a packet of first pages from actual manuscripts received over the transom. I ask the participants to determine two things based on the letters and sample pages: Would they invite the writer to send his or her work, and would they continue reading the novel based on the first page? In every workshop I've conducted, the students are in almost unanimous agreement about which manuscripts they wanted to continue reading and which letters piqued their curiosity.

Evaluating manuscripts, like grading papers, produces a bell curve of what appears to be natural ability. It quickly becomes clear which papers are the most accomplished, which letters the most inviting. Indeed, editors and agents alike enjoy nothing more than being startled awake by a particularly witty or moving letter or reading the fresh pages of an extremely well-written manuscript. "I try to remind my students that most of the editors I know are not opening that envelope hoping to find another story like the ten thousand they've already seen," said Michael Cunningham. "They're hoping to find something alarming, brilliant, and unprecedented."

Too many writers, in trying to secure the services of a literary agent or publisher, simply do not do their homework. The best way to get an agent's or an editor's attention is to write an intelligent and succinct letter. And then send it to the right person. Too many aspiring authors send blind letters of inquiry in the vain hope of piquing the recipient's interest. These letters, which we receive by the dozens, both depress and astonish me. What's depressing is how much misguided energy goes into these efforts. What's astonishing is the sheer industry. Because writing is such a personal endeavor for most people, some forget that they are entering a professional relationship. Editors and agents are turned off by letters chock-full of misspellings (including the recipient's name), or those that assume a relationship where none exists. Query letters that sound as if they were penned by the Unabomber instead of a thoughtful writer get automatically deep-sixed, sometimes after they are passed around for sport. Just as the reading public judges books by their covers, we judge manuscripts by the accompanying query letters. And if you can't write a good, crisp sentence by way of introduction, it's doubtful that you'll inspire any interest on the part of the recipient.

Over the years I have received any number of gifts or gimmicks included with query letters or manuscripts intended to butter me up, amuse me, or entice me, including chocolate cigars, a stained-glass pendant, baby booties, ribbons, flowers, a pair of dice, a five-dollar bill, a bottle of patchouli oil, numerous author photographs (sometimes topless of the men, bikini-clad of the women), a box of Band-Aids, a box of Kleenex, a pack of cigarettes, and a bottle of wine. Over one six-month period I received a monthly package of what looked like outsider art, usually a soda can decorated with clay, buttons, twigs, and so on. When no letter of explanation or manuscript arrived as part of what seemed like an elaborate scheme to get my attention, I was advised to call personnel and turn over each piece of "art" as evidence in case a crazed writer ever decided to come and claim his work or go postal along editorial row, blowing everyone away in a fusillade of pages and buckshot.

Just to make matters perfectly clear, please resist the temptation to do any of these outlandish things. Also, if you are sending your material in hard copy, do not use colored or scented paper, bind your manuscript in a three-ring notebook or any other way, attach stickers or drawings, or include a 9-by-11 glossy of yourself with too much teeth or cleavage. (At a previous job, there was a bulletin board in the kitchen of all the photos we received in the slush. It looked like a cross between a Most Wanted list and a dating service.) If you are submitting via email, most agents prefer you send the query without the attachment—only sending the material upon request. Do not allow the casual nature of email to confuse you—this is still a business letter. And in either kind of submission, no jokey, attention-getting first lines such as the one I recently received: "Have I got something hot for you!" Um, no. No crazy fonts or colors, no sob stories, no excuses, no overly long explanation of what your project is about, and no ridiculous or overstated marketing statistics. And if you're listing the competition, tell us why your book is different—no need to trash talk.

I am always struck by the writer who, with no credentials per se, blithely compares his work to any number of current or past bestsellers. Were you to believe the claims of query letters, every travel memoir would be destined to become the next *Eat, Pray, Love*. Every dog story, *Marley and Me*. Every cat story, *Dewey*. If you're mining the historical thriller genre, no doubt your book is the next *Devil in the White City*. Or perhaps you're the next Sebastian Junger or Jon Krakauer, who were each relatively unknown when their books reignited the action/adventure category with *The Perfect Storm* and *Into Thin Air*, respectively. Everyone in publishing knows that in order for a book to work (that is, sell) a great many factors must come together, including the quality of the book itself, publicity breaks, bookstore support, and so forth. It's too simplistic to claim that you or your project is the next anything, because books are made from scratch. If it were easy to copy John Grisham, every publisher would do so. And yet many of the query letters we receive about legal thrillers promise they will be the next Grisham. How many succeed? Just once I'd like to see a writer make a humble promise or estimation of his expectations. Just once I'd like to see a writer compare his or her work to a book that isn't a commercial blockbuster. Or better yet, let the publisher draw the conclusion, based on the quality of the work. I promise, a simple, dignified letter with a clear statement of your intent and credentials will win more affirmative responses than any gimmick or hype.

Don't address your query "Dear editor" or "Dear agent." Do your homework and find the right person's name. This is a much less daunting task than it used to be, when the best resource—scouring the acknowledgments pages of favorite authors to see whether agents or editors were thanked—was fairly hit or miss, and the *Literary Market Place* (known as the LMP), an encyclopedia of publishing information, didn't list agent or editor names. Now you can subscribe to PublishersMarketplace.com, a highly worthwhile investment. On this site, you can search by name or category. You can see which agents have sold, for example, health books or cookbooks or young adult novels. You can see everything an agent has sold, to determine if she might be right for you, and vice versa. If that isn't enough information, you can check out most agents' websites, search for them on Google, or read their blog (if they have one, ahem). There is no longer any excuse for not coming up with a list of agents who are appropriate for your project.

Even before all this technology, writers found their way. When Susan Sontag finished the first book she felt was publishable, *The Benefactor*, in 1963, she made a list of publishers.

"Farrar, Straus was my first choice, because they had just published *The Selected Works of Djuna Barnes*," she recalled in *Conversations with American Writers*. "New Directions was my second choice, because they published many more writers I admired, but somehow I had the impression that they were more inaccessible. Third was Grove Press, because they were publishing Beckett. I put the manuscript of *The Benefactor* in a box and left it at Farrar, Straus and Giroux. Two weeks later I got a call, was asked to lunch by Robert Giroux, who offered me an option that turned into a contract. I spent several months reworking the book and they published it."

Sontag's story of her first publication is made even more remarkable by the fact that she went on to spend her entire career with the same publisher. By seeking those whose work she respected and responded to, and leaving her small package without much flourish or craven exaggeration, she found herself a lifelong home.

Unfortunately, most of the unsolicited queries that editors and agents get come from people who clearly have not taken the time to research the playing field. In other words, if you go to the trouble of writing to editors and agents, at the very least target your search through some careful investigation of what the house publishes, what that editor has worked on, or whom the agent represents.

And then, don't call or email. I cannot emphasize this enough. Returning the email of an unsolicited author ranks very low. Yes, you can have the last laugh when your book stays on the bestseller list week after week, and those who once took weeks to return your calls are now fawning all over you. But as an unsolicited writer, you're at the bottom of the barrel. Plus, if you are calling to see if the agent or editor has read your work yet, I can promise you she hasn't. No one reads a manuscript, loves it, and doesn't call the author. She'll call if she's interested, or she will reject it. This may take up to six months. Unfortunately, it's a don't-call-us-we'll-call-you world until further notice. Exception to the rule: a polite nudge via email is acceptable four to six weeks after submitting your book. Sometimes a manuscript gets lost or mislaid; it doesn't hurt to check. More important, assuming you sent out your novel or proposal on a multiple submission (and you should), and one of the agents is interested, this would be the time to get in touch with the others. This, my friends, is called leverage, and it's your moment to exercise it. Let the other agents know that someone is interested in representing you and ask that they take a quick look and let you know their thoughts. This will shake a few rejections loose, but you will probably have more than one agent to choose from at the end of the day. The only other reason to get in touch while your work is under consideration would be to report something significant in your literary life. You won an NEA fellowship, the *New Yorker* accepted your first story, Stephen King gave you an endorsement, or similar. Do not "share" any news that is not germane, such as getting divorced, getting pregnant, getting hair extensions. When you become a client, you may confide in your agent, but for now, business as usual.

There is some truth to the old saw that the squeaky wheel gets the oil, but in my experience calling too soon or too often will have the opposite effect, and you'll be branded as a nudge.

All editors and agents already have enough nudgy authors to deal with. In addition, unless you were referred, the editor probably has no idea who you are. Most editors and agents don't read their slush or unsolicited query letters. They depend on their assistants to pass along anything that might be of interest. Dan Brown can be a nudge. You can't.

Writers always ask whether they should multiply submit. The answer is yes, unless you hope to work with an agent who has expressly stated that he or she will not read a multiply submitted manuscript. I recommend sending your work out to a half-dozen agents, unless you have a good referral or contact at an agency or house; otherwise you could spend a year making three or four single submissions. However, I also recommend that you make the most of your multiple submissions by paying keen attention to the responses. And I would mimic the strategy our high school guidance counselors suggested for applying to colleges: make two submissions that are a reach, two that are in range, and two you would consider "safety schools." Try an agent or two at one of the big firms, a couple at medium-sized agencies, and a couple who are out on their own.

The long silence that follows the submission of your work can be maddening; frustration and paranoia tend to run high. Every now and then an editor will receive a call from an extremely irate author who cannot believe that no one has jumped on his opus or that months have passed and his highly explosive nonfiction proposal remains on the unread pile. Many writers become agitated, and some turn hostile, as if those of us in the corridors of publishing were deliberately trying to sabotage their careers. Granted, nothing is more frustrating than waiting for a

response for weeks or months and then getting only a form letter. However, a form letter is all that any agent or editor owes
you. After all, you are seeking professional, not educational,
services.

If you receive only form letters in response to a query,
then you should take a good look at your approach. Chances
are that it needs serious refining, revising, or rethinking. And
before you waste any more of your own time, you should
consult any of the excellent books on getting published. For
nonfiction, I highly recommend *How to Think Like an Editor* by
publishing insider Susan Rabiner. It has an excellent chapter on
how to write a proposal. Or seek out educational services in
the form of a writing workshop, a course on proposal writing,
or perhaps a freelance editor or copyeditor to review your work
and offer specific help. If you do receive some personal notes
from editors or agents, take this as a very good sign. Perhaps
an agent has even offered to read a revision should you make
some changes. As with love, all you need is to find one person
who believes in you.

Edith Wharton confesses in her autobiography that when
she sent out her first tentative submission of a few poems to
the leading magazines of the day, she was clueless about how
to do it. "I did not know how authors communicated with
editors, but I copied out the verses in my fairest hand, and
enclosed each in an envelope with my visiting card!" After a
week or two, she received word that all three poems had been
accepted. "As long as I live I shall never forget my sensations
when I opened the first of the three letters, and learned that I

was to appear in print. I can still see the narrow hall, the letter-box out of which I fished the letters, and the flight of stairs up and down which I ran, senselessly and incessantly, in the attempt to give my excitement some muscular outlet." As if this weren't heart-stopping enough, the editor of *Scribner's Magazine*, Edward Burlingame, invited Wharton to share more of her work. As she recounts, "He not only accepted my verses, but (oh, rapture!) wanted to know what else I had written; and this encouraged me to go to see him, and laid the foundation of a friendship which lasted till his death."

❧

More than a few writers whom I've met at conferences have complained to me that it's more difficult to get an agent than it is to interest a publisher, which is surprising, given how many agents there are. Some tell horror stories of agents who agree to take them on but never return their calls. Agents who, after making a few submissions, lose interest if the project doesn't sell and stop submitting it. Agents who take months to read new work. Agents who care only about making the deal and don't act as advocates for the book. Agents who don't attempt to sell the author's foreign, audio, film, and serial rights.

The worst accusation I ever heard was of an agent who reportedly held on to an author's advance monies and royalty payments until the author threatened to sue. As in every pro-fession, there are a few people who give the industry a bad name, but unless you already have a publisher interested in your work, or believe that you alone or with a lawyer can negotiate best terms, and feel reasonably certain that you can handle any disputes that may arise, you should spend whatever time and energy it takes to secure the services of a good agent.

Do not, however, let an agent's interest in you or your work keep you from taking certain precautions. A writer is entitled to a reasonable amount of information when he or she signs on with an agent. You may ask to see the agent's client list (though most are now available on their website). You may ask what books he or she has sold and to what publishers, what his or her percentage or cut is (15 percent is standard), and what, if any, additional charges will be billed back to the client, such as the cost of messengers, copying, books, and foreign submissions. You need to know what the contractual obligation is between you and the agent and whether you are required to sign a contract. This agreement should outline your contractual responsibilities to one another, the commission structure, and, like a prenup, what happens in the event of a breakup. As a client you should also be apprised of the general game plan, including where the agent plans to send the book and whether he plans to send it out to just a few publishers or widely. If the first six publishers turn it down, will the agent give up, advise you to revise, or keep plugging until he finds one? What plans does he have for the exploitation of secondary rights, meaning film, foreign, audio, and electronic rights? I know some young writers who are afraid of their agents, who don't want to bother them or appear needy and insecure. It's understandable that they don't want to alienate the first person who actually seems to like their work. Still, you should feel a bond of trust with the person representing you and your work. If at all geographically possible, meet with any agent who expresses interest in representing you and bring a list of questions. Whether through letters, email, conversation, or an actual meeting, it should become clear if the agent is interested in your long-term career or just a one-night stand.

I will never forget an incident at the agency where I first worked. The owner, an extremely hardworking man with many successful commercial clients, loved literary fiction and went to great lengths to sign up writers of literary quality, even though their earnings were meager by comparison with others on his roster. After sending one young woman's first novel around for nearly thirty submissions over a two-year period (this goes back to when manuscripts were submitted one at a time), he persuaded her to write it from a different point of view, based on the advice of some of the more thoughtful rejection letters. The author spent a year on the revision, and the agent started to send it around again, first to the editors who had said they would reconsider the work if it was revised. And again he sadly began to rack up another pile of heartfelt rejections. He was nearly out of places to send to and about to give up when, late one evening, while I was putting in some extra hours in the back office, the phone rang. The agent had wandered downstairs with a pile of manuscripts and letters for the following morning, and I heard him take the call. Then I heard what sounded like sobbing. When I came down the hall to see what was wrong, my boss, who hadn't realized I was there, became flustered and embarrassed. Then he laughed and said, as he removed his glasses to wipe away an escaped tear with the heel of his hand, "We got an offer, we finally got an offer."

Writers complain that there aren't many agents left who will keep submitting a book with that kind of tenacity, though I would argue that those willing to stake their name and reputation on a piece of writing will go the distance. After all, no one takes on a quiet literary novel or memoir because he thinks it will make him rich. He takes it on because he loves it and hopes that the writer will develop over time into an author of some esteem. Some might argue that fewer agents take chances because fewer publishers take chances and because there are fewer publishers period, and all of this is true. Also, an agent in the business for many years probably has a full client list; she may take on one or two new clients a year, while a new agent is eager to sign up writers. I recently met an agent who put a highly successful client list together mostly from the discards of a well-established agent who offered to refer all her rejects. What's the expression? One man's slush pile is another man's Edgar winner.

Much of the unhappiness and pain that arises in an author-agent relationship seems to stem from a lack of trust or from frustrated expectations. Some writers only want their agent to sell their book and do their bidding. And yet they are always second-guessing the agent's strategy or choice of submission. Others crave camaraderie; but more than friendship, they sometimes want their agent to be all things: father confessor, brother, and champion. Some authors want their agents to be mind readers, offering help and encouragement when they need it, leaving them alone when they don't. Some authors want to belong to a certain agent's stable because his list is full of well-established, successful writers, but once there they feel like small fish in a big pond. Others want to be big fish, then wonder if their agent has enough clout to get the best deal.

Often the agent is the first reader of a writer's work, and the author relies on him as heavily as, if not more than, his editor for feedback. And some agents do indeed edit. Furthermore, editors tend to jump from house to house, and sometimes the only continuity a writer can hope for is from the relationship with his agent. It's extremely important to have an agent who not only knows your publishing history the way a doctor knows your medical history but who understands how you work, what you need, and how best to present your work. The best agents provide this service and then some. Some have even been known to lend money to clients in advance of their publishing payments, as agent Harold Ober often did with the wayward F. Scott Fitzgerald. But that is going above and beyond the call of an agent's duty. Still, no matter how many wonderful agents there are, their reputations, like those of mothers-in-law and pit bulls, are sullied. "Ten-percenters," as agents are referred to in *Variety*, aren't known as the world's great humanitarians.

Even the best agent/writer relationships can break down. Sometimes when a book doesn't sell, the author may feel the agent was at fault, or in any case that he needs a new start. A certain level of resentment can also accrue because the agent generally takes 15 (not 10) percent of the writer's earnings. Relationships can become strained when one party is somewhat beholden to the other. Every year we witness one or another high-profile defection of a writer to a new agent. Always the circumstances are acrimonious, as they should be; money, sometimes lots of it, and ego are at stake. One of the most notorious cases, and one that will take some doing to top, involves Martin Amis, whose highly entertaining novel *The Information* details the exceedingly healthy spirit of competition among writers. Taking top honors in the ever-amusing art-imitating-life category, Amis's much-publicized defection from his longtime British agent to an American agent kept writers, agents, and publishers on both sides of the Atlantic knee-deep in gossip for weeks. The *New York Observer* referred to the melee as "a stew of literary envy and bad karma worthy of the most stomach-churning, self-flagellating moments in *The Information*." The bad karma referred to the fact that Amis's longtime agent just happened to be married to Julian Barnes, Amis's oldest friend in the literary world. And ratcheting it up a notch from there, apparently Amis based the buffoonish bestselling writer at the novel's center on none other than Barnes. "The friendship did not survive the business rupture," editor Gerald Howard wryly noted in the *Review of Contemporary Fiction*, pointing out that "the novel might be described as a demonstration that hatred of one's peers is so powerful a force in the literary world that they can cause writers to behave approximately like Tonya Harding."

Sometimes agents jump ship, too, as in the much-publicized 1989 departure of Lynn Nesbit, the head of ICM's literary department, to join forces with lawyer Mort Janklow. A story entitled "Royalty Wedding of the Year," which appeared in *Manhattan Inc.* magazine, described the merger as the "marriage of Mass and Class." Nesbit is famous for her literary authors: Her first bestseller was *The Kandy-Kolored Tangerine-Flake Streamline Baby* by Tom Wolfe. Later, she sold Donald Barthelme's first short story

to the *New Yorker.* And in 1968, she took on an unknown first
novelist called Michael Crichton. Janklow's stable consisted of
Judith Krantz, Sidney Sheldon, and Jackie Collins. "Mort sells
the equivalent of heroin in books," commented his competitor
Andrew Wylie. "One damages the body, his books damage the
mind." But Janklow, as a result of having worked with some of
the bestselling authors of all time, was able to see, from what
Wylie dismissed as his beach-blanket perspective, the international and marketing opportunities for promoting authors.

"Publishing used to be a sort of mom-and-pop operation,"
Janklow commented. "It's going through a transitional phase.
It's becoming more international. There are big changes in the
retailing and distribution. The marketing side is vastly improved.
Publishing is becoming a very serious business. There is the
growth of the idea that it is not unliterary to sell the product."
And he said this long before the proliferation of superstores, coffee bars, Amazon.com, readers' guides, reading groups, before
Kindles and iPhones and print on demand, before Facebook
and Twitter and the most powerful mover of books in the land,
Oprah. What Janklow didn't say, but what he certainly must
have seen, during that decade when he brilliantly joined forces
with ICM's top agent, was that it would be the decade of the
agent.

No matter how many mega-agencies merge (the latest being
Endeavor and William Morris), or individuals (usually down-
sized publishing execs) enter the fray, there is still an art to
selling. And no agent exemplified said art better than Irving
"Swifty" Lazar, who, in his day, made deals for the likes of Noël
Coward, Tennessee Williams, Clifford Odets, Lillian Hellman,

and Ernest Hemingway. Acclaimed editor Michael Korda's reminiscence of Lazar in his *New Yorker* article "The King of the Deal" portrays a larger-than-life character whose business feats and philosophy were part Attila the Hun, part Yogi Berra. Lazar, one of the first truly bicoastal agents, became well known for his undaunted bravado and for making deals and offering projects by famous actors he didn't actually represent, then exacting a commission if his fishing expedition proved fruitful. Lazar had three advantages, according to Korda, that kept him on top for fifty years. The first was his extraordinary access to anyone and everyone; the second was his staunch refusal to deal with underlings, going straight to the top instead; the third was his insistence on a quick answer. "Even now, if I tell Irving that I want to think something over or discuss it with someone else," wrote Korda, "he will snap, 'Never mind, I can see you're not interested.'"

Sam Cohn, "a progenitor of the Hollywood superagent," according to his *New York Times* obituary, had an incredible roster of A-list writers, directors, and actors, such as Paul Newman, Meryl Streep, and Mike Nichols. He was a founding member of the mega-agency ICM and pioneered deals through creative collaborations previously unheard of. In a single year, at the height of his powers, he had ten movies and nine Broadway or off-Broadway plays open with his clients as actors, directors, and more. But the quote that stays with me, from Nora Ephron, describes what it felt like to have him in your corner: "When he got behind you, it was like an army of thousands." I don't think an agent could dream of higher praise.

I think every industry needs its Swiftys, its elder statesmen, its iconoclasts, its rising stars. We need people who defy convention just as much as we need those who uphold it. Every time an agent challenges conventional wisdom and gets a good deal for her client, whether it's better terms or a bigger advance, then she has moved her client's cause forward. Every time an agent discovers a new writer and through careful grooming and presentation offers publishers an absolutely irresistible property that sells for more money than anyone imagined, it's a victory. But most agents struggle along, just as everyone else in the industry does. While their financial risk is small in comparison with the publisher's costs of development, manufacturing, marketing, and distribution, their reputations are at stake, as is their livelihood—for their clients can walk out at any time. Few agents enjoy the luxury of having on their list what I call repeat offenders, that is, authors who reliably publish a book a year that automatically hits the list, such as James Patterson, Michael Connelly, and Janet Evanovich, or, more recently, J. K. Rowling, Stephenie Meyer, and Malcolm Gladwell. And like everyone else in publishing, agents deal with the residual effects of disappointing sales, bad reviews, selling slumps, loads of rejections, and unearned royalties. However, they can also profit from an unexpected windfall in ways that turn most editors green.

A fresh-faced college graduate might surmise that becoming an agent is a better goal than trying to become an editor, especially if he's intrigued by the financial incentive. There was a time when actors' salaries, ballplayers' contracts, and author advances were private matters. No longer. Whenever a large deal is struck, the story is all about the agent and the size of the advance. Who the writer is or what the book is about is often secondary. Everyone wants to report that his deal was the highest amount, as if book deals were sports records, there to be broken.

On the other side of the equation is the great story of the late golf pro Harvey Penick, who was considered the crème de la crème of golf instructors and who kept a lifelong record of advice in the form of homilies in a little red leather notebook. According to ICM agent Esther Newberg, writer Bud Shrake saw the potential in Penick's work and helped the golfer prepare the material. Newberg shared it with Simon & Schuster publisher Charlie Hayward, an avid sports fan. Hayward, she said, "took about twenty-five seconds and offered $90,000." Newberg called Penick's wife, since Harvey was nearly deaf by this point, and told her that Simon & Schuster was interested in publishing the book for $90,000. His wife said she needed to discuss the offer with Harvey. When she got back to Newberg, the golfer's wife said that they had talked it over and wanted very much to go forward with the book. She explained that they would get a second mortgage on their home to come up with the ninety grand. It's amazing that the news didn't kill Penick when he finally understood that the publisher was going to *pay him*. And as if that weren't enough, *Harvey Penick's Little Red Book*, published in 1992, went on to become one of the most successful sports books of all time.

But the day that stays with me as emblematic of the sea change taking place in the industry came when one literary writer whose work I loved was making the rounds of publishers with her agent. The agent planned to move her author from the small regional publisher where she had gotten her start to a major New York house. It was a bit of a coup for me to get the agent to send the new manuscript, as I was still relatively untested. I was more than a little excited about the meeting, which was to be attended by some of the company's brass. The writer was from the South, and after an exchange of niceties about the weather and how New York was a far cry from her hometown, she placed both hands on the table and asked if we could get down to business. Yes, of course, we told her; what was it exactly that she was looking for in a publisher? She told us she had had her share of editing, "The Maxwell Perkins stuff is great and all that," she drawled, "but what I want to know is how y'all are going to break me out?" This was ten years before the hit movie that made everything perfectly clear: Maxwell Perkins has been supplanted by Jerry Maguire. *Show me the money.*

8.

REJECTION

REJECTION IS A FACT OF WRITING LIFE. IF
you are still unpublished, you probably suffer from the misconception that publication in and of itself will cure everything
that ails you. But the pain of rejection doesn't stop the day a
contract arrives. In fact, when you sign your name on the bottom line of your publishing contract, you may be signing up for
more disappointment than you ever dreamed imaginable. Saint
Teresa's dictum "More tears are shed over answered prayers than
unanswered ones" should be hung on the wall over every writer's desk. Sometimes being rejected may mean being spared.

If you are just starting out, try to look at rejection as a ladder. The first rung is made up of form letters that offer some
trite condolence about why your work isn't right for the literary journal, magazine, or publishing company. The next rung
might still be form letters, but now an editor has scrawled a
note: *Try us again!* Usually the signature is illegible, a common
tactic to keep the writer from getting his hopes up by imagining

that he might actually develop a relationship with the editor. James Dickey, in a *Paris Review* interview, said that the world of publishers and agents might just as well have been in the outer part of the solar system, so foreign were they to him. "I just knew that I liked to write and I had some ideas that I thought might work out as poems. So I wrote them, then sent them around. As they say, I could have papered my bedroom wall with the rejections. . . . I sent poems in and I kept getting back these form rejections. In 1948 or 1949, I remember with wonder I saw a true human handwriting on a rejection slip. It said, 'Not bad.'"

The next rung may seem like a small step, but it is the equivalent of a moon landing: the personal letter. At this stage it may be a very short letter, but the point is that it is absolutely *not* a form letter. They don't want this story or project, but the editor or agent is actually inviting you to send more work! Fourth rung: bull's-eye! Then those magic words: *We are pleased to inform you . . .* Very few writers are catapulted into the land of publication without amassing rejection slips. If you are not one of those fortunate few, take heart as you climb. As frustrating as a close call can seem, it does mean that you're on the right track. And chances are, if you stick with it, that close call will eventually become a full-fledged acceptance. Unfortunately, it's easy to become agitated and lose heart, especially when you drop back a rung. For instance, after receiving personal notes for a while from a book or magazine editor, you may suddenly find a form letter in the mail. Or worse, just as you have finished the sixth draft of your novel and are preparing to send it to the editor who had sent you a few encouraging notes or provided some editorial advice over the years, you discover when you phone the publishing house that she has joined the Peace Corps. The one person who had appreciated what you were up to is off somewhere in Somalia. No note, no call. Just up and gone. *Somalia! Somalia!*

These things do happen, and often it is a matter of luck, good or bad, that appears responsible for any given access or denial. Luck isn't a concept that interests me. I see publishing as more like a game of odds in which you increase your chances of acceptance simply by doing more than the next guy. It wasn't about being in the right place at the right time but about being in a lot of places at a lot of times, showing up even when the odds seemed lousy. How this applies to writers is somewhat obvious, but I'll belabor the point: submitting your work fifty times or revising it as many times as you have to may be what separates the sung from the unsung.

There is no better story in publishing history than that of mega-bestselling writer John Grisham. His first novel, *A Time to Kill*, which he wrote in the predawn hours over a three-year period while he juggled a high-stress sixty- to eighty-hour workweek as a lawyer with a young family, was rejected by dozens of agents before he found one who would take it on. His agent then submitted the book for a year, also amassing a pile of rejections, before finally placing it with the now defunct Wynwood Press for an advance of $15,000. The book had a five-thousand-copy first printing. "I bought a thousand, and another thousand were sitting in a warehouse," said Grisham in a 1993 *Publishers Weekly* interview. "So you know not many were out there." Not exactly an auspicious debut.

But as is his habit, Grisham started his next novel the day after he finished *A Time to Kill* (and more important, long before the world responded with its resounding yawn). That next book, *The Firm*, had a rather different publishing trajectory. While it was on submission to publishers, a copy "leaked" out to Hollywood, and Paramount paid $600,000 for the movie rights before a single publisher made an offer. "News of the deal lit up phone lines on both coasts," reported *Publishers Weekly.* "Within two weeks, Grisham had a contract with Doubleday, one of the many houses that had passed on *A Time to Kill* two years earlier."

Grisham's success looks like the stuff of fairy tales. Twenty years and twenty books later, every new book of his debuts at number one on the bestseller lists, and his novels have sold more than 250 million copies worldwide as of this writing. You might say that John Grisham got lucky, but I would posit that hard work, persistence, his habit of starting a new book the day he finishes his last, as Anthony Trollope always did, account for Grisham's success. Luck is winning the lottery. Writing draft after draft, and sending them out over and over again, is sweat.

In a witty and useful essay in *Poets & Writers* magazine, author Bill Roorbach puts it this way: "Luck is a fine thing for a writer, but take note: Good writing creates luck. . . . By the time most good writers start to publish work regularly, they've amassed many hundreds of rejection slips, in all shapes and sizes. . . . Ping-Pong, my writer friend Bob Kimber calls it. You shoot a manuscript out, they shoot it back; you whack it back out there, it comes back. As long as you've done the honest work and know that what you're offering is good stuff, you have every reason to play the game." So why do people stop whacking their pages out there? Do you get discouraged, depressed, distracted? Do you feel the odds are stacked against you? Did three or ten or thirty agents or publishers reject your work? Are you willing to revise, possibly start all over? Just remind yourself, each time you catch yourself thinking that the bestsellers and prize winners of the world are merely lucky or well connected, each time you begrudge others their success, feeling that you are once again outside the sweet-smelling bakery with your nose pressed up to the glass: the sticky buns are within reach.

❦

No one is as tormented as the rejected writer. If he isn't beating himself up, he is expending a fair amount of energy feeling slighted and neglected and in some cases downright robbed when a writer of similar age or background makes it. He doesn't stop to consider that the other writer may be worthy; the very fact that others are able to get published is like salt in the wide-open wound of a writer's psyche. I meet a lot of people at writers' conferences who exude woundedness. I can tell they have made an attempt to get published and have failed thus far. They are full of yearning yet have not perfected their craft. Some would rather talk about writing than write. Some are desperate for contact with other writers. Others are suspicious, guarded, or weary, and a few are downright hostile. They seem to think that the publishers and agents present are on enemy ground; who wouldn't feel that way after being rejected time and again?

After attending one such conference, a group of editors and agents gathered for dinner, and naturally we started to gossip about the attendees, those who showed promise and those who seemed hopeless. I felt implicated in the judgments we so easily tossed off; after all, I had been one of those seekers who had attended writers' conferences before throwing in the towel and going into publishing. I took workshops, even got my MFA, though a part of me felt that writing programs were a joke, just a place to bide your time and stave off entering the real world. One of my literary heroes, Truman Capote, said in an interview, "The last thing in the world I would do was waste my time going to college, because I knew what I wanted to do. . . . The only reason to go to college is if you want to be a doctor, a lawyer, or something in a highly specialized field. . . . If you want to be a writer, and you are a writer already, and you can spell, there's no reason to go to college."

Much as I agree with Capote's sentiment in theory, I still feel a huge compassion for those seeking the community of writers and advice about getting published. The fact is that many students of writing programs get invaluable advice about their work and even direct access to agents and editors. However, any statistics would show that most of the people attending any conference or writing program will never become published writers. Even if your portfolio gets you into a writing program, once there you have only entered another Darwinian system that will naturally weed out the weak from the strong. Not the better writers per se, but the ones who won't quit.

When Gordon Lish (aka Captain Fiction), famous for his outrageous conduct, used to harangue the students in his marathon-length writing classes about their staying power, sometimes even mocking the rare student who'd dare to get up to go to the bathroom, calling him a puppy who couldn't hold his water and piss with the big dogs, many of the attendees thought him certifiable. Others let their bladders nearly burst during the six-hour marathon sessions. The method may have been mad, but Lish treated his job as seriously as a drill sergeant's. He knew that most of us were likely to get killed out there, that the world of ten thousand things, as he called it, was indifferent to our sentences, and he wanted to toughen us up. He scrutinized our sentences with all the coldness and lack of interest of the real world. His was not a workshop, it was boot camp, and more than a few grunts couldn't hack it.

I think the best advice to writers attending a conference or beginning a writing class is to ascertain where you stand in relation to the other participants and learn from those who are a step or two ahead. Like finding a tennis partner whose ability is a notch above your own, you will play better if your partner's game challenges yours. All you really need during those long years when rejection may get the better of you is one friend with whom you can share your work, one fellow writer with whom you can have an honest exchange. Just as Wordsworth befriended Coleridge, as Hemingway used Fitzgerald, so did Welty rely on Porter, and Kerouac on Ginsberg—writers need one another. Some have formed loose associations, such as the Bloomsbury writers, the Algonquin Round Table, or the Beats, thus establishing powerful networking channels, a literary manifesto, and a platform from which to be heard. For a number of years following graduate school, some friends and I put together our own magazine and held monthly poetry readings. Eventually we all became too busy, and our mutual purpose eroded as we made diverse career choices. But for that brief period we felt as if we were part of something important that involved our identity as writers.

If you don't have a writers' group, start one. You can't expect the publishing community, either agents or editors, to stand in for personal instruction and feedback. Some writers, even those who are quite accomplished, rely their whole lives on a person or a small group of trusted writing friends for feedback and support. I was shocked when I discovered that an established writer whom I had signed up relied on no fewer than five writing friends for a critique of her manuscript before turning it in to me, her editor. And as she started refuting some of my editing, she'd recall the comments of one friend or another. I wanted to tell her that I didn't edit by committee, that too many chefs spoiled the word soup, especially when she'd cite an exboyfriend's reaction. As if he'd tell her the truth! But I was also aware of how important this circle of friends was to her survival as a working writer; they were more than readers, they were also engaged in the struggle and thus provided shelter.

Still, no matter how valuable I think a writer's conference can be, especially for a writer who has yet to find a community, when I attend as a representative of the publishing world I automatically feel on edge. Suddenly I am staring at all those rejection letters I dinged back, in the flesh. Week after week we churn them out: *Not right for our list, Not our cup of tea, Better luck elsewhere, Good luck with your work.* And suddenly we're face to face with the cup of tea. Better luck elsewhere is sitting in the front row and asking if I'd be interested in her memoir. What the hell am I supposed to say? I want to row everyone to safety, but the goddamn raft will sink.

❧

Writing is nothing if not a long-distance race. The same kind of hubris that can cripple a runner who doesn't properly train can also derail a writer from reaching his goal. And just as the expert runner can tell the novice from a mile away, usually from his spanking-new running suit, the editor can spot the writer manqué. These are the people who invariably give editors the most trouble, who badger us constantly to help them, who make a million excuses or apologies for their work, or lack of work, and whom we wind up carrying down the mountain in a body bag. These are the writers who want to sell us on a book idea but balk when we suggest that they first try it as a magazine-length piece. It's like wanting to get married without having gone on a date.

Before attempting to publish a book, you can do any number of things that will help make your work more rejection-proof. If you are a nonfiction writer, try placing op-ed pieces on your topic, or publishing a magazine piece, or better yet, a series of articles. Perhaps you could get a regular column in a local newspaper. If you want to be recognized as an authority, you probably need to get an advanced degree and publish in the professional journals in your field. Think about offering classes to gain a local following. At the age of twenty-nine, a young man without a college degree started to work as a spiritual counselor and teacher in London, according to his website. Eventually, he would publish a book based on those teachings with Namaste, a small spiritual press. That book would come to the attention of a major trade publisher through the efforts of an editor browsing in a tiny bookstore on an island off Vancouver—where the writer also happened to live. To say that his ideas caught fire would be an understatement. Since then, Eckhart Tolle has dominated the mind/body/spirit section of the bookstore. *The Power of Now* became a *New York Times* number one bestseller and has been translated into thirty-three languages. His next book, *A New Earth*, was selected by Oprah for her book club. Sales are reported at ten million copies. Tolle continues to speak and teach extensively throughout the world. Most impressive, if you ask me, he has an iPhone app with original text and graphics from his books. (I want an app!)

I doubt Tolle had much of this in mind when he had his "awakening" in London. He took his ideas to a certain level, began teaching, and found a small press for his work. Some writers even go so far as to self-publish, so determined are they to spread their word. And in some cases, major publishers have gotten wind of successfully self-published books, have acquired the rights, and have published them nationally. Whether through determination, elbow grease, or missionary zeal, the authors kept the dream alive long enough for someone else to finally pick up the ball and run with it.

Blogging is the latest iteration of this phenomenon. Agents and publishers have seized on a number of writers whose blogs caught their attention for their growing popularity and the voice or unique idea behind them. Julie Powell started a blog about her mission to cook every one of Julia Childs's recipes in *Mastering the Art of French Cooking*, as a way of warding off ennui from her day job. The idea and winning voice attracted a food columnist from the *New York Times*, whose article attracted an agent, who then sold the book handsomely. And next, as you know, *Julie & Julia* was adapted for the silver screen, with the inimitable Meryl Streep in the title role.

A blog titled "Stuff White People Like" was the subject of a debate on NPR's "Talk of the Nation." Was the site racist or satirical? I know NPR can be a bit dry, but hello? Later, Random House signed up a book based on Christian Landers's clever photos and super-snarky commentary on consumerism and culture. I'm sure the title alone went a long way in attracting attention, millions of blog followers, the NPR "controversy," and finally the $300,000 book deal.

In 2001, a blogger who wrote negative posts about her employers landed in the unemployment line. Where some might have permanently logged off, Heather Armstrong found she had hit a nerve and mined it in a series of brilliant posts that would eventually become a daily chronicle of every aspect of her life, marriage, and motherhood in one of the most popular blogs today: Dooce.com. When her book, *It Sucked and Then I Cried*, was launched, hundreds of fans showed up at her readings, many bearing gifts, many buying multiple copies. The book jumped onto the *New York Times* bestseller list the first week out.

When I address writing conferences I always ask the participants to think about how badly they want it. Is having a book published worth taking out a second mortgage, filling up the trunk of your car, and schlepping books from mall to mall? Novelist E. Lynn Harris self-published his books about relationships among straight and gay African Americans after the major publishers had turned him down. He loaded his car with copies and brought them to local beauty salons, where he rightly guessed he might find an audience as well as a pretty good word-of-mouth network. His books caught the attention of a local bookseller, who in turn mentioned them to a publisher's sales rep, who brought the novels back to the home office. The company took up Harris's novels, all of which have gone on to become national bestsellers.

If you insist that you want to write only in book-length form, that writing magazine articles, running workshops, or blogging doesn't interest you, then write your book proposal or even the complete manuscript and see what happens. Perhaps the power of your ideas, the strength of your prose, the irresistible appeal of your style will garner you a publisher. A *Newsweek* article featured the nature-versus-nurture debate and used as its centerpiece a book called *The Nurture Assumption* by Judith Rich Harris. "This petite, gray-haired grandmother hardly seems the type to be lobbing Molotov cocktails at one of the most dearly held ideas in child development," the article explained. What fascinated me was that the sixty-year-old author had no academic affiliation and no PhD. In fact, she was thrown out of Harvard in 1961 "because her professors believed she showed no ability to do important original research." Thirty-eight years later, Judith Rich Harris saw her work published *and* graced the cover of *Newsweek*. Naturally, her adversaries claimed that her work was irresponsible. Still, Harris, who clearly never gave up, had the satisfaction of seeing her ideas disseminated and debated.

There is always more than one way to skin a cat, as the expression goes, and if you've got great writing/communication skills, something new or necessary to say, focus, drive, and a certain amount of quixotic self-belief, then I believe you will be heard. Obviously, writing a novel and writing a self-help book are entirely different endeavors, but as an editor I will venture to say that all authors, at heart, are not so different from one another. All are driven by a desire to share their stories and ideas and to connect with people. All believe in the power of the written word and in the power of the book. The novelist wants to change people's lives by transporting them into a story; the journalist wants to find the story hidden in plain view; the self-help author wants to help people effect change in their lives. The greatest compliment any writer can hear from a reader are the words *Your book changed my life.*

As much as writers and agents complain that the publishing industry is interested only in the "slam dunk" bestsellers, most of us live for discovering original voices and unexpected runaway successes. Nothing compares with discovering a first-time writer and seeing her book come to fruition and meet with success in the marketplace. Consider *Reading Lolita in Tehran*, Azar Nafisi's memoir of the secret classes where she taught forbidden books by Western authors. The book was published modestly, which is a polite way of saying relatively few copies were printed and distributed. Word of mouth began to build and it was taken up by book clubs (a more perfect selection hard to imagine). But it was also the confluence of world events that largely accounts for the book's success. The beginning of the Iraq war gave the book tremendous currency and urgency, if born of dire circumstances. *Reading Lolita in Tehran* would stay on the bestseller list for more than one hundred weeks and was translated into thirty-two languages. The gratification of seeing a book break out is enormous, especially when it sparks a national conversation, or in today's parlance, when you've got the "It" book.

Whenever I used to lift the top off a new manuscript box, listen to its cardboardy hiss, and take my first intoxicating whiff of the fresh pages within, there was, if only momentarily, that renewed hope that this one could be it. Unfortunately, the pressures of the publishing world too often diminish that feeling of hope, and editors, in dealing with the sheer number of submissions alone, don't have time to stop and smell the pages.

We rely on a body of conventional and received wisdom about what sells and doesn't sell (which is thankfully proved wrong from time to time) and develop a shorthand to evaluate and reject projects. Rejecting a project is easy; taking on a project is complex. In most of today's publishing companies, it has to jump through many hoops after an editor shows interest. Sales, marketing, and publicity often have a significant voice in the acquisition process and can shoot a project down. I'm not saying their voices and viewpoints aren't valuable, only that an editor's passion or expertise no longer carries the day alone in most publishing companies.

It is incumbent on you to make your proposal or novel as bulletproof as possible. Anything can sink it, so take precautions, go the extra mile. Have it professionally copyedited if you're nervous about grammar, punctuation, spelling. Nothing makes a writer appear less professional than not knowing whether to use *it's* or *its*. Try to get endorsements from experts in the field before you seek a publisher. If your project comes with a blurb or introduction by a nationally regarded specialist, it will naturally attract more attention and appear more viable. Get feedback from other writers. If you're pitching a nonfiction idea, it's important to study the competition and in your proposal explain why your book is different, better.

Sometimes the title alone will distinguish your book from the rest of the pack. Sometimes a catchy, clearly targeted title can make a project almost irresistible. Enticing readers is the Holy Grail of titling: a good title will go a long way, and if the book's contents live up to the promise of the title, you just may have something destined to sell for years. Lots of books are acquired without a title or with a bad title, but a brilliant one can improve its chances of acceptance. A nonfiction title that includes its own hook or conveys the concept in the nanosecond it takes to digest is a great title. Think of *The Tipping Point*, *Freakonomics*, and *Fast Food Nation*. One of the best titles is now a bona fide brand: *What to Expect When You're Expecting*. Fiction is, of course, much more subjective, but a memorable title is the starting point from which you introduce your work. It's like your face: the first thing people see. Among recent memoir titles, I love Nick Flynn's *Another Bullshit Night in Suck City*, Dave Eggers's *A Heartbreaking Work of Staggering Genius*, and *Me Talk Pretty One Day* by David Sedaris. Each is audacious, funny, edgy, unique. For fiction: Alice Sebold's *The Lovely Bones* for its haunting quality, Cormac McCarthy's *The Road* for its stripped-down, iconic power, and *Pride and Prejudice and Zombies* by Seth Grahame-Smith because it's so silly. I hear many writers say they couldn't think of a good title, so they planned to wait until they had a publisher, because the title would probably change anyway. If this is you, please turn around and go back to the drawing board.

Also, don't make the mistake of writing in what I call a proposal voice; this isn't a grant you're applying for—there's no need to pad the thing with high-minded promises. Editors and agents primarily want to know whether you can write and what the voice of the book will be. Write the proposal in the voice and style in which you have written or plan to write the book. Over the years I have witnessed too many writers who take the opposite approach, believing they must compose their ideas in the most basic terms. They are writing, they tell me, for the lowest common denominator. When I ask who they imagine reading their book, they invariably reply: everyone. No one seems to think that his subject matter is limited. Rather, everyone thinks that Oprah, if only she heard about the book, would plug it, no matter if it is about vegetation along the Merritt Parkway, the power of wishful thinking in Jane Austen's novels, or overcoming halitosis. The desire to popularize your ideas is neither uncommon nor wrong-spirited. It becomes problematic only when you imagine yourself somehow above your constituency in the process. So where do you pitch your book, or rather what is the right pitch? My advice is to write the book you want to read. Write the book that takes everything you've got. Don't imagine an audience of more than one. Don't dumb down, and don't try to outsmart the market.

On the fiction side, the same holds true. Whether you are writing literary fiction, a potboiler, a thriller, or a romance, you must appeal to something real in the body of human experience. Always write with an ideal reader in mind. No writer was more blunt in her appreciation of her audience than Jacqueline Susann, who said that she wrote for the women who read her on "the goddamn subways." "I know who they are," she continued, "because that's who I used to be." Susann understood that the fantasy she created fed an intense envy and curiosity on the part of her readership, women who dreamed of expensive jewels, star-studded parties, and suave men with slow hands. But she also gave her readers what they needed by making all her rich and beautiful characters suffer. "That way the people who read me can get off that subway," she said, "and go home feeling better about their own crappy lives."

Susann's own life was more than a little crappy, though she worked hard to conceal both her personal suffering from breast cancer and the challenge of having an autistic son. Some people might dismiss Jacqueline Susann as just a trashy writer, but I believe her success is underlined by her identification with her audience. She never wrote down; rather, she wrote her heart out.

I like to tell people to write for their mentor or their fiercest critic. Write to the very top of your form. When rejection comes, and it will, at least you will know that you did your best work. Every moment you spend explaining away the hurt of a rejection, telling yourself it wasn't your best work, is a moment that fails to advance your cause.

If a wad of rejection letters is all it takes to get you to quit writing, then accept the consequences, but understand that it was you who gave that wad its power. While it is true that some editors get off on rejecting people, showing off their smarts and exercising their power, most are truly uncomfortable saying no to people. I've often suspected that part of the reason why editors take so long to decline on projects, apart from never having enough time to consider them, is how uncomfortable they are rejecting and disappointing people, whether it's the agent who has submitted the work or the unknown soldier who wrote it. Plus, we've all seen our share of books that have been notoriously and strenuously rejected throughout the industry that nevertheless go on to bestsellerdom or critical acclaim.

Every now and then an editor will get an irate letter from a writer for whom the rejection letter was the straw that broke the camel's back. The writer will rail against the rejection, quote the editor back to himself, and insist that the criticism is misguided. Some writers question whether the editor actually read the book, noting that the pages barely look riffled through. Some will demand a rereading, so convinced are they of the editor's subterfuge. According to Robert Hendrickson's wonderful book of literary anecdotes, *The Literary Life and Other Curiosities*, one author wrote an editor who had recently turned down her story, "Sir, You sent back last week a story of mine, I know that you did not read the story, for as a test I pasted together pages 18, 19, and 20, and the story came back with these pages still pasted; and so I know you are a fraud and turn down stories without reading them." The editor replied, "Madame, at breakfast when I open an egg I don't have to eat the whole egg to discover it is bad."

Accusatory letters from rejected writers are depressing. It's impossible not to feel for the writer, to empathize with the helplessness, the depth of despair. Yet to answer these letters would be to invite madness. Still, I like to believe that writing the letter and shooting it off in anger at least reclaimed some piece of dignity for the writer. The author must know on some level that an angry letter won't get him anywhere; but I like to imagine that it helps him get through another day, that it enables him to reclaim his writer's soul by saying, *You cannot erase me—I reject the rejection.*

Naturally, editors prefer to get letters thanking us for our time and asking if we might be willing to look at some future work. This, dear reader, is a better strategy. Unless you have received a form letter, it doesn't hurt to write a thank-you note. However, do not mistake a polite letter of rejection for a letter of encouragement. Every editor has experienced the sad submission of a writer who includes the rejection letters of other editors, all of which are clearly kiss-off letters, as proof of the project's appeal. The writer imagines that the sentences of faint praise are actually words of encouragement.

Just as you shouldn't take a polite letter for an encouraging one, don't let a harsh letter do more damage than necessary. Maybe the editor writing it was just dumped, or acquired more than her share of projects, or was reprimanded by her boss for poor showings. It's hard not to focus too deeply on a rejection letter, or any correspondence from an editor, because it's often the only feedback you have, but I beg you not to spend more time with rejection letters than the time it takes to read and file them away. Do not paper your bathroom walls with them, as one woman I went to writing school with did; do not wear them down to a fine talc with your worrying fingers. Do not study them like the I Ching, hoping to draw symbolic meaning from the arrangement of letters on the page. Trying to figure out what the editor or agent *really* meant or felt is not useful unless she has offered some specific constructive criticism that resonates with you. Even if it is shattering to learn that the editor whose response encouraged you to totally revise your novel is now in the heart of Africa, you should have revised it only if you believed it was the best way to fully realize the story.

Never do anything just because an editor tells you to. I have heard too many writers complain to me or absolve themselves of responsibility for a bad idea or a revision by saying that an editor told them to do it that way. No matter how desperate you may feel in your efforts to secure an agent or editor, don't go along with their advice unless you believe that it is right and sensible. That said, don't be stubborn or stupid; decide when to stand your ground and when to capitulate. Most writers work in isolation for so long that they no longer have perspective. What's most important in the dance of submitting your work and getting it rejected is figuring out how to use the process to improve your material, and thereby your chances of having it published. "It is not too much to say that how well a writer copes with rejection determines whether he has a genuine literary vocation or just a literary flair," wrote esteemed editor Ted Solotaroff in a superb essay called "Writing in the Cold." "Rejection along with uncertainty are as much a part of the writer's life as snow and cold are of an Eskimo's: they are conditions one has not only to learn to live with but also learn to make use of. . . . The gifted young writer has to learn that his main task is to persist."

The only writers I ever feel contempt for are those who announce that unless their work is accepted for publication they won't keep writing. Perhaps they save themselves lifetimes of grief, but I find the attitude astonishing in its arrogance and naiveté about what the world wants or owes anyone. The world is a mysterious place, and as far as I can tell, no one really knows why we all dance around certain texts and parade them through our streets. One thing, however, is certain: no matter how many people return your work, the only one who can send you packing is yourself.

9.
WHAT
EDITORS
WANT

ASKING WHAT EDITORS WANT IS A LITTLE like asking what women want. While particular editors become known for loving and choosing certain kinds of books, an extraordinary number of variables affect any editor's taste, judgment, and response, and these are subject to change based on everything from her workload, the support or lack thereof from her colleagues, her track record, and the length of time since her last acquisition.

Some editors are hired with a particular mandate: to bring in celebrity books, sports books, business books, commercial fiction, health, or how-to. And some publishers' lists are likewise focused. But for the average editor who works for a trade press, chances are she is a "generalist" and edits a variety of books in what we call the adult trade. An editor will become known as an expert in a certain field after she has a certifiable hit, a book that either sells exceedingly well or that walks away with one of the big literary prizes. An editor does not exist without her authors; as the coach of any championship team acknowledges as he enters the winner's circle, he's only as good as his players.

When I started as an editorial assistant at Simon & Schuster, I was fortunate to be a fly on the wall of a publishing house that still had at its editorial helm two editors whose reputations were built on books that inspired awe. At one end of the corridor was Alice Mayhew, who shepherded the publication of one of the century's most important political books, Bob Woodward and Carl Bernstein's *All the President's Men*, a book that electrified the nation, if not the world. The other end of the hall was occupied by a man of slight build with a showman's glint in his eye, and I soon discovered that Michael Korda had edited an extraordinary spectrum of authors, from Jacqueline Susann to Carlos Castaneda. As far as I was concerned, these two editors were living legends, and I felt both shy and giddy when our paths crossed in the long corridor known as editorial row (also known as Death Row, as the house was famous for its swift removal of any editor who didn't pull his weight and for its tyrannical leader who, fortunately, was housed many floors above).

Everyone who works with books is in one way or another attempting to become a part of publishing history. Just as the author hopes for immortality through publication of his book, most people in publishing hope to work on a book that touches people, entertains them, enlightens them, or changes them, a book that shapes the national dialogue or becomes a part of the lexicon. Over time, many book people become disenchanted and cynical about the business, but even the most hardened tend to soften when their company produces a runaway best-seller or a prize winner, a book they feel proud to be associated with.

During that same first year as an editorial assistant, I watched as Simon & Schuster discovered one such book on its list. It was by an academic from the University of Chicago, and it went against the grain of the political-correctness movement that was mushrooming on American campuses. Even more sur-prisingly, the book's initial printing was so small that when a rave review by Christopher Lehmann-Haupt in the daily *New York Times* vaulted it onto the bestseller list, no one was more astonished than the publisher. "Allan Bloom fools you in his remarkable new book, *The Closing of the American Mind*, which hits with the approximate force and effect of what electric-shock therapy must be like," began the critic. "By turns pas-sionate and witty, sweetly reasoned and outraged, it commands one's attention and concentrates one's mind more effectively than any other book I can think of in the past five years." Lightning had struck!

It was very exciting to be at Simon & Schuster during that time, even though I obviously didn't have anything to do with the book or its success. There was a palpable sense that a book could still be a force of nature. It was 1987, and the American public was obsessed with *Fatal Attraction*, Black Monday, and the Iran-Contra affair. And in the midst of all that, this little flare from the pristine campus of a Midwest-ern university was making headlines. One late night during a Scrabble game that I played each week with two other editorial assistants, I wondered aloud if the editor was enjoying his suc-cess, imagining what it might feel like to have a book on the bestseller list and stirring national debate. "He didn't bring it in, you know," one of the assistants retorted with a sneer. I didn't understand—he was the editor of record. My friends, who had been assistants for a year or more before I arrived, filled me in. The acquiring editor, the man who had signed up the book, had left the company to run his own division at another house. We debated whether the editor who inherited the book was any less important than the one who brought it in, especially since he had done all the editing. Finally, the assistant with the most seniority explained with an air of great wisdom and world-weariness that ultimately it was the person who signed the book, the acquiring editor, who mattered.

Vying for credit and credit-mongering are mainstays of the editorial ranks. Except for the fortunate few whose contribu-tions are both recognized and rewarded, most editors jump from house to house either for better opportunity or because they were pushed, and as a result they often leave much-loved or potentially lucrative projects behind. I wonder if an editor today would be able to stay employed at a single publisher long enough to build the kind of list assembled by Nan A. Talese, whose eponymous imprint at Doubleday has published such celebrated authors as Pat Conroy, Margaret Atwood, and Ian McEwan for the length of their careers. Alice Mayhew at Simon & Schuster still works with Bob Woodward, twenty-five years after *All the President's Men* was published, as well as nonfiction superstars Doris Kearns Goodwin and Taylor Branch.

Signing up authors or acquiring projects is ultimately what

separates the assistant who gets promoted from the one in the next cubicle who winds up going to law school or getting that graduate degree after all. The aspiring editor has to acquire a project of her own if she ever wants to be promoted, just as an editor has to produce in order to keep her spot in a publishing climate that resembles the elimination game of musical chairs. What does it take? If you were to survey a random group of editorial assistants, it quickly would become clear which ones are secret writers, hoping to use the job experience as a jumping-off point for their own careers; which ones, too in love with literature or some romantic notion of how the world should work, will never cut it in a grueling, competitive environment; and which ones bring just enough book smarts, good taste, social skills, marketing savvy (and by that I mean social-networking Internet wizardry), to succeed in the age of corporate publishing. If she can hold her bourbon at a *Paris Review* party, that's also a plus.

The year I entered publishing, 1987, an article entitled "Nobel House" appeared in *New York* magazine, about the estimable publishing firm of Farrar, Straus & Giroux, still independent at that time. (Even the name sounded more like a tweedy old law firm than a book publisher.) Most of my favorite poets were published there, and I salivated as I read about the care with which the house treated its authors, its commitment to quality and literature. According to the article, the firm took an almost perverse pleasure in publishing books with little or no audience. According to the article, Roger Straus, the publisher, was famous for "barb-trading" with Dick Snyder, the head of the house where I worked, saying that "he cried for the trees sacrificed to produce Snyder's books." In describing FSG's appeal, various authors weighed in with praise, remarking on the accessibility of everyone who worked there. Scott Turow, who published his first few books with FSG, said, "Everyone there is a standout, from the amazingly literate salespeople to the publicity department. Long before my book was a success, they were all spectacularly kind to me at every turn." Walker Percy said of cofounder Robert Giroux, "He's a man of great good taste. One writes with a sense of who your reader is, and Bob Giroux is my imaginary reader." But the quote that really impressed my youthful, idealistic soul came from the production director, who explained that FSG still used metal type to set their books instead of film, which is less expensive and the way all the other houses had gone. "We feel typefaces in metal have a nicer look, more expressive," she explained.

Everyone who comes into book publishing has a special relationship to books, understands their mystery and their power, even if their careers take unexpected turns and don't end up the way they had planned. In certain respects, the climb up the editorial ladder is not unlike the writer's quest for publication. The apprenticeship is long. Many, if not all, of the ideas and manuscripts a young editor brings to the attention of his superiors are rejected. He often wonders if it's worth it, especially when he watches a fellow assistant who seems to be the soul of corruption get a leg up. Advancement is not guaranteed, and whether an aspiring editor sticks with the long hours and largely uncertain future often depends on whether he is encouraged by more senior people in the company.

I had the good fortune of finding a mentor, either directly or from afar, at every publishing house where I worked, and from each I gleaned some inspiration. One boss was universally considered a control freak, but he taught me how to think like a publisher. You couldn't acquire a book unless you could envision all the steps necessary to launch it. At most companies you had to run a profit and loss statement, but he made us get sales figures for comparison titles, imagine a jacket, come up with a list of potential blurbers, think about who in the media might cover it, and finally figure out how you would present the book at sales conference. My next boss had a laissez-faire style; if you wanted a book he'd encourage you to chase it. Left to our own devices, some editors unraveled, others took the ball and ran. At Houghton Mifflin I had the privilege of working with Ruth Hapgood, a beautiful woman with nearly translucent skin and long white braids that were always neatly pinned into a bun. Ruth, far ahead of the curve, introduced any number of health gurus to the public long before alternative medicine took off. At her retirement party, Ruth, never long-winded (a virtue in and of itself in the publishing business), thanked people for their friendship and collegiality. She told us not to worry about her, she had enough dreams for six people. But then she became quiet, searched out our faces as she scanned the room, and said in a lowered voice, "All of you are the children of the book. Remember who you are."

I never forgot the admonishment, though it's easy to lose heart when you sink your all into a book that vanishes without a trace, or when a beloved author gets a hideous review in the paper of record and you want to rail against the powers that be for giving your kid a bad grade: *She deserves better than that! She worked so hard!*

❧

As a junkie craves a fix, an editor gets off on the thrill of finding a new writer or winning an auction. There is even something vaguely amatory about the whole mating dance when an editor is in pursuit of an author, especially one who is being vied for. I have heard authors complain of editors who were far more attentive before they signed them up than after, almost as if the conquest were the point. Sometimes an editor will go for months without reading anything that inspires him, that makes him stay up past his bedtime or miss his bus stop. Whenever a fellow editor starts to complain about how long it's been since he's acquired a book, it reminds me of how my friends and I used to lament how much time had transpired since we last got laid. And as with sex, the longer you go without it, the greater the chances are that you'll lower your standards. Acting out of desperation—whether with partners or projects—all too often ends badly.

After an editor has won the hot project being offered around town, she's a bit like a lioness after capturing her prey, lazily chomping on the spoils from the kill, her tail absently smacking flies off her rump as she surveys the savanna, certain no other game is on the horizon. But the editor who loses one project after another, either because she can't find support in-house or because the advance goes higher than she is allowed or willing to bid, starts to feel and act just a little too hungry. After a few months of this, she will jump on anyone's bones, all judgment and per-spicacity out the window. When I left one publishing house for a decidedly more commercial company, the editor-in-chief who had been my boss for four years took me aside as I was packing up my office and said he would like to offer one small piece of counsel. "One word," he said, leaning in: "patience."

An editor newly arrived at a publishing house feels enor-mous pressure to make that first buy, to plant the flag, and this means trying to acquire a big-ticket item. And competition is fierce. When I worked at the agency off Gramercy Park, manuscripts were submitted to editors one at a time, and the editors' names were logged on index cards. It could easily take a year to place a novel. Then, the multiple submission gained acceptance and copying machines fired up all over town. The acquisition process was no longer a gentleman's game. Editors were now reading submissions from certain agents overnight, such was the power of their influence and the fear of missing out. Think about it: if Dan Brown's agent sent you a novel and said it was the most exciting thriller he'd read since *The Da Vinci Code,* you'd be a fool or fired not to start reading the moment it hit your desk.

Now, with electronic submissions (which have become stan-dard), the process is even more accelerated—and often paperless. A writer sends his agent his proposal in a Word file. Agent, in turn, sends it to fifteen editors, electronically. Most of those editors download the document on their Kindle or preferred e-reading device, and a book can be acquired without so much as a single piece of paper exchanged. This is fine if it achieves efficiency, if it spares trees, and all that. But no matter how fast we can transmit material, the fact is that writing and editing, if done well, are extremely slow processes. And it strikes me that taking a certain amount of time to consider a project is warranted.

The editor who nurses a Maxwell Perkins fantasy of discovering great authors, having three-martini lunches, and making gentleman's agreements will be sorely disappointed to discover that in today's publishing climate it's eat or be eaten. Publishers themselves recognized that they must merge and solidify operations and distribution lines or risk disappearing altogether. Just ten years after the *New York* magazine article about Farrar, Straus & Giroux, the house that prided itself on its independence was bought by the German conglomerate Holtzbrinck. About the same time, Bertelsmann bought Random House; Hachette bought Little, Brown; Pearson bought Putnam and merged it with Viking Penguin; HarperCollins bought William Morrow; Houghton Mifflin bought Harcourt; and then, as in the Agatha Christie title, there were none.

Now more than ever, editors are under tremendous pressure to acquire. The editor who can find a project of quality or commercial potential and edit it well will no longer survive on those skills alone. She has to be faster, more clever, and more resourceful than the editor next door as well as the editor across town. She needs to secure blurbs, cultivate reviewers and booksellers, attend readings and parties; she needs to get her colleagues to pay attention to her titles even though there are fifty others on the list. But first, she needs to have the clout to convince her publisher to pay as much money as will be required to win the next big book at auction when the asking price escalates in a competitive bidding war. It's tremendously exciting to be a part of such a feeding frenzy, raising the bid with every round like a poker player pushing all his chips to the center of the table. And yet, as we see over and over again, when one too many of those big books bombs, heads tend to roll to get budgets back in line.

Some editors feel perfectly at ease in this gambling game. *It's not my money*, they tell themselves. Others get nervous spending a lot of money on a project as if the money were their own. But it's not as if an editor has free rein to spend; editors have to have the publisher's authorization to make even a modest offer. Some editors are more fiscally responsible than others. Others think an editor has to spend big to earn big. It's a great theory if everything goes right.

While editors are often lambasted for not editing, heavy-duty editing is a fairly modern phenomenon. Before Maxwell Perkins came along, very little was done to manuscripts. The policy at Scribner's, where Perkins worked, was decidedly hands off. In a letter from senior editor William C. Brownell to Edith Wharton, the company's editorial policy was made clear: "I don't believe much in tinkering, and I am not suffisant enough to think the publisher can contribute much by counselling modifications." So it was more than a little unorthodox for the young Perkins to respond to an unknown writer's novel, entitled *The Romantic Egoist*, with extensive suggestions for revision. This was a manuscript that had bounced from editor to editor, each of whom had found it unpublishable and attached his opinion: "Couldn't stomach it at all," said one; "Hard sledding," wrote another.

As Perkins's biographer Scott Berg explains, editors at Scribner's felt it beyond their purview to offer criticism of manuscripts they declined. "But Perkins's enthusiasm impelled him to comment further." After one revision, the writer paid a visit to Perkins, and while it is not known what transpired, the young writer set off and began another round of changes, including switching the narrative point of view from first person to third. Seven months later a complete revision landed on Perkins's desk. Every one of his suggestions had been taken, including the transposing of the story's point of view. The title page, also revised, now read *The Other Side of Paradise*. According to Berg, Perkins brought the novel to the monthly editorial meeting for "his third assault." Once again the editor was met with a dismissive attitude by the more senior staff, and it looked as if he was going to give up when Charles Scribner entreated him to explain his point of view. "My feeling is that a publisher's first allegiance is to talent. And if we aren't going to publish talent like this, it is a very serious thing." Perkins argued that Fitzgerald would get another publisher and attract other young writers to that firm. "Then we might as well go out of business," he said. "If we're going to turn down the likes of Fitzgerald, I will lose all interest in publishing books." Smart young editors have been using the same argument ever since to convince the old fogies that they risk losing business if they lose touch with the next generation of readers.

If editing has become a luxury in today's world, because of the accelerated pace of publishing and the pressures on editors to spend their time acquiring, it is no less important in the life of a book. No matter what anyone may ascertain about an editor's abilities, it is finally the writer who knows whether his editor has a gift for language, an understanding of structure, a grasp of the dynamics of plot, pacing, tension, and resolution. Only the writer knows if his editor edits. The best editor is a sensitive reader who is thinking with a pencil in her hand, questioning word choice, syntax, and tense. An editor is someone who probes the writer with insightful questions, who smooths transitions or suggests them where none exist. A good editor knows when the three pages at the beginning of a chapter are throat-clearing. *Start here*, she'll mark in the margin. *This is where your book begins.* And she'll know when you should stop, spare your reader being hit over the head as if your point were a two-by-four.

In a 1946 speech to welcome and introduce Maxwell Perkins to the students in NYU's publishing course, Kenneth D. McCormick, then editor in chief of Doubleday, described the great editor as more a friend to his authors than a taskmaster; by his own admission, Perkins was a terrible speller who used punctuation idiosyncratically. He helped them structure their book, if help was needed; thought up titles, invented plots; he served as psychoanalyst, lovelorn adviser, marriage counselor, career manager, moneylender. Few editors before him had done so much work on manuscripts, yet he was always faithful to his credo, "The book belongs to the author."

A good editor should be able to go as many rounds as a writer needs to get his manuscript just right, though an inverse equation often rules: those books that require the most work may be least improved by editing. Often the editor has to work hardest on a book that was mediocre to begin with, and, after she labors over everything from structure to grammar, soup to nuts, the book is still only readable. The finest writers, often perfectionists, tend to require the least amount of an editor's time. I think most editors would agree that nothing is more satisfying than working with a writer whose quality of mind and ability with prose are exquisite and well matched. As the first editor I ever worked for said, after finishing his line-edit on a very fine biography that was eleven years in the making, "It was like polishing silver."

Editing is a science and an art. There is a basic architecture to every book, and if the author has a wobbly narrative leg or an insufficient thesis to stand on, the editor must find the blueprint or create one. What an editor learns as she gains experience is that while no two manuscripts are exactly alike, certain predictable patterns crop up, and as with math problems, the more experience you have, the more readily the solutions appear. As a young editor, I often applied my understanding of the formal structure of poetry to the books I worked on. At the beginning of my career, I found it difficult to hold an entire book in my head, but when I imagined each chapter as a stanza and used my understanding of how a metaphor builds throughout the argument of a poem, it was easier to keep the bigger picture in mind as I helped the writer shape sentences, paragraphs, chapters. Every prose writer has his own rhythms, from sentence structure to the length of paragraphs and chapters, and the editor must help him use that form to its most powerful effect, just as Perkins was able to see that Fitzgerald's novel would work when written from a different point of view.

The art of editing is a dance one engages in with the author to help him achieve the best results. Before an editor can cut a paragraph or a page, she must establish trust. This is best accomplished by showing the writer what works, taking time to pepper the manuscripts with appreciation: *lovely phrase, great word, nice transition.* An editor builds trust with an author through careful attention to his pages. Suggesting that a writer delete his words is excruciating for some, and the excision must be made with delicacy. Sometimes this means the use of lightly penciled queries in the margins: *awk? right word? believable? trans? rep?* Of course, what the editor means is: *totally awkward, terrible word, completely unbelievable, how the hell do you expect the reader to make a transition when you haven't,* and *this is so damn repetitive I feel like killing myself.* The comments and queries become a net beneath the writer so that he feels emboldened to risk the high wire, to the thrill of the crowd below. The editor says, *I will catch you.*

The editorial dance between author and editor isn't complete until the author takes the marked-up manuscript away and goes back to work, taking, the editor hopes, her suggestions and improving upon them. When editors talk about percentages, they mean how much of their editing the writer took. According to the editors I speak with, the percentage varies greatly, though I think it would be very difficult to continue editing if you didn't feel that writers were relying on your judgment.

❧

Only a writer knows for sure whether an editor is making a serious contribution to and improvement of his work. Only the writer really knows how good an editor is on the page. While industry watchers are eager to point out how few editors edit, they never report on those books that were nearly rewritten by editors or that were cut to within an inch of their lives.

The reason is twofold: First, once the book is published, the editor's marks are invisible. Second, the idea of authenticity is central to our literary culture. Don DeLillo rightly counseled his friend Gordon Lish, whose editorial contribution to Raymond Carver's success has been hotly debated, to take a big step back from the fray: "There is no exposing Carver," DeLillo wrote. "Even if people knew, from Carver himself, that you are largely responsible for his best work, they would immediately forget it. It is too much to absorb. Too complicated." He further explained that readers wouldn't fault Carver for relying so heavily on his editor as much as they would resent Lish for sharing the credit.

For a *New York Times Magazine* article about the true provenance of Carver's work, writer and former editor Dan Max visited the Lilly Library at Indiana University to see firsthand the extent of Lish's editing in the archives. "What I found there, when I began looking at the manuscripts of stories . . . were pages full of editorial marks—strikeouts, additions and marginal comments in Lish's sprawling handwriting. It looked as if a temperamental seven-year-old had somehow got hold of the stories." Max charted what reads like a classic father-and-son story through the correspondence between the two men, in which the son, suffocating under the father's controlling hand, yearns to break free. While the father, astonished at the son's lack of appreciation, asserts more control. At first, Carver is deeply grateful to Lish, telling his editor in a 1971 letter, "Took all yr changes and added a few things here or there. . . . You've made a single-handed impression on American letters. . . . And, of course, you know, old bean, just what influence you've exercised on my life." Ten years later, when Carver is at the height of his fame and struggling to wrest his sentences from Lish's mighty blue pencil, he finally writes, "I can't undergo that kind of surgical amputation. . . . Please help me with this book as a good editor, the best . . . not my ghost."

"An editor does not add to a book," Perkins warned a group of students toward the end of his career. "At best he serves as a handmaiden to an author. Don't ever get to feeling important about yourself, because an editor at most releases energy. He creates nothing." It's hard for an editor to remember that all he has done is release a little energy when he has discovered a writer, nurtured him for years, rewritten him in some cases, and gotten him ready to meet the world. It's hard to remember that $e = mc^2$ when the writer in whom the editor has invested the breadth and depth of his creative attentions and on whom he has staked his reputation says, *Stop, you're suffocating me.* Perkins, too, had learned the hard way.

It was during the writing and editing of Thomas Wolfe's second book, *Of Time and the River*, that the relationship with the brilliant and complicated writer began to devolve. Wolfe was adding fifty thousand words a month at a fevered pitch, and Perkins apparently pulled the book away from him, fearful that the writer was on the brink of breakdown. Years later, in an article for the *Carolina Magazine*, Perkins wrote, "I, who thought Tom a man of genius, and loved him too, and could not bear to see him fail, was almost as desperate as he, so much was there to do. But the truth is that if I did him a real service—and in this I did—it was in keeping him from losing belief in himself by believing in him." Perkins read the manuscript in its entirety—one million words—and set about delineating the two separate story cycles within. The work they did together was legendary, and in thanks, Wolfe dedicated the novel to him, despite Perkins's attempt to discourage him from doing so:

> To Maxwell Evarts Perkins
> A great editor and a brave and honest man, who stuck to the writer of this book through times of bitter hopelessness and doubt and would not let him give in to his own despair . . .

Two years later that dedication would be used against Wolfe in a piece that ran in the *Saturday Review* called "Genius Is Not Enough," attacking Wolfe for not having the "critical intelligence" to have pulled off his novel without the help of his editor. Scott Berg suggests that even as Wolfe lashed out against critic Bernard De Voto to anyone who would listen, the piece struck the very deep vein of his terrible insecurity, and he grew to resent Perkins for being the bearer and enabler of his terrible secret. The relationship never rebounded; the two exchanged letters that suggest the emotional wreckage of a love relationship come undone. No writer, no matter how grateful, wants his mother forever straightening his lapel as he gets up to accept his prize.

❦

No reviewer ever says, "By God, this book was well edited," though reviewers seem to have no compunction about slamming editors for not doing more, when they have no idea how hard an editor may have tried to eliminate a character or help an author with his tone. If a book is basically solid and the author insists on keeping certain elements his way, the editor usually accedes. It's the author's book after all—though some editors will make a last attempt to get the author to make changes, even going so far as to pull what I call the Jewish Mother caveat, insisting, *The changes are for your own good*, or *We just don't want you to get hurt*, or *I won't say I told you so*. Still, it doesn't make it any more pleasant when the reviews come in exclaiming, *This book sure could have used an editor*. Once, after a book I worked extremely hard on received such a notice, even my own mother called and asked why I didn't edit it. *Mom!*

One of the great thrills for an editor is to have a revision come in that feels transformed. It may be the result of a complete overhaul or of just getting a whole lot of tiny details fine-tuned, but suddenly the writing sings where before it had only hummed. In describing the editorial process, editor and writer Charles McGrath said of Robert Gottlieb, an editor who worked with some of the finest writers of the last few decades both in publishing houses and at the helm of the *New Yorker*, "Bob has an uncanny knack for putting his finger on that one sentence, or that one paragraph, that somewhere in the back of your mind you knew wasn't quite right but was close enough so that you decided to worry about it later. Then you forgot about it, or you convinced yourself that it was okay, because it was too much trouble to change. He always goes right to those places. It's an instinct. He and I share a belief that if you take care of all the tiny problems in a piece, all the small attention will somehow make a big difference. Sometimes I think that's just a touching faith of ours, and that, in fact, nobody ever notices whether, say, you use the same word twice in a paragraph. At other times I'm convinced that the details are all that matter."

Editors and authors are happy to crow about their successful unions. One rarely hears about the books that didn't live up to expectations, the relationships that fell apart or ended badly, as the Perkins-Wolfe collaboration eventually did, and the Carver-Lish affair decades later. For every author devoted to his editor, many more feel shortchanged, cheated, slighted, forgotten. An editor's stable of writers tends to resemble a family of siblings in which a clear favorite emerges: the hardworking, dutiful ones never feel appreciated enough, and the charismatic and erratic ones who drive their parents to distraction often win their hearts.

I have learned from experience that the only way to deal with sibling rivalry is not to engage. For instance, when a writer asks what else I'm working on, I try never to tell him. In the first place, he doesn't really want to know, and in the second place it's a trick question. What he's really trying to determine is whether his book is the most important on my list.

Authors know that their editors are working with a number of other writers at the same time, but they still want to feel unique, and in this way being an editor is not unlike being a shrink. You know your therapist has other patients, but you're the most interesting, right? She likes you the best. And just as a shrink sees a person at his most vulnerable, editors see a side of authors that no one else ever should: we see them at their most needy, their most egomaniacal, delusional, paranoid, insecure, and arrogant. We are on the receiving end of false flattery and buttering up, as well as tantrums and sulks.

Still, there can develop a unique bond between authors and editors—the editor's joy of discovery, the author's happiness at being found. No matter how beleaguered the world of editing has become, no matter how short a book's shelf life in today's market (Calvin Trillin's now-famous line is that the life of a book is somewhere between the milk and the yogurt), no matter how Kindled, downloaded, or digitized, none of us can ever forget the feeling of first discovering the majesty of reading. (Roger Straus III, son of the co-founding father of Farrar, Straus & Giroux, claims to have had his first "literary orgasm" at fourteen while away at boarding school, when he discovered "The Love Song of J. Alfred Prufrock.") The best part of being an editor is the promise of making those discoveries again and again.

*

Every now and then everything works out: everyone at the company loves a project as much as the editor does; she is allowed to make the high bid and wins the book at auction.

The author turns out be a lovely, hardworking person who takes all editorial suggestions, including a new title that everyone agrees is brilliant. The art director presents a jacket that is so beautiful and original and right for the book it takes everyone's breath away. The editor introduces the author to the director of publicity, who then wants to pitch him to every media outlet and send him to every bookstore in America—he's that promotable.

When the editor sends the manuscript to key people in the marketing department and on the sales force before the sales meeting, it is met with universal approbation. Marketing wants the author to meet with key booksellers in advance of publication and decides to make up T-shirts and posters for key buyers. The sales force recommends the book to all their accounts and requests extra galleys to get booksellers excited. First serial rights are sold to the *New Yorker*. Barnes & Noble selects the book for its Discover program. Borders writes it up in its newsletter. It's a staff pick at many independent retailers and the blogosphere is starting to buzz. Steven Spielberg buys the movie rights. All the top newspapers give the book glowing reviews. Oprah selects it for her book group (the grown-up equivalent of getting a gold ticket in your Willy Wonka chocolate bar). The book appears on the bestseller list, climbs, and stays there for a record-breaking number of months. The book is nominated for this, shortlisted for that. The editor signs up the author for his next two books. She gets a big bonus at the end of the year and feels like Cinderella at the ball, with midnight nowhere in sight. And for a brief while, she doesn't wake up in a cold sweat wondering when she's going to be fired. This, too, is what editors want.

Every year one or two books seem to have their stars thus aligned, and all of us in publishing watch as that much-longed-for ideal, a book that achieves both critical and commercial success, materializes. Wally Lamb became known as the only author to have not one but two of his novels selected by Oprah for her book club. The publisher of Charles Frazier's *Cold Mountain*, ten years in the making, famously defied pressure from a national chain to change its impressionistic jacket to a classic Civil War treatment, and the book went on to win a National Book Award, sell more than a million copies, and be made into a feature film starring Nicole Kidman and Jude Law. When Alice Sebold's searing memoir about her rape, *Lucky*, failed to sell many copies, the author had to find a new publisher for her first novel about a teenage girl, abducted and killed, who narrates her story from heaven. This beautiful literary treatment of a brutal and terrifying topic caught the attention of a key buyer at one of the national accounts. A strong endorsement by Anna Quindlen on the *Today* show followed, as did that rare thing: a rave from *New York Times* book critic Michiko Kakutani. Word of mouth and book club adoptions further fueled the success of *The Lovely Bones*, which would eventually sell more than ten million copies worldwide and be made into a feature film, directed by Peter Jackson. And on the heels of the novel's success, *Lucky* would also become a bestseller. Stephen King sent in a surprise prepublication endorsement for a first novel: "I flat out loved *The Story of Edgar Sawtelle*, and spent twelve happy evenings immersed in the world that David Wroblewski has created . . . I didn't want it to end." He had no connection to the author; this was not a case of logrolling in our time. But the publisher made hay with the quote and worked hard to get the book in front of every book enthusiast until it found its way onto the bestseller list and into the favor of the most powerful enthusiast of all: again, Oprah. More than a million hardcover copies sold. Last, and even more mind-blowing, is the story of a Mormon stay-at-home mother of three young sons. According to her website, she had a vivid dream: "Though I had a million things to do, I stayed in bed, thinking about the dream. Unwillingly, I eventually got up and did the immediate necessities, and then put everything that I possibly could on the back burner and sat down at the computer to write, something that I hadn't done in so long that I wondered why I was bothering." Three months later she finished her first novel, *Twilight*. Three. Months. Maybe you can hurry love. The book was discovered in the slush pile of a literary agency and the rest is history. According to *USA Today*, "One in every seven books sold last quarter was a Meyer book—16 percent of all books sold in the first month of 2009." And since it's not a competition, the article also allows, "Meyer's domination of the list for the past twelve months has smashed records that until now had belonged to J. K. Rowling."

People in publishing are students of the industry, watching these seemingly blessed publications and keeping tabs on them the way a veteran gambler plays the ponies. We know the history of every book that breaks out and track its rise on regional, chain-store, and distributor bestseller lists. We know the amount of the advance, the editor, the agent, the number of copies the publisher first printed. We track the ad campaigns, roughly tallying how much the publisher is spending. We read the reviews and debate whether a good review is also a selling review, whether a negative review has any impact once the book has momentum. Sometimes we even make time to read the book amid all the submissions we have to read and manuscripts we have to edit just to see what all the fuss is about.

We tend to feel kindly and generous toward some successes, deeply chagrined and mingy about others, depending on who is involved. We are nothing if not competitive, which is why you used to be able to find us crowded around the fax machines on Wednesday nights, waiting for the advance copy of publishing's ultimate report card: *The New York Times Best Seller List.* Now, of course, we check our BlackBerries for the weekly ratings like rats on crack.

It's easy to forget, in this ultra-accelerated culture of ours, where even fusty book publishing is caught up in the national fervor for celebrity and where the value of all things is equated with their dollar value, that what most editors truly want is a book they love. No matter how much it may seem otherwise, no matter how many mediocre or just plain bad books get fed into the great machine, most of us are in awe of a brilliant manuscript and will do everything in our power to see that it reaches readers. No matter how competitive editors may be with each other; no matter how little or how much they edit; no matter how beleaguered or esteemed—editors are a breed apart. And in our brave new electronic world, those of us who have begrudgingly forsaken pencils and Post-its for "track changes" and email attachments can seem quaint, with our fixations on serial commas and dangling modifiers. But editors are still the world's readers. And thus the eyes of the world.

10.
WHAT
AUTHORS
WANT

"MY DEFINITION OF A GOOD EDITOR IS A MAN I think charming, who sends me large checks, praises my work, my physical beauty, and my sexual prowess, and who has a stranglehold on the publisher and the bank," said John Cheever, in what might be the truest words ever uttered by a writer when asked what he wanted from his editor. All writers have a fantasy of who their editor will be and what the relationship will be like. In the best cases, the pairing is as mutually agreeable as a good friendship, in which each party feels ennobled by the other's company. And in some cases the relationship does grow into a friendship and may become intimate or personal. After all, when an editor gives a writer a contract, the effect can be no less intoxicating than the words every lover hopes to hear: *I choose you.* Not only does the editor want you, he is staking his reputation on you. Unfortunately, many such pairings do not survive the first rush of excitement, when the thrill of acquisition is overshadowed by the reality of day-to-day work. More than a few author-editor relationships have fallen apart when disenchantment sets in. But in the best of all worlds, somewhere between Cheever's fantasy and reality, a mutually beneficial relationship is forged.

"The first thing writers want—and this sounds so basic, but you'd be surprised how un-basic it is in the publishing world—is a quick response," said Robert Gottlieb in a *Paris Review* article entitled "The Art of Editing," which serves as a case study on the editorial process from the author's point of view. A number of Gottlieb's authors were tapped for accounts of their experiences working with him. Most editors would cringe at the thought of being thus dissected by their authors, but the comments from this roundtable of literary lights make it clear that Gottlieb has in abundance both the gift of language and the psychological acuity to handle each author's individual needs. In simply understanding the need for a speedy response and providing one, Gottlieb lays the foundation for trust, which is the basis of any healthy working relationship with a writer.

Most writers are simply too paranoid and prone to magical thinking to imagine that silence from an editor is anything but a death knell. Writers are desperate to hear from their editors once they've turned in pages. Some even try to force their way into the office and have the editor read their pages while they wait. This way madness lies. In my very early, inexperienced years, I once let a writer pull this stunt. I proceeded to read while she sat across from me, pretending to be distracted by the other books on the shelf and the collage of pictures on my bulletin board. But every time I so much as twitched my lip, she burst out of her seat and demanded to know what had made me smile. If I furrowed my brow, she'd lunge across the desk and demand an explanation, as if I were a suspect in a major crime. At one point I laughed, and when I looked up in anticipation of her inquisition, she just smiled and gazed out the window, as if suddenly supremely confident of her powers. Only ten seconds later she asked, "Where are you now?" and "What was the line that made you laugh?" Since then, when others have tried to get me to read in front of them while they waited, I have flatly refused, explaining that they won't be able to sit with every person who buys their book, and gauge the reactions. Reading, I like to remind them, is not a team sport.

"Once they've finished a new manuscript and put it in the mail," continued Gottlieb, "they exist in a state of suspended emotional and psychic animation until they hear from their editor, and it's cruelty to animals to keep them waiting." Most writers become fairly agitated awaiting a response from the editor. Some have been known to decompose completely during the waiting period. They are parents anxiously pacing outside the intensive care unit, who care about just one thing: *Is my baby going to make it?* What they often don't realize is that in today's publishing climate, editors are required to do far more than edit their books. They must serve as mini-publishers for each of their titles, which means that their time and energies are always stretched exceedingly thin. As a result, taking on a new author can sometimes feel like adding an eleventh child to a family of ten. Happy as Mom is for the new baby, she's not sure where she'll find the time to nurture her or the food to feed her. The new baby doesn't give a fig for the ten before her, she wants all of Mom's attention now.

When editors sign up a nonfiction project, they usually give the author twelve to eighteen months to finish the book. During this time some authors want or expect a great deal of attention, even when they aren't producing any pages. As I grew more experienced with writers, I realized that like small children, they work best with some guidelines and goals. To that end I hold fast to two rules. The first: no pages, no lunch. Having concrete work to talk about is by far the most productive use of an author-editor meeting. Second: call before sending chunks of manuscript. Forewarned, I can give an author a reasonable estimate as to when I will get back to him. There is nothing more disconcerting for an editor than to have four hundred pages of a manuscript show up without warning. It's not that we don't want to edit the manuscripts; it's just that it's like having out-of-town guests show up uninvited for the weekend.

Editing requires a kind of deep immersion, a total concentration, and the best among us average five to ten pages an hour. It's possible to pick up some speed if the manuscript is really clean, but it's slow, painstaking work that demands complete concentration. In addition to the actual time it takes to edit, time that few of us can take during the workday, one needs to create the mental space. And sometimes an overanxious author can unwittingly crowd that space by calling too often. I am completely sympathetic with the anxious writer, and doubtless there are editors who are negligent in the extreme, but if you basically trust your editor and are impressed with the authors and books she has worked on, try to defuse your anxiety in some other way.

Not all writers are so dependent on their editors for assurance; some are even disdainful of any interference. The master himself, Vladimir Nabokov, was more than dismissive in describing how he felt about editors and their services. "By 'editor' I suppose you mean proofreader," he said. "Among these I have known limpid creatures of limitless tact and tenderness who would discuss with me a semicolon as if it were a point of honor—which, indeed, a point of art often is. But I have also come across a few pompous avuncular brutes who would attempt to make a 'suggestion' which I countered with a thunderous 'stet.'"

Some authors crave the blue pencil. They seek out those friends or readers who are unafraid to be completely honest, whose opinions lead to improvements in the work. Edith Wharton described one friend with whom she had a lifelong literary affair whose critical response she credited for both sharpening her prose and helping her see the world anew. "I suppose there is one friend in the life of each of us who seems not a separate person, however dear and beloved, but an expansion, an interpretation, of one's self, the very meaning of one's soul," she wrote. "Such a friend I found in Walter Berry. . . . He alone not only encouraged me to write, as others had already done, but had the patience and the intelligence to teach me how. Others praised, some flattered—he alone took the trouble to analyze and criticize. . . . Once I found my footing and had my material in hand, his criticisms became increasingly searching. With each book he exacted a higher standard in economy of expression, in purity of language, in the avoidance of the hackneyed and the precious."

I have known authors who were truly dependent on and grateful for feedback, while some paid only lip service to the editorial process. No matter how much bluster a writer produces, he still wants to be loved, to be read, to be praised. Sometimes a famous older writer is assigned to young, eager editors. At the end of their careers, these writers are often resistant to any editorial suggestions, but they still need someone to kick around. And no one on earth is more slavish than an eager associate editor newly assigned to a literary lion. Until, of course, he gets eaten for supper.

Writers want to be catered to. And who can blame them? Having survived the deprivations and degradations of being an unpublished aspiring nobody, why shouldn't you hope for a little . . . respect? Eliciting revisions requires more than delicacy; it requires a certain understanding about the writer's general temperament and well-being. Some writers will defend each word. Some are deeply analytical and need only be presented with reasons to make changes. Others work on instinct and feeling; they traffic in nuance and tone. Some authors are humorless. I usually like to have a trial run of editing around seventy-five pages to see how an author responds before continuing on the entire text. Almost in a reversal of the authorial anxiety that attends handing in pages, I'm always anxious about the author's response. *Will he or she take to my editing?* When I hear about author-editor relationships that have run aground, it is usually the author who is cited as the malcontent. But it is also true that some editors fail to realize that an author needs more than the benefit of line-by-line editing; he needs someone who has the sensitivity to build confidence in the writer as he revises his text. Is this a writer who just needs to be pumped up with encouragement? Or does he prefer to work with the

Devil's advocate? Does he need to be read the riot act, or will a measured response convey the problem? In describing her editorial relationship with Gottlieb, Cynthia Ozick identified the unspoken transference that tends to occur between a writer and an editor. "An editor is often a father figure, a mother figure, a kind of ministerial figure . . . someone who stands in authority over you and has something to tell you."

For me, as an editor, the transference was often mutual. More than once when a writer, especially a first-time author, handed in his pages, I felt they were presented with the innocent hope and pride of a small child offering a first art project. Or sitting amid a sea of folding chairs at a reading, watching my author read from her book, I often felt that she was giving her first recital, my heart in my throat as she worked her way through the sections that I alone knew had given her trouble.

Writers sometimes need an hour of an editor's time, and what they want has very little to do with fixing sentences or correcting proofs or requesting ads. They want and need handholding, and no matter if they have loved ones, friends, esteemed colleagues, and extremely expensive psychotherapists, few people understand what they are going through or share the same level of investment as the editor or agent. "Sometimes I feel like I'd make a lot more money," said agent Eric Simonoff, "if I charged an hourly rate, like a psychotherapist."

"An editor has to be selfless," says Gottlieb, "and yet also has to be strong-minded. If you don't know what you think, or if you're nervous about expressing your opinion, what good is that to a writer? I remember working on a book of John Cheever's and feeling there was a minor problem with the ending. At first I thought, *Who am I to be telling John Cheever to change the end of his novel?* And then I thought, *Well, I'm the editor he chose, and I can't, out of cowardice, withhold what I think. I'm not forcing him to do anything. I'm saying, This is what I think is wrong, and it's up to him to decide whether to take my advice or not.* As it happened, he immediately got the point and found a solution."

What goes on between a writer and an editor is as mysterious and alchemical as a marriage. Some relationships are terrifically sadistic, abusive, and malcontent, while others are filled with mutual respect, adoration, and appreciation. But what most writers want, it seems to me, is to feel secure. They don't want surprises. They don't want to be kept waiting. They want their criticism meted out along with praise. They want to know why you don't like this, and some want to know how to fix it, while others want to be left to their own devices. Most have such deeply ambivalent feelings about what they deserve and how good they are that they are often bouncing between their desire for approval and fear of rejection. Then again, if they didn't struggle with issues of need, attention, disapproval, isolation, and social life, chances are they wouldn't be writers.

"It took me some time," said Gottlieb, "when I was a very young man, to grasp that a writer—even a mature, experienced one—could have an emotional transference on me. But of course, it makes sense: the editor gives or withholds approval, and even to a certain extent controls the purse strings. It's a relationship fraught with difficulty, because it can lead to infantilizing and then to resentment. Somehow, to be helpful, an editor has to embody authority yet not become possessive or controlling." Novelist James Salter explained in a *Publishers Weekly* interview that he and his Random House editor, Joe Fox, became friends over the years. "I found him authoritative, but he also had that nice quality of saying, 'All right, if that's what you feel.' I think a good editor does that, unless you're obviously headed for the cliffs."

Writers want to know that they are not alone. After the long struggle to find an editor and a publisher, a writer wants to feel that finally he has found some protection, some support. A contract is symbolic of many things, not least of which is the implied commitment of another person to see you and your book through, to walk you down the aisle the way a father walks his daughter on her wedding day. The writer wants a relationship with his publisher, and the physical embodiment of that relationship is usually the editor. Cynthia Ozick describes her editor as a combination of muse and guardian angel. "Now, very often when I am writing, I have something like a bird sitting on my right shoulder, a watchful bird looking over my shoulder at what I am doing. I want that bird's approval—I have to get it. It is a very critical bird, who is in a way a burden, but also grants me *permission*." Most writers want that bird to help. To tilt its head this way or that as they peck out their pages. They want their editor to leave bread crumbs, Hansel and Gretel–like, a trail that shows the way but that vanishes as surely as those scraps of bread across the forest floor.

✤

The best editors call attention to those parts of the book that have been bothering the writer, if only on an unconscious level. In my experience, most writers are happy to follow the crumb trail, especially if the manuscript is in some kind of trouble. Almost every book I have ever worked on needed help with the pacing and structure. The challenge of sustaining a certain pace and rhythm throughout an entire book can be staggering, and most writers are too involved with the details to see where the story flags. I like to imagine the narrative as a trip. Just as the ride feels shorter on the way home, a phenomenon all school-age children remark on, even though it is exactly the same number of miles as the trip away, the reader expects that time will pass more rapidly as the book heads toward the finish. Once we know the way, the scenery rolls by like so much wallpaper. Your editor should help you see when the writing has turned into wallpaper.

When readers speak of being hooked from the first page, what they most likely mean is that the writer has earned their trust. It's a silent and immediate pact that the reader doesn't even realize he is making. In just a few introductory sentences the authorial voice is established and we know whether we are traveling by Concorde or ocean liner, whether we need seat belts or life preservers. And more important, whether we want to go along for the ride. No matter what genre you are working in, keeping the narrative moving will keep your reader, and it is the editor's job to address those sections where the tire is leaking or, worse, is completely out of air.

Questions of how to handle the passage of time are easier to cope with once a structure has been decided on. Like the foundation of a house, a book's parameters, once set, dictate only so many ways to build. Usually within the first two or three chapters, all the major decisions of any consequence have been made, whether or not the writer is aware of his choices. Matters of tone, tense, point of view, time frame, syntax, style, and narration are like the pipes and electrical lines: you may not see them buried beneath floorboards and behind Sheetrock, but you can depend on them to bring you light and water. Books tend to be constructed either chronologically or thematically, with many variations on the theme. But even if you don't have a narrative per se, your book needs to find its inner logic so that the reader does not feel she is entering a hall of mirrors. Beginnings, middles, and ends, no matter how they are shuffled, are the ways in which we organize our lives.

Not all writers have an innate sense of structure. As a young editor, I used to think that those who couldn't structure their books were somehow inferior to "real" writers or people with "natural" ability. I imagined that skill in the handling of time was akin to having an innate sense of rhythm in music, and that you either had it or you didn't. I've since revised that notion, having worked with brilliant authors over the years who committed all kinds of time crimes and didn't see the structure their own sentences and paragraphs suggested. I have also worked with writers who were flummoxed when it came to connecting two scenes or collapsing a week's events into a day to advance the narrative more swiftly. Whether you want to chronicle a lunch hour, as Nicholson Baker did in *The Mezzanine*, or have your main character worry about a single dinner party, as Virginia Woolf did in *Mrs. Dalloway*, or concern yourself with a single day—June 16, for instance—you must find and adhere to a specific structure. If you plan to write an epic covering many years and many lands, such as the *Odyssey* or the

Ramayana, you will need to chart an entirely different course. Are you concerned with one terrible century, one terrible summer, one terrible night?

In her collection of essays and reviews *The Eye of the Story*, Eudora Welty articulates the importance of time and how it functions: "Time can throb like a pulse, tick like a bomb, beat like the waves of a rising tide against the shore; it can be made out as the whisper of attrition, or come to an end with the explosion of a gun. For time is of course subjective, too. ('It tolls for thee.')" A good editor—whether for fiction or nonfiction—crouches like a coach on the edge of the track, his stopwatch grasped tightly in hand, clocking a writer's progress as each sentence strides toward the finish. Sometimes merely breaking a long paragraph in two can take a few seconds off a writer's time. Sometimes breaking apart a long chapter can give a feeling of movement and breadth. A writer can use paragraphs and space breaks the way a poet uses stanzas, each one setting forth a new beginning, signaling to the reader that we are going through another door. A good editor knows that paragraphs, space breaks, new chapters, and part divisions are far from arbitrary. Just as a driver uses directional lights to signal his turn, a writer uses these devices to say, *Here, this way, come with me*, or *Take a breather, refill your glass, get into your pj's and then we'll read one more chapter*.

Any writer doing work of real interest is by necessity going out on a limb, taking chances with either the content or the style of his material. Does the limb hold? Will the writer wish, months or years from now, that someone had stayed his hand? Of course, the writer must decide what to include and what to leave out, but a trustworthy editor can make all the difference. John le Carré said of his novel *A Perfect Spy* that it was his most autobiographical novel and the one closest to his heart. "It skates along the edge of a great deal of childhood pain and stuff. Bob [Gottlieb] pointed out the places where he felt that the fiction became so autobiographical that it became embarrassing—where he felt that I had really spilled into private experience and had thrown away the mask. He was terribly good at that. What we left on the cutting room floor still makes me blush."

When Paul Theroux's editor took him out to lunch to turn down his seventh novel, he told the young writer that he didn't believe in the book and couldn't publish a book he didn't believe in. As Theroux describes the scene in *Sir Vidia's Shadow*, he lashed out in response, "You publish lots of crappy books. If you turn this down you'll lose me as an author. I'll go to another publisher. I'll never let you publish another book of mine. And all it's costing you is two hundred and fifty quid. This lunch is costing you thirty!" When the publisher replied that he'd publish the book if Theroux twisted his arm, Theroux snapped, "That's it, then. That's all. Forget it—I want my manu-script back." Then he confessed to wishing he could shove his publisher in the path of a moving car.

Theroux's response seems healthy to me—healthier, in any case, than letting one editor shatter your belief in yourself. Some writers, angry at the powerlessness of their situation, especially when no other publisher is waiting in the wings, begin to feel that editors are arrogant at best, sadistic at worst. But the truth is that most editors fear confrontation of any kind and feel terrible about turning down an author, especially one with whom they've developed a relationship. And though few admit it, an editor may begin to question her taste and judgment in light of these decisions, especially when, after letting a writer go, she sees his next book break out. When the new publisher makes a success of a writer who has been languishing, the feeling industry-wide is often one of astonishment. Turning a writer's career around is extremely difficult, given how much an author's previous sales track dictates the level of support bookstores are willing to give. But sometimes a new team of publishing people can, with the right book, relaunch a writer with savvy and brio and make lemonade where others saw the pits. It must feel like sweet revenge to the writer, and sweet revenge is something nearly all writers want as well.

Still, an editor's good bedside manner cannot be overvalued. After I had been editing for half a dozen years or so, I found myself spending countless hours at the computer trying to explain in detail why a beloved author's book wasn't "cohering" and thus why I had to reject it. It was an exercise in the gravest diplomacy. A much more senior editor stopped by my office and noticed my agitated state. When I explained what I was facing, he ran to his office and returned with an envelope, which he flipped onto my desk. Then, without a word of explanation, he ducked out again.

The letter inside, a single-spaced carbon copy typed on a manual, was dated nearly thirty years earlier. It was the most moving, generous, and intelligent editorial letter I had ever read. It explained in exquisite detail why certain characters in the novel were not believable and how the writer might make critical changes to ensure their verity. It spoke of pacing, setting, and style. It spoke of bringing the book's deepest themes into relief through the restructuring of flashbacks. The editor also felt that the book needed to be told in the third person so that the novelist could make the wife's point of view more convincing. He spoke of the beauty of the prose but wondered if it wasn't overshadowing the simple human gesture at the book's core. In essence, the editor had opened the chest cavity and held the heart of the novel, carefully outlining the necessary surgical procedure to repair it. But more important, he wrote in a spirit of friendship and respect for the author's great literary accomplishments and beseeched him to consider his advice so that this book would maintain the author's reputation in the literary world. In closing, the editor harked back to the half-dozen books the two had already worked on together and hoped that this novel, with the major overhaul he was suggesting, would be his best yet.

After I finished reading the letter, I returned to the senior editor's office and slumped down in the chair facing his desk, which held little more than whatever the editor was reading at that moment, a pencil, a dictionary, a shabby lamp with a wooden base, a box of cough drops, and the manual typewriter on which the letter had presumably been composed. Most editors of his accomplishment surround themselves with walls of books and framed jackets of the renowned titles they have worked on and the bestseller lists they have climbed. His modest furnishings and half-filled shelves betrayed none of his extraordinary experience in publishing some of the greats. I told him the letter was the most amazing editorial response I had ever read. I said I was humbled by how much I still had to learn in terms of corresponding with writers and how this editor had walked that very fine line of telling a writer his book was deeply flawed while filling him with hope and ideas and confidence to tackle the revision.

Finally I asked what happened, whether the writer took his suggestions. As it turned out, he had taken his book elsewhere and gotten it published on the strength of his name. The book was a colossal failure and the two men never spoke again. I asked the older editor if he felt vindicated. In answer, he lowered his eyes, shook his head, folded the letter, and returned it to the drawer. I ventured that the writer was a fool for not taking his advice and reiterated that I had never read anything like his letter. "Well," he explained with his characteristic wit, "I guess it's a little like telling a guy you think his wife is ugly."

❧

The only thing writers want more than getting into print is staying in print. No matter how well your book is received, there are no guarantees that it will have staying power or will not be supplanted by the next big thing. Martin Amis, in a *Paris Review* interview, summed up the attitude of most writers toward their fellow authors. "I feel generally resentful of younger writers," he said. "You're not thrilled to see some blazing talent coming up on your flank. Dislike and resentment of younger writers is something fairly universal among writers." As one of the most successful of those upstarts, Amis of course upstaged not only the older generation of writers but his own famous father as well. Even when a writer's stature and currency are as assured as anyone's can be—and Amis certainly enjoys more literary distinction and reported financial gain than many—I find it fascinating that his eye would still be trained over his shoulder. "The older writer," he elaborated, "at some point, is going to lose touch with what the contemporary moment feels like."

Writers want justice. I remember one writer guiltily confessing to feelings of sheer joy when he heard that someone with whom he felt highly competitive was suffering from an extended bout of writer's block. Another writer told me that she couldn't write for three months when a rival novelist's book was in the spotlight. She felt she was by far the better writer, but knew that the other's work would always prove more popular with the critics and enjoy better sales. Her jealousy was killing her.

Writers want some insurance that their craft and drive, their will and hard work, and finally their fierce self-belief and gift will produce work of lasting value. What writers want is to be taken on their own terms, to have their books praised or panned according to their own stated or implicit goals, not according to the whim and prejudice of critics who say they should have attempted something different, more in keeping with the critics' ideals or notions. "Writing a book is a horrible, exhausting struggle, like a long bout of some painful illness," wrote George Orwell. "One would never undertake such a thing if one were not driven by some demon whom one can neither resist nor understand. For all one knows that demon is simply the same instinct that makes a baby squall for attention."

No matter how lonely or driven the writer, no matter how many others he would gladly trample or shove in front of an oncoming car so that his own words could emerge triumphant, what writers finally want more than good editing and smart marketing and ten-city tours and two-book contracts and appreciation (make that worship) and lucrative movie deals and hoity prizes are readers. Loyal, avid readers.

11.
THE
BOOK

THE PUBLISHING PROCESS MIGHT BEST BE described as everything that happens between the writing of the book and its reading by the public. No matter how well or poorly a publisher readies a book for the marketplace, there are finally only two people, the writer and the reader. It is easy to forget how truly intimate the encounter is between them.

Most first-time authors are woefully unprepared for what to expect when they're expecting to publish. Some publishers prepare a booklet about the process that they give their authors along with the contract. But somehow even the best author's guides, with their descriptions of clearing permissions, formatting text, and reviewing page proofs never fully convey exactly what happens once a book is accepted for publication. Some writers, so grateful for a publishing contract, are reticent about asking what the process entails. Others, full of information from writer friends or expectations nursed over those many months and years waiting for publication, come with a good deal of knowledge, as well as a lot of misinformation heavily laced with fantasy.

Journalists, who are used to speedy responses, especially if they work on dailies or weeklies, are often shocked when they discover how slowly the wheels of book publishing turn, from editorial responses to production schedules to selling cycles. Publishers ideally like to have nine months from the time the book is completely edited to its publication date, during which time the book is copyedited, designed, typeset, proofread, cataloged, jacketed, and manufactured. At the same time, sales representatives are crisscrossing the country taking orders, publicists are attempting to get advance bookings, and marketing people are working with bookstores and other distribution outlets through which to sell or market the book.

Most of the disappointment that a writer experiences in having a book published can be traced back to his initial expectations and how well he was informed about the publisher's plans. One doesn't have to work in publishing for very long to know that a great deal of time is spent in letting people down gently. I had been an editorial assistant but a few weeks when I fielded my first author-in-distress call, from a woman in her midthirties whose first book had been published about six weeks earlier. She wanted to know what was "happening" with the book. I told her I'd pass her message along and gather what information I could. What I discovered after talking with her editor, my boss, was that the first printing was very small, that the sales force didn't feel it distinguished itself enough from other books in an already crowded category, that publicity had been able to get only a couple of local radio interviews, and that reviewers weren't biting. All told, the book was DOA. When I asked my boss if there was anything we could do for the author, he shrugged. It wasn't that he didn't care; it was more that as a seasoned professional he knew when and how to call his shots. Much as he liked the author and this project, he understood that its viability in the marketplace was negligible unless something truly miraculous happened. When I asked why he had signed it up, he explained that he had believed in it, the author's credentials were solid, and she had a worthwhile message. Unfortunately, that message did not translate to a wider audience.

At the time I was extremely upset by all of this. The woman had sounded desperate on the phone, and I had promised to call her back with an update. I pressed my boss about how to handle it. He explained that her expectations were out of scale for a book on early childhood psychology. It was a good and important book, but as the sales force and publicity departments had discovered, there wasn't much of a market outside of educators and psychologists. The book clearly wasn't going to "crossover" sell to parents. It didn't take much to realize that all efforts had ceased. DNR.

When I finally screwed up the courage to call the author back, I told her, as I was instructed by the publicist, that the publicity department was still trying to get reviews and that we might get a break in one of the professional journals. Like many authors I've worked with since, she believed that the critical silence in response to her book was personal. "They hate me," she cried. "I can't believe no one's going to review it. I put four years into this book." Not knowing what to say, I asked her about her research and about the process of putting the book together. (In college I had been good at talking people down from bad acid trips, and my skill returned in force.) As she calmed down, she began to tell me how she had gotten a promotion as a result of the book. And she had been invited to speak at major conferences in her field, also because of the book. Even she had to admit that the book had clearly done more for her than she realized. Most of all, I told her, you did it. For every person who writes a book there are thousands who believe they could. She seemed buoyed by our conversation. I've had dozens of conversations like this since, as has every editor or agent—all painful, as a writer comes to grips with the fact that the *New York Times* isn't reviewing his book, an interview with *People* is cancelled without explanation, he can't find his book in any store, or a total of two people showed up for his reading (and one was his mother). I like to tell first-time authors that Rome was not built in a day, that most careers are built slowly over time, but expectations in a Twittery world are more accelerated than ever.

Somewhere between the acceptance of a manuscript and actual publication, a great deal happens, or doesn't happen, that greatly influences how well the book will be received, by both critics and consumers. What most writers don't understand, but learn all too quickly and painfully, is that landing a contract and being published do not guarantee the fulfillment of all their hopes and dreams. In fact, getting onto a publisher's list just means that your book will be physically produced and cataloged for booksellers to evaluate. Whether booksellers actually order your book depends on a great many factors, most of them not in your control, such as what other books are being published that season, whether booksellers perceive the category as glutted, whether they are skeptical about the author's credentials or ability to interest the media, and sometimes whether they hate the jacket. They know they can always order the book after publication if they discover that they've passed on something that is gaining momentum. But an initial lack of interest will affect how the book initially is perceived and performs. No matter how many times an editor walks a new author through the process, until he finally goes through it there is little the editor can do to quell his fears. And in many cases, authors' fears are justified, especially when they begin to sense that getting published may not be everything they had imagined.

The unpredictability of the business—whether reviewers or bookstores support the book, whether it will get a break or remain ignored—is what makes the process both maddening and thrilling. Still, if publishers didn't think they knew what they were doing on some level, paralysis would ensue. There is a famous story of an expensive consulting firm coming into a publishing house in the mid-eighties, just as the merger fever of that decade started to have its impact on the book business. The consultants spent six months interviewing employees at every level, analyzing distribution lines, warehouse systems, accounting practices, and profit-and-loss statements. After crunching numbers and systematically breaking down operations, they came up with the following recommendation: Since 10 percent of the titles account for 90 percent of the revenues, why doesn't

the company publish only the 10 percent that are profitable—
that is, only the bestsellers. A clever-sounding strategy. The
problem, the publisher explained to the consultants, was that
we never actually know which is which.

Although some publishers improve their odds by special-
izing in particular categories and becoming extremely adept
at packaging, marketing, and distributing one kind of book,
most of the trade houses still produce a fairly eclectic list every
season, with a range of fiction, literary and genre, and a range
of nonfiction, including self-help, how-to, narrative nonfiction,
biography, history, pop culture, and so forth. Most publishers
take their cue from the marketplace and produce books according to current trends and tastes in everything from jacket design
to trim size—that is, the height and width of the book. There
are a handful of tried-and-true formulas for packaging books
that seem to have currency. Go into your bookstore and examine a dozen books in any given category: parenting, business,
health, literary biography, and you will easily ascertain how
a certain look dictates the general style in which the titles are
presented. Most publishers adhere to tried-and-true formulas.
For instance, a health title will usually have an all-type jacket
on a white background, lending it an air of seriousness and
authority—the idea being that people looking for medical advice
want a package as reliable as an aspirin bottle. Some publishers will depart from the conventional look in an attempt to set
a book apart or break it out, while others leave well enough
alone; if it ain't broke, blah, blah.

All of these decisions fall under the general heading of

positioning. And as publishers prepare a book for the market-place they engage in a series of meetings to focus that effort. Once an editor has a complete manuscript, or one that is close enough that the book will make it into the next catalog and selling season, she prepares a variety of materials about the book, such as sample pages, author credentials, and tip sheets with marketing handles and comparison titles. These are circulated to key people in various departments within the company, such as sales, publicity, and marketing, to acquaint them with the project. This process varies from publisher to publisher, but all follow the same general trajectory. Having worked at four different companies over the course of my career, I have learned that the particular emphasis in a house generally emanates from the publisher's own career path. In other words, if the publisher worked her way up through sales, she will tend to put the most emphasis on selling. If she came up through publicity, she will tend to focus on how the media will react and how to secure promotion for the book; if the publisher has an editorial background, he will focus on the book itself and on the writer. This is what people mean when they call a publishing house sales-driven, or marketing-driven, or editorially driven. There is always an emphasis on one part of the process, and that emphasis influences everything from the size of the first printing to the jacket.

🌿

One of the most visible ways in which a book reaches its market is through its jacket, and the jacket or packaging meeting is usually the first in the process. In some publishing companies the art director won't even think about starting the jacket until he has a manuscript to read. Other publishers begin work on their jackets with nothing more than an editor's description of the material and a title. I used to think it was blasphemy for an artist to work on a book without having read it, but sometimes reading the manuscript can be a hindrance, leading to a jacket that is too literally conceived. Other times, a small detail, say the charm fashioned from the Monopoly piece of the little house in *The Lovely Bones*, will serve as inspiration for a jacket.

Everywhere I've worked, I have witnessed the most acrimonious behavior surrounding a book's jacket art. While most people are somewhat circumspect about commenting unfavorably about the content of a book (especially to the editor of the project), everyone has an opinion on the jacket and feels perfectly qualified to offer it. Usually, when a jacket is displayed at this first meeting there's an immediate rush of enthusiasm or adverse reaction. The worst, however, is when the unveiling is met with silence. A famous art director at a major company was known for ripping jacket comps in half when an editor took too long to respond.

Jackets, like faces, can tell you quite a bit about what's inside. When an editor and author see a jacket for the first time, it's like looking in the mirror. If the reflection doesn't radiate the qualities you believe your book possesses, it will be disappointing, maybe worse. Some authors don't care what is on their jacket as long as their name is prominent. Others take the art personally and cannot separate from it. One author, in a moment of supreme anguish over a jacket image she hated, threatened to pull her book from publication. As her editor I completely understood her dilemma; I take supreme pleasure in the presentation of books, so much so that if the jacket on a book I am reading strikes me as wrong, I have to remove it. Other people cannot even tell you what the jacket of the book they are reading looks like. They don't judge books by their covers because they are interested only in the content.

The person who walks into a store or shops online with a specific subject in mind—a book on accounting or bed-wetting or flower arranging—shops with diligence. Another has either read a good review or perhaps had a book recommended to her, and she will likewise make a fairly concerted effort to find that specific title. But many people just want to look around. They are vaguely hungry though uncertain what they're in the mood for: Chinese, Italian, maybe a burger. They look around. Sniff. Hover over the display table stacked high with its spanking-new offerings or scroll through page after page of recommended titles in one of Amazon's best features, "Customers Who Bought This Item Also Bought." A jacket, a title, an author—some combination of these elements will beckon and the prospective buyer will pick up the book. He may examine the back, the flaps, he might even read a first line or paragraph—a browsing experience that can now be cleverly simulated online. In the end he may not buy the book, but the packaging did its job by enticing the browser.

Why are so many authors unhappy with their jackets? And why are there so many bad jackets? The two main reasons involve the usual suspects: time and money. As soon as a publisher comes up with the first pass at a jacket design, he has started to spend money. The meter is running. The editor hopes against hope that the first few designs will come close to some ideal in her mind's eye, because once that clock starts, the options shrink. If the author hates the jacket and the publisher loves it, or if the budget and deadlines are used up, the editor can be in the unfortunate position of having to convince her author that it's a great jacket or, taking a more politic stance, that it's *right for the book*.

When it came time to jacket Lucy Grealy's book, *Autobiography of a Face*, the challenge was enormous. How to depict the author's childhood struggle with cancer and the resulting disfigurement? Given the quality of her prose, it was never a question that we would seek a literary treatment. Our art director farmed out the job to a top designer. He returned with three mock-ups: One incorporated a mask, which had been an element in the story, but here it made the book look like a thriller. The other jackets used bandages in different collagelike patterns, which made me think of mummies. Time was growing short, and we had spent a small fortune with no jacket to show for it. Then I returned from lunch one day to find a photographer's portfolio on my desk. I didn't see any note attached, and I opened the box. Staring up at me was a black-and-white photograph of a young girl, her face obscured by the piece of cellophane she was looking through. I knew in an instant that this was the image we had been looking for. It perfectly captured childhood and loss in a hauntingly beautiful way.

As it turned out, the photographs were part of a submission by an Irish photographer who collected the tales of tinkers in the Irish countryside. Although I was unable to convince my company to publish the book of pictures, I did persuade the photographer to contribute his photograph for my author's jacket. The little tinker girl was often mistaken for the author herself, so perfectly did the image convey the book's interior.

Publishers do not as a rule rely on any kind of market testing, apart from showing the jacket to various people in the office and canvassing their reactions. Unlike the magazine world, where marketing has been known to test jackets in different geographic regions, publishers make their decisions either on their own or by some quorum of their choosing. Needless to say, sometimes the process works, sometimes it's disastrous. The most obvious but most overlooked reason why so many authors complain about their jackets is that an art director is generally responsible for anywhere from fifty to a hundred titles per season. It's not like marketing a new low-fat tortilla chip or breath freshener: every book is a product unto itself and requires a unique package. Art directors are under tremendous pressure to produce an enormous amount of original artwork, and often they work with small budgets—without a manuscript to read, with an editor who may not provide clear direction, with an artist who may be temperamental or blocked, and with a publisher who may be completely inarticulate about why he doesn't like a design yet has no ideas to offer.

In a letter to his editor, F. Scott Fitzgerald complained vociferously about the jacket for his novel *Taps at Reveille*, which followed *Tender Is the Night*, citing no fewer than six people who commented on its awfulness. Having spent so much time trying to create charming characters, he said it was "discouraging" to be stuck with an artist who couldn't draw better than his five-year-old daughter. He added that he didn't want to sound ungrateful or be a pest but was writing on the "off-chance" that what he had been shown was a sample and that there was still time to try again. It may prove comforting to some writers to know that authors at every level and for all time have felt themselves ill served by their jackets.

The best way to avert jacket disasters is for an editor to glean from an author what exactly is in his mind's eye and to have some discussion before a line is drawn or penny spent. As the author's in-house advocate, the editor can communicate the author's wishes to marketing and the art director as well as quash any really stupid ideas on the author's part. It's hard to let go and trust that you will like your jacket and that everything will be okay. Find out from your editor when the process starts and tell her what jackets you like and give a rough idea of what you envision. If you actually have a photograph or a piece of art in mind, share it with your editor. If there is a style of type or a color you absolutely hate, let her know. Publishers prefer their authors to be happy. But they don't have the time or resources to give an author an endless number of choices, unless that author has clout. I promise you, Stephenie Meyer, Malcolm Gladwell, and David Sedaris aren't crying about their jackets.

❧

Once the jacket art is under way, the next series of meetings involves marketing, publicity, and sales, and this is often where an editor can "make or break" a book. Sometimes the attendees have been given some sample material from the book, but more often than not the editor's presentation of the book and the author are all they have to go on. The editor will have produced a title sheet with biographical information, a brief description of the book, competitive titles, the author's track record if there is one, marketing ideas, and probably the most important element: the sales handle. This is your whole book boiled down to a sentence. Many writers balk at the idea of their books being boiled down to a single sentence. After all, they have often spent years writing. Still, and this is truly where you need an editor to help you see the forest, it's critical to be able to pitch your book in a sentence or two. All along the food chain, a succinct description of your book will garner more interest than a lengthy plot summary, whether you are pitching an agent, your agent is pitching to editors, editors to salespeople, sales to book buyers, publicists to producers, and so on.

Sometimes even the editor is too close to the book to make a good, clear presentation. If she is mired in editing it, she may give a long-winded, confusing plot description when all that's called for is a witty anecdote and some salient points that are not on the fact sheets. The best presenters I have seen either have breathtaking erudition, making whatever they talk about seem highly intelligent and worthy, or they are showmen, with vaudeville cunning in their blood.

During my Simon & Schuster internship, I had the privilege of watching each of the company's editors present his or her books at a presales conference. Each editor clearly had his own style and ability to communicate the value of the books, but some of the presentations seemed to implode. Unfortunately, most editors aren't showmen. They wouldn't be editors if they were. Editors tend to be introverted and self-conscious. But in today's world, where presentation, spin, and perception seem more important than anything else, a book may hit the skids in a meeting if the editor can't put it across. There's nothing worse than the dead silence following a botched presentation for a book.

On the other hand, I will never forget the feeling in the room when S&S editor in chief Michael Korda—king of the showmen editors—arrived to present his list. The room came to attention. I had only glimpsed him in the halls until then, but every time I saw him, either turning a quick corner or disappearing behind closing elevator doors, like Willy Wonka zinging his way around the chocolate factory. As he entered, it was clear that he relished the moment, taking his seat and smoothing his pink silk tie as he surveyed the room the way an actor assesses the crowd. He was there to present one of his bestselling diva authors. "Look, folks," he finally said, smiling with the impish grin of a schoolboy caught red-handed. "I haven't read a word of it yet. I doubt she's written one. But it's going to be fabulous. And it's going to sell." And of course, it did.

❧

Most people know a good title when they hear one, but as publishing wisdom goes, a good title is one that sold. Sometimes, as the writer is working, the right title can help bring the entire work into focus. In Larry Dark's anthology *Literary Outtakes*, which collects a wonderful variety of life on the cutting-room floor, Amy Tan tells how she originally thought to use the title *Wind and Water* for her first book, after the Chinese belief in feng shui, the balance of the elements. "The words 'The Joy Luck Club' had never struck me as unusual or remotely literary. It was a social club my father had named and to which my parents and their friends belonged for as long as I could remember." It may have sounded ordinary to Tan, but upon reading her manuscript, her agent seized on the name of the club and sold the book with the title *The Joy Luck Club*. Tan found that as she continued to work on the book, the club and its members became increasingly vivid to her. "I sometimes wonder what would have happened if I had not changed the title. Because now I realize that a title is not simply an ornament that graces a book jacket. For me, the title gave shape to the stories, provided the necessary force to pull the whole book through from beginning to end."

It's at the publishing meetings that titles and subtitles are tested. This is about as close to market research as publishing gets, when the various departments, including sales, publicity, and marketing, react to a given title. One person or another may voice a complaint about a title or ask for a new subtitle sending author and editor down the rabbit hole. Again, study the competition if you are seeking a title. If the book is self-help, the title or subtitle should offer some promise or hope. If it's a how-to book, the gimmick should be part of the subtitle. A survey of diet books shows that most put the message into the title, such as *Eat More, Weigh Less, The Carbohydrate Lover's*

Diet, Sugar Busters! and so on. Only then a diet book called *The Zone* became a huge bestseller. That title could have been used for a thriller, science fiction, science—almost anything. It was a gutsy move not to put the diet concept in the title. I think a lot of publishers would have rejected the title because it didn't follow the formula. Perhaps one of the reasons *The Zone* worked so phenomenally well, especially among male consumers, who don't generally talk about diets and dieting as much as women do, was that it deemphasized dieting and had a macho ring. *The South Beach Diet* took an entirely different approach; now dieting was all about aura, milieu, and real estate. It's astonishing we haven't seen spin-offs like *The Aspen Diet* or *The 90210 Diet.* Location, location, location. My favorite entry in the category is the in-your-face *Skinny Bitch.* The promise goes far beyond the shedding of pounds; it's about gaining an attitude along with your size o True Religion jeans.

Sometimes getting the title right comes down to the wire. Peter Benchley claims to have tried more than a hundred titles before settling on *Jaws* twenty minutes before going to press. As he tells it in *Literary Outtakes,* "I had toyed with a lot of Françoise Sagan–like stuff, such as *A Stillness in the Water.* My father goaded me onward with splendid solutions like *What Dat Noshin' on My Laig?* Then there were *The Jaws of Death* and *Leviathan Rising* and *White Death* and *The Jaws of Leviathan* and *Death in the Water* and *Shark!* and (the French used this one for their version) *The Teeth of the Sea,* and *Summer of the Shark* and on and on and on." Finally, Benchley and his editor decided that they should pick a single word. The only one they agreed on

was *Jaws*. "I ran the title by my family and my agent. Everyone
hated it. I didn't think much of it either. But what the hell. . . .
Nobody buys first novels anyway."

Bestselling author James McBride struggled to find a title for
his memoir about being a black son raised by a white mother
who kept her Jewish roots secret. After his editor rejected his
suggestion *A Bird Who Flies*, he wondered, in a letter to her,
how much the title mattered. If it's good, won't people buy the
book? he asked. As the press date for the publisher's catalog
approached, McBride and the editor brainstormed. The laundry
list they came up with included the usual range of dull solutions (*My Mother's Life*) and occasional howlers (*Bagels and Blues*)
born of complete exhaustion. At the last moment, however, the
title appeared. It came, as some of the best do, from a line in
the text, a beautiful snippet of dialogue that captured both the
big picture and the nuances within the memoir. Once, when
the young McBride had asked his mother what color God was,
she replied, "The color of water."

After books are titled and jacketed, the next major meeting
in the publishing cycle is called presales, and once again it's a
gathering of all the departments, but now the in-house sales
people are joined by the regional sales representatives from
around the country. Once again each book on the list is presented, and this time the various parties have a chance to read
some of the text and react to what we call the numbers—the
planned first printing or number of books the publisher hopes
to advance in the marketplace.

The sales conference, the culmination of all the planning

and preparation of the list, is a bi- or triannual meeting at which all the reps come together with the publishers and the heads of the various departments, such as publicity, marketing, and so on. Usually, the editors present the next season's list of books and attempt to communicate what is best and most distinctive about each of them. Today, most of these conferences have been cut back and many are conducted via teleconference. I was fortunate enough to come of age in the days of gala conferences, often held at swanky resorts. The day-long meetings were followed by equally long nights of roasts and banquets, service awards and special author appearances, all-night poker games, extramarital affairs and brawls. The abstemious drank and the nonsmokers smoked. After long days of presentations and computer training, and longer nights in the hospitality suite, many people, battle-fatigued, let their hair down. It was during those late nights that I learned how reps were engaged in their own negotiations between the bookstores they sold to and the expectations of the publishers. The best reps understood their accounts and knew how and when to push. They knew, too, when a book had struck a nerve or when it fell flat. "It's where the rubber hits the road," an old-timer said to me. It didn't matter how much effort we put into the catalog copy and jacket and even the text. If it didn't appeal to a buyer, if they didn't see a market for it, they weren't going to order it. I knew a rep who worked for a big commercial house that had a roster of bestselling thriller writers. I imagined that the responsibility of selling those big guns was huge. On the contrary, selling them was a "no-brainer." It was wedging a few copies of a literary memoir into an account that took time and massaging.

Just as the author faces rejection by editors, agents, and reviewers, the sales rep is on the front lines at the doors of the marketplace, whether he is selling to the largest chain in the country or trying to persuade a independent bookstore to take a few copies of a first-time author, or to take copies of a second novel after the first has tanked. Until 2001, no one except the publisher really knew how many copies a book had sold. Then Nielsen, of ratings fame, launched BookScan, publishing's equivalent of the guillotine. Now, any publisher or bookstore could, with a few strokes of the keyboard, find out more or less how many copies any title had sold. It's like the whole world finding out you've been padding your bra. All the finessing and passion and magical thinking in the world can't change the numbers. And it's the rare bookseller, chain or indie, who will ignore the "track record." BookScan numbers will influence the advance you receive from a publisher for your next book as well as the bookstore's support. It's like a credit rating.

Now, most catalogs are electronic, and orders are put through on computers. When I was a young editor, I went on a few sales calls back when the buyer had a hard copy of the catalog and sat face-to-face with the rep, going through it. In addition to the catalog, the rep generally came equipped with galleys, sometimes there'd be other swag—a button, a tote bag, a T-shirt. Most important was key selling information that could boost a buy, such as a guaranteed appearance on the *Today* show, or the author's having won a Pulitzer Prize. The more ammunition the rep has, the more likely a store will take a quantity of books. It's not enough to say something is beautifully written—a literary writer need not put pasties on her tits and dance around a pole, but it will help her cause if she has published in the literary journals, has won a prize or grant or fellowship, or has an endorsement from a prominent author. Because there is nothing worse, after all the effort that goes into a book, than for a buyer to utter the one word you never want to hear: *skip*.

In response to the changing face of the industry, independent booksellers collaborated to find ways to speak with one voice—albeit a characteristically idiosyncratic and feisty voice. In 1999, the American Booksellers Association launched Book-Sense to promote independent booksellers. BookSense has morphed into IndieBound; its mission to promote books and help stores market to their customers through a series of programs. IndieBound highlights books on a monthly basis—and getting on the Indie Next list is one way for a quiet or first book to get on the radar of booksellers. Likewise, climbing the Indie Bestseller list can help stimulate sales across the country.

In our accelerated culture, where there's so little time to read and digest books, it's no wonder that authors, especially literary writers, fear that their books will get lost in this process. It's important to remember that most people fall in love with reading through fiction and that most people in publishing love great writing. First novels still hold out that promise of first love. And contrary to popular opinion, if a sales force lights on a first novel or a work of literary nonfiction and feels passionate about it, the book can get an incredible push backed by genuine enthusiasm, even when the monetary commitment seems relatively small. "Money doesn't necessarily matter," explained agent Lynn Nesbit in a *New York* magazine article entitled "How to Make a Bestseller." "There has to be a buzz within the house, and of course, they might only get behind one book a season." That buzz usually starts with the sales force. The rep with his ear to the ground is the closest link between the publisher and the reader.

✤

While all the meetings are going on, the manuscript is also being physically prepared for publication. It will be copyedited, a process that the best writers appreciate. I have authors who insist on using the copyeditor they worked with previously, so profound is their respect for that person's careful eye and command of grammar, punctuation, syntax, and other nuances of language, and so deep their gratitude for having been spared embarrassing errors. For the writer who truly loves language, a trip to the copyeditor is like a week at a spa. You come out looking younger, trimmer, and standing straighter. It is true that some copyeditors will, in their efforts to bring a piece of writing into accord with house style, fail to appreciate a writer's particular quirks of style, and in these instances, the editor needs to step in and referee. In general, however, copyeditors are unsung heroes, the men and women who stand as the last line of defense against the fall of civilization, so fierce and exacting is their protection of the English language.

After the author reviews and corrects the copyedited manuscript, it is designed and set in type. Page proofs, the typeset pages, is a stage that never fails to excite me, no matter how many times I shepherd a book through production. Usually, one of the company's designers consults with the editor about the typeface, the design of the title page, and the page layout, and the editor in turn shares the designed pages with the writer. But it's not until the entire manuscript is set in type that one truly senses the book coming into being. Type is a powerful element. In his remarks on receiving the 1998 National Book Foundation Medal for his distinguished contribution to American letters, John Updike paid tribute to the typeface used in his books, explaining that his editor, Harry Ford, was "a perfect knight of the print world, an editor and designer both, who gave me a delicious striped jacket and an elegant page format, in the typeface called Janson, that I have stuck with for over forty books since. To see those youthful willful hopeful words of mine in that type, with Perpetua chapter heads set off by tapered rules, was an elevated moment I am still dizzy from. The old letterpress Linotype had a glinting material bite that all the ingenious advantages of computer setting have not quite replaced."

There is nothing more disconcerting than finding a typo in a book. It's an affront. We all hope that the proofreader who is paid to comb the book for errors is meticulous, but the author also has this last chance to read his pages and make minor changes and corrections. There are many stories of writers rewriting their books in the final hour of the page proof stage, causing great unhappiness all around. Once a book is typeset, any major changes, especially those that affect pagination, are costly and time-consuming to fix. It can be disastrous if a book "slips," meaning it was scheduled to publish in a certain month but because of production delays, often caused by heavy or late author changes, is pushed back a month or more. By this time the book has been sold to the stores, it's on their computer systems, and it's scheduled for warehousing and distribution. If delayed, it may be bumped from special in-store promotions, and media engagements may not be rescheduled unless the author is a powerful person or celebrity. All told, a delay in a book's production usually puts it on a roller coaster of potential disasters.

The final addition to the jacket is the flap copy—the description of the book, written by either your editor or an in-house copywriter—and the blurbs, which have become de rigueur for the backs of jackets, even though almost everyone knows that the business of blurbing is a game of six degrees—or fewer—of separation.

The reason blurbs won't go away is simple: consumers inherently distrust manufacturers. Why should anyone believe the publisher? Of course we're going to tell you that the book is good and, more important, that you should buy it. No matter how much money is spent on advertising, Americans tend to trust personal experience or expert endorsement; we've been ripped off too often. While some consumers are among the literary cognoscenti, know who's slept with whom, and thus can deconstruct the connections that bind a book with its blurbers, most readers don't know that A is friends with B, who was taught by C, who was married to D, who went to school with E, and so forth.   •

Sometimes the blurbs are most effective in-house before the book is even published, which is why editors circulate the blurbs to everyone in the company in the months before publication. When an editor can show his or her colleagues that an extremely famous author has endorsed his first-time novelist, people take notice. A domino effect is created as the blurb is then forwarded to bookstores and the media as a way of saying: *Pay attention!* No matter how much any editor hates sending bound galleys to famous writers, trolling for blurbs (it is, after all, a huge imposition and favor), it's thrilling to actually land the endorsement of a famous writer, especially when he or she doesn't know the author from a hole in the ground. And there's nothing like a good blurb to settle the nerves of a prepublication author. *You like me, you really like me.*

The blurbs, the flap copy, the author photo—all these elements join the jacket art to create an overall effect that the publisher hopes will attract and intrigue the consumer. Using an author's physical beauty to sell his book is not beneath most publishers. Never was this more apparent than in the author photo for Truman Capote's first book, *Other Voices, Other Rooms*, which has been called the most famous book-jacket portrait in contemporary letters. It certainly was at the time, featuring the young Capote stretched out on a divan, his bedroom eyes drawing you in, his mouth a perfect pout. According to George Plimpton, author of an oral biography of Capote, "It caused as much commotion as the book itself. Truman, dismayed by the negative comments, said he had been cajoled into the languorous pose, which in fact he had suggested himself."

If an author looks like George Eliot, chances are her

picture won't be emphasized on the jacket. However, when an author's photo is incorporated into an ad campaign, it's usually because he or she is stunning. Sebastian Junger, author and hunk, once complained bitterly that people were focusing on his looks. Somehow it was hard to feel sorry for him after he posed open-shirt, his torso extended in all its washboard definition over the prow of a ship, for *People* magazine's "Most Beautiful People" issue.

A brilliant young photographer began taking pictures of writers in 1983, and her work has found a cultlike devotion. It became a badge of pride to be photographed by Marion Ettlinger, who works exclusively in natural light. Each of her deeply textured black-and-white photos seems to uncannily capture the essence of the author. In 2003, she published a book called *Author Photo*, and it includes such portraits as Capote himself, Cormac McCarthy, Ann Patchett, Jhumpa Lahiri, and Richard Ford. Oh, and Sebastian Junger as well.

When all is said and done, there is nothing quite like seeing your book for the first time. Whenever the first copies of a book from the bindery arrived in my in-box, I always took a few minutes to examine them, carefully removing the jacket to make sure that the spine had the right title and name. I'd check the endpapers, the title page, a few sample pages. Then I would write a note to the author, urging him to take a moment before the world reacted and take pride in his accomplishment and in the thing itself. No matter how many compromises were made along the way, no matter what happens in the future, a book is a thing to behold.

12.

PUBLICATION

"MOST BOOKS COME INTO THE WORLD WITH the fanfare of a stillborn," wrote James Purdy, in a line so dark and forbidding one feels the need to avert one's eyes. Publishing a book can be a cruel joke on the uninitiated. Every author hopes that publication will improve his life, if not transform it in some miraculous way that usually never materializes. Many think that the publication of a book will help them get or keep a job, win respect from friends and family, get laid. "A book is a pussy magnet," said one of my young writers. "The equivalent of a Mustang to a high school senior." No matter how realistic authors claim to be—and many do try to appear rational—Zen, even—all harbor dreams of greatness. This quixotic belief in oneself is critical for a writer's continued existence; as we all know, for every book that wins the National Book Award or hits the bestseller list, thousands disappear without a trace.

When I entered the industry, one writer epitomized the story of the girl with the glass slipper. Consider Alice McDermott, whose first novel, *The Bigamist's Daughter*, was glowingly reviewed on the front page of the *New York Times Book Review* by Anne Tyler—a dream come true for any first novelist. In most cases, a writer would pay for such good fortune by having her second book savaged by critics. But McDermott's second novel, *That Night*, was again praised on the front page of the book review—lightning had struck twice—this time by David Leavitt, who claimed the novel had a "sense of almost Shakespearean tragedy." It was nominated for a National Book Award and made into a feature film. Novel number three, *At Weddings and Wakes*, made the bestseller list, and McDermott's fourth, *Charming Billy*, won the National Book Award *and* hit the bestseller list. The story of her success is devil's candy for those whose wish is to emulate her, just as surely as it was salt in the wounded egos of those who would begrudge her. (And there's nothing like the National Book Award to stir up grudges.)

Perhaps even more extraordinary was the fate of a first short-story collection, published in trade paperback in 1999, that went on to win the Pulitzer Prize. Received wisdom in publishing asserts that short story collections don't sell, and books published in an original trade paperback format will not get the serious review attention usually afforded to hardcover books. When Jhumpa Lahiri's collection, *Interpreter of Maladies*, won the Pulitzer, it was a triumph on many levels: a first-time author, a collection, a paperback. The cards couldn't have been stacked more against her. When she published her third book, *Unaccustomed Earth*, also a collection of stories, it went right to number one on the *New York Times* bestseller list. Hail the short story! Hail Jhumpa Lahiri! A year later, *Tinkers* by Paul Harding, another original trade paperback from Bellevue Press, a five-year-old publishing company, also won a Pulitzer Prize. Not quite a trend, but hopeful news that some amazing and original new voices are being recognized with the highest honors.

The first misnomer most writers encounter is that highly charged day known as publication day. One seasoned novelist with six books to her credit described the excitement and anticipation she felt as publication day neared for her first novel. She spent the days before her book came out cleaning her apartment like an expectant mother in nesting mode. When I asked her why she was so frantic, she said that on the physical level it was pure nerves, but somewhere in her imagination she dreamed of serving tea to a bevy of journalists who would stop by for a chat about her novel. "I almost bought a tea set," she said, laughing at the folly of it all. "Then the big day comes and nothing, I mean nothing at all happened. The phone didn't even ring. Finally, at four o'clock in the afternoon I put on a hat, scarf, and sunglasses as if I were Greta Garbo and ducked out into a bookshop, didn't see my book anywhere, and skulked out feeling totally mortified."

Tom Wolfe may get a caviar extravaganza at the Pierre Hotel to celebrate the arrival of his newest novel, but most authors have to throw their own book parties or finagle friends into marking the occasion with a celebration. If they are lucky, the publisher will offer to print the invitations and contribute a case or two of wine. But the days of big publication parties are largely over, because they're expensive and don't usually help the sales of the book. My advice to writers is to press friends and family for a fete. It isn't every day that you write a book, even if your publisher hardly notices. In Michael Korda's memoir of publishing, *Another Life*, he tells of the hilarious gaffe made by publisher Max Schuster when he ran into his author Gypsy Rose Lee at 21, where she was enjoying a celebratory meal for her book. Simon & Schuster had not thrown a party for the famous stripper, and as Korda tells it, when Lee spotted her publisher at the restaurant, she felt awkward about approaching him. Finally she worked her way over to his table. "Max beamed up at Gypsy, and before she could say a word, stammered out to her: 'Gypsy, how nice to see you! You know, I've been thinking about you a lot lately. . . . One of these days, you ought to write a book.'"

If your publication day doesn't mean anything to Jon Stewart or Stephen Colbert or Michiko Kakutani, if Charlie Rose and Chelsea Handler aren't sparring over who's going to get that exclusive interview, you're not alone. But it doesn't mean you should spend the day skulking around bookstores in dark glasses. (Though after a few weeks of having a book out most authors become heat-seeking missiles, checking every store within driving distance for stock.) In actuality, publication day is a technical term for booksellers. It refers to the on-sale date in the stores and is meant to be coordinated with the timing of reviews. There is almost nothing more frustrating than a fabulous review that runs weeks before a book is available in the stores. Still, publication day sounds like a birthday to most writers, and it's impossible not to have one's expectations aroused, especially after the long months of waiting. This is the time when most writers go into some kind of free fall.

I urge all my writers to get to work on their next project before publication. Working on a new book is the only cure for keeping the evil eye away. After publication, the writer opens himself up to reviewers and critics—or to their glaring silence— and is extremely vulnerable. Even when the press is good, it can be subverting. Scott Spencer, in an interview, recalled that "the public reaction to *Endless Love* immediately put me into competition with myself—'I sure hope the next one meets with that kind of success.' And with that bald-faced utterance, I ripped the pen from my fingers, broke it in half, and basically didn't work for about a year." The great poet Pablo Neruda lamented the effect of criticism in a *Paris Review* interview: "Oh! My critics! My critics have almost shredded me to pieces, with all the love or hate in the world! In life, as in art, one can't please everybody, and that's a situation that's always with us. One is always receiving kisses and slaps, caresses and kicks, and that is the life of the poet."

The more you are able to do on your book's behalf, the better shielded you will be from bad reviews or random acts of cruelty. And I cannot reiterate this enough: get to work on your next project before the reviews begin to come in on the first one. In publishing circles, the inability to come up with a second book is blithely referred to as the sophomore slump, but for the writer in the slump the pain is excruciating. There is no way to predict how attention or the lack thereof will disrupt your ability to work.

✦

The first signs of how a book will be received are in the pre- publication reviews from the trade papers, namely *Publishers Weekly* and *Kirkus Reviews*, as well as *Library Journal* and *Booklist*.

These unsigned, paragraph-length reviews are often harbingers of reviews to come. There is no better feeling for an editor than when sending off a positive early review to an anxious author and her agent with a quick note: *Congratulations on the great review—a sure sign of good things to come.* It's more dicey when the review is lousy. Some editors deep-six bad prepublication reviews altogether. Some call the author and commiserate about the stupidity of the review. Often, it's a good occasion for an editor to ask an author if he or she wants to see all reviews, come what may, though most authors have themselves on Google alert and regularly check Amazon for any new reviews posted by readers. I've known more than a few writers who claim to want to see all reviews, no matter how bad, only to change their minds when they actually get bludgeoned. I always think it's a healthy choice not to read the bad ones, but many writers are nothing if not masochists.

When Bernard Malamud was asked whether criticism of his work affected him, he replied, "Some of it must. Not the crap, the self-serving pieces, but an occasional insightful criticism, favorable or unfavorable, that confirms my judgment of my work. While I'm on the subject, I dislike particularly those critics who preach their aesthetic or ideological doctrines at you. What's important to them is not what the writer has done but how it fits, or doesn't fit, the thesis they want to develop. Nobody can tell a writer what can or ought to be done, or not done, in his fiction. A living death if you fall for it."

Unfortunately, for some writers, the experience of publication is a living death, or hell, that offers little or no catharsis. Rather than acknowledging the accomplishment or feeling a degree of mastery over a body of material, the writer seems to have opened a Pandora's box of anxiety, guilt, and shame. Feelings of fraudulence continue to haunt some writers throughout their lives. Some writers I have worked with explain that it took three or four books before they stopped feeling like an impostor, and felt they could actually call themselves writers. In her autobiography, Edith Wharton describes her own impostor complex. "I had written short stories that were thought worthy of preservation! Was it the same insignificant I that I had always known? Any one walking along the streets might go into any bookshop, and say: 'Please give me Edith Wharton's book,' and the clerk, without bursting into incredulous laughter, would produce it, and be paid for it, and the purchaser would walk home with it and read it, and talk of it, and pass it on to other people to read! The whole business seemed too unreal to be anything but a practical joke played on me by some occult humorist; and my friends could not have been more astonished and incredulous than I was."

Wharton goes on to describe the feeling of reading her reviews, most of which, she happily reports, were kind and generous. But one eventually came along, she says, that "stiffened her limp spine." This reviewer took the tack that maddens writers most, that of schoolmarm, firmly correcting the writer as if she were some grade-school student. "'When Mrs. Wharton,' the condescending critic wrote, 'has learned the rudiments of her art, she will know that a short story should always begin with dialogue.'" Though Wharton heartily rejected the critic's formulaic approach as entirely bogus, she deeply pondered the critic's response, concluding, "This egregious commentary did me an immense service. . . . In an instant I was free forever from the bogey of the omniscient reviewer."

In Rilke's *Letters to a Young Poet*, he warns his correspondent with the following: "Read as little as possible of aesthetic criticism—such things are either partisan views, petrified and grown senseless in their lifeless induration, or they are clever quibblings in which today one view wins and tomorrow the opposite. Works of art are of an infinite loneliness and with nothing so little to be reached as with criticism."

One bridge that spans the infinite loneliness between a writer and the abyss comes in the form of something far less public than reviews but no less meaningful: author mail. I am always astonished at the depth of feeling conveyed in some of the fan letters my authors have shared with me. One of my authors, who was excoriated by the press for her memoir, never traveled without a suitcase full of mail by individuals who were touched by her work. Years after publication, the letters and emails keep coming. Another writer, who was severely criticized in the local press for exposing the foibles of a handful of small-town folk, continues to receive letters from people there, thanking her for finally telling the truth about their lives. One husband-and-wife team with whom I worked canvassed the country to gather stories about girls and sports. The book received only a handful of reviews—parenting titles and sports books rarely get review attention—but they received daily email and letters from parents who felt their efforts were acknowledged in the stories portrayed in the book. One letter enclosed pictures of a woman's little slugger; the mother described how grateful she was for the book's assurances in support of raising an athletic and competitive daughter.

For those who keep living it, the writing life, though never secure, becomes somewhat more predictable. Once you've done enough interviews and read enough of your own reviews, you can begin to predict how your work will be received. "You know, all of this is such a bore," said Philip Roth in a 1990 *Los Angeles Times* interview following the publication of *Deception*. "I wrote a book about adultery and people are very sophisticated about that subject until they're involved in it. So I upped the ante and got a little reckless. I wanted to capture the dangerous sense of being in an affair, and that's why I put myself into the book. You'd think people would strike out more independently when writing about my books. Instead of writing what everybody's been writing about for 15 years." What most aspiring authors would give for a taste of such boredom!

❧

Publicity is the key to getting attention for a book. This was not always the case. In his wonderful *New Yorker* article "Wasn't She Great?" Michael Korda describes publishing in 1958, when he began, as "a respectable profession." The business was being run, "for the most part, by men in suits or in donnish tweeds, with pipes, who were either Ivy League Wasps or Jews whose highest ambition was to be mistaken for Wasps." This would all change forever, according to Korda, with the 1966 publication of *Valley of the Dolls* by Jacqueline Susann. "It brought together for the first time the worlds of Hollywood, gossip, and Broadway press-agentry, to sell a novel whose subjects included all those things. Jackie, then forty-seven, had spikey false eye-lashes, a chain-smoker's gravelly voice, and glittery dresses; her feisty, tough-broady image seemed to many like the beginning of the end—show business vulgarity at the door of the temple of culture."

Korda goes on to describe the particular magic that was Jackie, but also points out how she and her husband created a new way of selling a novel that included shameless self-promotion, personal appearances, and celebrity tie-ins. Even the word *launch* was new to publishing. But beyond the glitz, Korda also describes a woman who understood that she had earned her success by working it from the ground up. Jacqueline Susann was zealous in getting to know booksellers; apparently she even noted their birthdays in her Rolodex and sent affectionate, handwritten notes to the people who rarely get any attention or thanks: the clerks and managers.

Thirty years later, writers of every stripe, from romance to postmodern, want their fifteen minutes, and they want their books to sell. Jonathan Franzen will likely go down in history more for having turned down Oprah than his brilliant novel *The Corrections*. Most authors check their Amazon.com ranking much the way a stockbroker reads the Nasdaq or an inveterate dieter jumps on the scale. *Am I up? Am I down?* Sales figures are to authors what batting averages are to baseball players. Sure, you can have great form, but can you hit it out of the ballpark? Or to put it more succinctly, as Andy Warhol, the deceased priest of the cult of fame, used to say, "Success is what sells"— though I prefer to recall Bob Dylan's Möbius strip of a lyric, "There's no success like failure, and failure's no success at all."

We expect our writers, like movie stars, to be equipped to handle any kind of scrutiny or attack. Most first-time authors have no experience with handling publicity of any kind and are often caught terribly unaware, both of how to handle the media and of how to deal with the feelings stirred by those attentions or dismissals. If your book is likely to come under attack or is provocative, it is extremely worthwhile for you to spend time being either professionally or casually coached. A good publicist will prepare questions for interviewers and rehearse with you. You can be taught how to steer questions and talk about those parts of the book that put it in its best light.

Few writers are truly gifted at giving readings, and most have panic attacks before doing an interview, whether for radio, print, or television. And nowadays an author who isn't deemed "promotable" can be a liability. I worked with a brilliant academic who couldn't answer a question in less than ten minutes, so accustomed was he to elaborating on his ideas in scholarly journals and among graduate students. When his book came out, he was asked to appear on a few television shows, because the subject of his book intersected with some timely news events. Unfortunately, he failed each pre-interview. One producer summed it up thus: *He doesn't give good sound bite.*

It's important to plan your readings and selections before you speak in public. Long descriptive passages usually put people to sleep, as does staring down at your book for twenty minutes and reading either too fast or in a monotone. Your publicist or editor should help you select a few sections from the book that will be effective for the format. I have always loved poetry readings for all the anecdotes that poets share between poems, and I counsel my authors to do likewise and provide some meaningful stories. After all, anyone can read the book at home. If an audience has come out to see you, give them something they won't find in the book.

All authors expect to be sent out "on tour" with visions of green rooms and limos and long lines of devoted readers dancing in their heads. Writers still want to tour, though most have heard the war stories from the front. Annie Proulx, in a hilarious essay in *The Writing Life* called "The Book Tour," describes a reading in Wyoming where the relatively small crowd appeared rather agitated and kept sneaking looks at papers in their hands. After reading for fifteen minutes, Proulx gave up and headed for the wine and cheese at the back of the room. Immediately "a young woman who had been sitting in the front row got up and read a poem about her first airplane ride, a poem that went on for frozen centuries of time. She barely finished when another one jumped up and launched into a searing description of sex with a teenage cowboy. And so it went, until the entire audience, made up of local writers, had read their stuff."

Reports from the road are laden with tales of woe: the packed bookstore that never received the books, or the radio interviewer who keeps calling you by the wrong name or confesses during the commercial break that he hasn't read the book and badgers you to supply him with questions so that he can fill the airtime. Then there is the pleasure of landing in a new city the day your book is panned on the front page of the local paper, or the advertisement for your appearance is printed with the wrong date or time. There are the endless flights, the lost luggage, the escort who talks incessantly about her divorce—or worse, the book she'd like to write, the hotel that's lost your reservation, and the final insult: a minibar with no gin.

And yet, for the author who is scheduled to do only a local book signing, the book tour beckons; almost every author wants to go out on the road. When Terry McMillan discovered that her publisher had no plans to tour her first novel, she loaded up the trunk of her car with books and hit the pavement, making friends with booksellers across the country. The rest is history. Today the touring circuit is more crowded, with some stores hosting three or four authors in a single day. But just as McMillan refused to let her publisher limit her appearances, writers today have many new ways to provide exposure for their work.

Just a few years before the explosion of social networking sites, I met two poets who set up a thirty-city tour for their self-published books. The only criteria they had for choosing cities was that they know at least one person who lived there. This "point person" would help them come up with an invitation list and find a bar to host the event. They each nearly sold out their first printings and had a blast reading poetry to lots of non-poetry types (whatever that means!), and one of the women met a regional publisher who would go on to publish her next book and eventually become her husband.

No matter how much time we spend clicking and sending, people still need to get out, if only to see friends, get laid, find love. But for you, the writer, it's also about word of mouth, building an audience, and in some cases "branding" or "extending your brand," to borrow from the business lexicon. What every publisher wants is a "brand name" author, someone who consistently sells in mega-bestselling quantities, such as John Grisham, Stephenie Meyer, Malcolm Gladwell, J. K. Rowling, Mitch Albom, and the newly anointed, Dan Brown. One thing you will notice about these authors is that, whether their new book is a sequel or not, the packages all look like their previous bestselling books. If you can "brand" an author in this world of a billion things, you are that much closer to keeping a reader, a much more difficult challenge than getting a consumer to stick with Heinz ketchup or Diet Coke.

The author who might be considered the mega-brander of all time is also the minister of his mega-church, Saddleback, in Lake Forest, California. According to *Publishers Weekly*, Rick Warren is the bestselling hardcover nonfiction author of all time. After seven years in print, *The Purpose Driven Life* has sold more than 52 million copies. Better yet, and this is where "brand extension" comes in, you can also purchase, among many other items: *The Purpose Driven Life Journal*, *Daily Inspiration for the Purpose Driven Life*, *The Purpose Driven Life Deluxe Journal*, *A Catholic Perspective on the Purpose Driven Life*, *The Purpose Driven Life for Commuters*, and my personal favorite, *The Purpose Driven Life Camouflage Edition*. Is this for when you're in a foxhole in Afghanistan, or when you don't want your friends to know you're getting in touch with your spirituality? Warren began his church with two hundred congregants—it now averages twenty thousand in attendance each week. Bottom line: word of mouth is still the most powerful way to sell books. Clearly, the success of *The Purpose Driven Life* emanated from Warren's huge constituency, built over twenty-five years. Rome, again, was not built in a day.

In 1998, a beautifully designed new literary journal appeared on the scene. It was extremely hip, showcased some great young writers, and would likely last a year if that—such is the lifespan of most literary magazines. The magazine has more than lasted; and the editor at its center, Dave Eggers, has gone on to create his own publishing empire in the ten-plus years since he started *McSweeney's Quarterly*. The magazine, now produced as a hardcover book with superb production values and exquisite design—each edition a collector's item—is nationally distributed. Eggers has also published or copublished more than fifteen books under four imprints; his list has been recognized by the National Book Critics Circle and others. A monthly magazine, *The Believer*, is another thriving Eggers publication, and *Wholphin* is a quarterly DVD magazine that features short films, animation, and more by filmmakers such as Spike Jonze, David O. Russell, and Miranda July. *McSweeney's Internet Tendency* provides original daily writing along with events listings, and was awarded a National Webby Award for Best Writing. Eggers is also the author of his own successful books including his audaciously titled *A Heartbreaking Work of Staggering Genius*, which went to number one on the *New York Times* bestseller list and was nominated for a Pulitzer Prize. His 2009 book, *Zeitoun*, published by his own outfit, also made the *Times* list. If that isn't enough, Eggers cowrote with his wife the screenplay for the Sam Mendez–directed *Away We Go*; wrote a novelization of Maurice Sendak's *Where the Wild Things Are*; and founded 826 Valencia, a nonprofit writing and tutoring center for kids ages six to eighteen that has grown into a national organization. Did

I mention that he operates a pirate store in San Francisco and a superhero store in Brooklyn? That's right, a pirate store and a superhero store. I've been to the latter. It's awesome.

I think of Eggers as a literary P. T. Barnum, impresario extraordinaire. I'm not saying that everyone can or should be creating a personal literary dynasty, but it's essential to be creative in thinking about how to market yourself. "Without promotion something terrible happens . . ." said Barnum. "Nothing!"

According to Malcolm Gladwell, the critical difference behind something that "tips" or that reaches epidemic proportions is people. He identifies three types: the connectors who have huge social networks, the mavens or specialists who share information, and the salesmen who persuade you. Today's word of mouth may be communicated over a cup of chai latte or via text or Twitter, but the fact remains, people influence other people. It's still word of mouth that drives people into bookstores or to Amazon. It's still a human being who tweets. An "Influentials" study by Word of Mouth Marketing found that 72 percent of consumers have recommended at least one book to a peer within the last thirty days, There are hundreds of websites devoted to recommending favorite books, from well-established sources such as NPR to passionate individuals who simply want to talk about books.

Some publishers have figured out early on how to tap into social networks and help books go "viral," exponentially increasing sales. At first this meant a recent college grad surfing the web and sending out galleys to sites likely to talk about the book. Now we're seeing books with interactive components, especially in the young adult and fantasy categories. For certain

books and authors, publishers are creating fan sites where readers can find additional material, including author interviews and
teasers from forthcoming books. Hyperion launched a memoir about a woman's battle with breast cancer—a topic I was
repeatedly told didn't sell when I was an editor—with a video
of the author reading an essay she wrote for the women who
supported her during her struggle. The video has been viewed
more than 4.5 million times and the book, *The Middle Place* by
Kelly Corrigan, has spent more than twenty-seven weeks on
the *New York Times* bestseller list.

Bloggers with large enough readerships can sometimes get
their books on the bestseller list by simply announcing the
on-sale date. One of the best examples of growing a readership through a website and blog is "The Cult." Chuck Palahniuk's site gets more than seven hundred thousand page views
a month and has more than thirty thousand registered users
on its forums. A component of the website is devoted to helping aspiring writers, and elsewhere on the site you can buy the
very sexy *Fight Club* T-shirt for just twenty bucks. Palahniuk
has maintained the website for more than a decade. I've been
told his "followers" paper their cities with Palahniuk posters on
the eve of his latest publication. A major investment, a major
return. The potential for innovating marketing and publicity
efforts for books through technology is boundless. Author loyalty: priceless.

A few years ago, all writers wanted to know if they had to
have a website. Now, they want to know if they should blog,
be on Facebook, or create a video about their book to post on
YouTube. To tweet or not to tweet; this is the kind of question

I'm most frequently asked. I'm still waiting for a world where babies are born with bar codes on their butts, their consumer preferences handed out with their birth certificates. Don't get me wrong: I think all these new ways of reaching people are amazing. I personally love blogging and have watched my "readership" grow exponentially because of links and tweets and recommendations. But I also know that much of this technology distracts writers from their primary goal. You have to be honest with yourself and do a cost-benefit analysis: How much time are you spending genuinely extending your so-called brand, and how much time are you just wasting online? Remember when email was a writer's primary form of distraction? How quaint!

Writers clearly have to be proactive when it comes to selling their work. In some respects, the new technologies make it easier than ever to find your potential audience. What most writers don't realize is that you can't, upon finishing your book, start a blog and expect it to drive sales. It takes time to build a real following. The typical writer has a few hundred followers on Twitter, or a website he hasn't updated in a year. None of this is going to drive serious sales. However, if you are blogging the entire time that you are researching your book you may begin to develop a niche audience particularly interested in your subject that you can tap for your book. Likewise, if you've been using Faceboook to find poets and poetry lovers all over America, this will help you when you publish your next collection. Some writers are freaked out by the prospect of doing online networking; some are so busy scurrying between blog, Facebook, Twitter, YouTube, and website that they never get around to writing a new proposal or selling a book. I hate to counsel balance because I don't think writers can or should lead balanced lives, but you need to be smart about what the web can do for you. For instance, a nonfiction writer with a particular niche can target organizations, institutions, clubs, and so on using the Internet, in ways that were not feasible when I started this book. This is a boon. A literary writer with a big Twitter account can tweet about her next reading and fill a bar in San Antonio with a click. But again, it takes time.

Many authors are crestfallen when their first book doesn't "hit." A writing career, a shelf of books with your name on them, doesn't happen overnight. Likewise, even though the Internet feels like it can provide instant results, it also takes time, care, grooming, attention. I think it's better to kick ass on Facebook or build up a corps of 6,000 Twitter followers than have a little of everything. It will take time to find your audience online, just as it does for your books.

✻

The best advice I can give any author on the verge of publication is: treat your publicist like gold. While most books published by trade houses do get sent out widely for review with a press release and are assigned a publicist, authors are often unrealistic about how far those efforts can go. Too many authors imagine that having a publicist means having a press secretary, a personal secretary, and a travel agent all rolled into one. Intellectually, most authors know that their publicist is also working on a half-dozen other titles, but emotionally they want total attention. Unless the company has paid a great deal of money for your book and plans to expose it widely through touring and promotion, it is unrealistic to expect your publicist to do much more than send out the book and make some follow-up calls. A publicist's job is thankless. And if lightning strikes, if a publicist lands you on *Oprah* or secures a high-profile interview, or schmoozes a book editor until he finally decides to review a book he has been on the fence about, few authors remember their publicist's efforts. Editors are thanked, spouses are thanked, publishers are thanked, but all too often the publicist gets lost in the crowd.

Though few people acknowledge her importance, the publicist is truly on the front lines of any publication. She can hear the distant thunder and knows before anyone else whether producers and reviewers and critics and pundits are clamoring or clamming up. I always instruct my authors not to abuse their publicist if they have to blow off steam. What most writers don't understand is that when they alienate their publicist, they're essentially cutting off their own nose, as the expression goes, because the publicist's job is all about going the extra mile: mentioning *your* book when a book review editor is calling about something else, bringing a copy of *your* galleys to lunch with a top magazine editor, bringing up *your* book to a producer trolling for a good segment for her newsweekly. If an author continues to annoy the publicist, harangue her with requests, condescend, or in any other way disrespect her job and position, it is unlikely that that author's book will be on the tip of her tongue when opportunity knocks. There are authors who send multiple emails to their publicist, then call minutes later to see if she's received them. Authors will tell you that their emails seem to go into the void, forgetting that the publicist has to balance any number of requests and pitches and calls and rejections in the course of her day. She will do a better job if you let her do it. Every minute she is on the phone with you is a minute she is not on the phone pitching your book.

True, not all publicists are created equal. Some have an astonishing depth and wealth of contacts and creativity. I have seen publicity campaigns that equal Sherman's March in fortitude and persistence. I have seen creative and strategic planning that has launched a book into the stratosphere. Unfortunately, publicity departments also have high turnover and a high burnout rate. Often publicists leave, as do editors, midproject, and it's extremely disconcerting for an author who has spent years on his book to discover that it is being reassigned to someone who doesn't seem to have any connection to the material. Yet even if you really bond with your publicist and feel that she will do everything short of selling her own mother to get you exposure, you can't expect the world to flock around when you publish your book. Just because reviewers aren't biting doesn't mean your publicist isn't out there pitching. Think twice before you vent your frustration on your publicist.

I learned from one of the first books I worked on, *Guerrilla Marketing*, that publishing a book is like starting a new business. Just setting up the store isn't enough. People aren't going to come in and shop just because you've put an Open sign in the window. It would be very nice indeed if you didn't have to do anything besides write the book. But if you want it to sell and to reach people, you have to be creative, whether your publisher is willing to push the book or not.

In some cases, it's a good idea to hire your own publicist,

especially if you feel that the market for your book is still untapped in the media. I worked with a woman whose book came out between Thanksgiving and New Year's, and for some reason we couldn't get her a shred of publicity, though we tried. Sometimes the holiday season is impenetrable for all but the big-name books. The following April the author hired her own PR firm for an additional three-week push. We supplied books and PR materials, and the extra effort yielded a few front-page lifestyle articles, a segment on the TV news program *48 Hours*, and a few more reviews. Though sales didn't improve much, when her paperback appeared the following fall, the enhanced press kit and tape from the television program helped pitch her, and as a result she got on another nighttime newsweekly and received some higher-profile coverage in the print media. Her paperback outsold the hardcover, and her next book was a *New York Times* bestseller. Again, Rome, not built in a day.

Whether or not you choose to spend your own money on publicity is a personal decision. For those who will never be satisfied with the publisher's efforts, I think it's a good idea. This way you will at least feel that you tried everything and that your book was given a full-court press—though you should be forewarned that your efforts might not result in more than a sales blip. We've also seen the proliferation of lecture agents whose role is to obtain paid speaking engagements for writers. In addition to earning extra income for writers, speaking engagements are also a great way to sell books. Almost every trade publisher has followed suit by opening an in-house lecture department to tap into this market, that is, nonbookstore venues such as universities, religious groups, corporations, and so forth.

❧

Everyone is dancing as fast as he can. Print media is retracting, major newspapers are folding, book pages and book reviews are endangered, some of the big chains are teetering, and too many of the best-loved independent bookstores have been shuttered. E-books, still a relatively small percentage of book sales overall (1 to 10 percent, depending who you ask), are threatening to change the entire pricing structure of books, and then there are piracy issues to contend with. Publishers are concerned that the business model that has long served their business will no longer work. All this is disheartening for writers. It's no wonder that some are tweeting for their supper. Sometimes, at publishing parties, throwing back a room-temperature Chardonnay, I fear that we are dancing on the deck of the *Titanic*.

For the first eleven years of my daughter's life, part of our bedtime ritual was curling up and reading a book. This year, on more than one occasion, we have gotten into bed with her laptop and looked at Facebook, cool websites, and YouTube. I imagine by the time she goes to college, she will download most of her coursework on to her Jetson-reader and text me through a chip implanted in her eyebrow. And when she stares at our beloved library—a collection that tells its own life story, volumes whose provenance we can trace to moments in our lives, vividly recalled by the spine of a dust jacket, a note in a margin, a letter tucked between pages—she will shake her head.

Relics. Dust-gatherers. Didn't we get rid of our LPs, our cassettes, our CDs? Why are we holding on to our books? Perhaps only for sentiment.

When asked whether literature as we know it is an anachronism, Isaac Bashevis Singer, in a *Paris Review* interview, replied, "I don't think that literature, good literature, has anything to fear from technology. The very opposite. The more technology, the more people will be interested in what the human mind can produce *without* the help of electronics."

Most of us are still attached to books. I can think of no better content delivery system. But it's more than that: Books have soul. And they have lasted a very long time. That, too, says something. I believe in change, and if I have to read a book off the head of a pin, I will, so long as it's a good book and a decent pin. For me, the bottom line is writers. Will I still get to agent and edit them? Encourage them, provide ballast, hear them roar? Hear them roar.

BIBLIOGRAPHY

Amis, Martin. "The Art of Fiction CLI." *Paris Review* 146, Spring 1998.

Archer, Ellen. "Viral Campaigns." *Publishers Weekly*, October 5, 2009.

Atlas, James. "The Fall of Fun." *New Yorker*, November 18, 1996.

———. "Speaking Ill of the Dead." *New York Times Magazine*, November 6, 1988.

———. "Stranger Than Fiction." *New York Times Magazine*, June 23, 1991.

Auletta, Ken. "Publish or Perish." *New Yorker*, April 26, 2010.

Beardon, Michelle. "John Grisham." *Publishers Weekly*, February 22, 1993.

Begley, Sharon. "The Nurture Assumption." *Newsweek*, September 7, 1998.

Berg, A. Scott. *Max Perkins: Editor of Genius*. New York: E. P. Dutton, 1978.

Blades, John. "Lorrie Moore: Flipping Death the Bird." *Publishers Weekly*, August 24, 1997.

Blythe, Will, ed. *Why I Write*. Boston: Little, Brown, 1998.

Brent, Jonathan. "What Facts? A Talk with Roth." *New York Times*, September 25, 1988.

Capote, Truman. *Answered Prayers*. New York: Random House, 1987.

———. *Music for Chameleons*. New York: Random House, 1980.

Carvajal, Doreen. "Read the True (More or Less) Story! Publishers and Authors Debate the Boundaries of Nonfiction." *New York Times*, February 24, 1998.

Cerf, Bennett. *At Random*. New York: Random House, 1977.

Cheever, Benjamin, ed. *The Letters of John Cheever*. New York: Simon & Schuster, 1988.

Cheever, John. *The Journals of John Cheever.* New York: Alfred A. Knopf, 1991.

Chernow, Ron. "Stubborn Facts and Fickle Realities." In *The Writing Life: National Book Award Authors.* New York: Random House, 1995.

Cheuse, Alan, and Nicholas Delbanco. *Talking Horse: Bernard Malamud on Life and Work.* New York: Columbia University Press, 1996.

Clarke, Gerald. *Capote: A Biography.* New York: Simon & Schuster, 1988.

Coffey, Michael. "Michael Cunningham: New Family Outings." *Publishers Weekly,* November 2, 1998.

Conant, Jennet. "Royalty Wedding of the Year." *Manhattan, Inc.,* January 1989.

Cowley, Malcolm, ed. *Writers at Work: The Paris Review Interviews.* New York: Viking Press, 1957.

Dark, Larry, ed. *Literary Outtakes.* New York: Ballantine, 1990.

Dickinson, Emily. *Final Harvest.* Boston: Little, Brown, 1961.

Didion, Joan. *Slouching Towards Bethlehem.* New York: Simon & Schuster, 1961.

Dostoyevsky, Fyodor. *Notes from Underground/The Double,* trans. Jessie Coulson. New York: Penguin, 1972.

Duras, Marguerite. *Writing,* trans. Mark Polizzotti. Cambridge, MA: Lumen, 1998.

Eliot, Valerie, ed. *The Letters of T. S. Eliot.* San Diego: Harcourt Brace Jovanovich, 1988.

Ellmann, Richard. *James Joyce.* New York: Oxford University Press, 1959.

Emerson, Ken. "The Indecorous, Rabelaisian, Convoluted Righteousness of Stanley Elkin." *New York Times Magazine,* March 3, 1991.

Ferguson, Andrew. "A River of Chicken Soup." *Time,* June 8, 1998.

Fitzgerald, Sally, ed. *The Habit of Being: Letters of Flannery O'Connor.* New York: Farrar, Straus & Giroux, 1979.

Garis, Leslie. "Susan Sontag Finds Romance." *New York Times Magazine,* August 2, 1992.

Getlin, Josh. "Sparring with Roth." *Los Angeles Times,* April 15, 1990.

Gillespie, Elgy. "Carol Shields." *Publishers Weekly,* February 28, 1994.

Ginzberg, Natalia. *The Little Virtues,* trans. Dick Davis. New York: Arcade, 1989.

Giroux, Robert, ed. *Robert Lowell: Collected Prose.* New York: Farrar, Straus & Giroux, 1987.

Goffman, Erving. *The Presentation of Self in Everyday Life*. New York: Anchor, 1959.

Goldberg, Natalie. *Writing Down the Bones*. Boston: Shambhala, 1986.

Goldstein, Bill. "King of Horror." *Publishers Weekly*, January 24, 1991.

Gottlieb, Robert. "The Art of Editing." *Paris Review*, Fall 1994.

Grealy, Lucy. *Autobiography of a Face*. Boston: Houghton Mifflin, 1994.

Green, Jack. *Fire the Bastards*. Normal, IL: Dalkey Archive Press, 1992.

Grimes, William. "Frank McCourt, Whose Irish Childhood Illuminated His Prose, Is Dead at 78." *New York Times*, July 19, 2009.

Hendrickson, Robert. *The Literary Life and Other Curiosities*. San Diego: Harcourt Brace, 1981.

Howard, Gerald. "The American Strangeness: An Interview with Don DeLillo." *Hungry Mind Review*, Fall 1997.

———. "Slouching Towards Grubnet: The Author in the Age of Publicity." *Review of Contemporary Fiction*, 1997.

Hughes, Ted. *Birthday Letters*. New York: Farrar, Straus & Giroux, 1998.

Hughes, Ted, and Frances McCullough, eds. *The Journals of Sylvia Plath*. New York: Dial Press, 1982. Reprint, Anchor Books, 1998.

Ishiguro, Kazuo. *The Remains of the Day*. New York: Alfred A. Knopf, 1989.

James, Caryn. "Auteur! Auteur!" *New York Times Magazine*, January 19, 1986.

Jamison, Kay Redfield. *Touched with Fire: Manic Depressive Illness and the Artistic Temperament*. New York: Free Press, 1993.

———. *An Unquiet Mind*. New York: Alfred A. Knopf, 1995.

Johnson, Denis. *The Incognito Lounge*. New York: Random House, 1982.

Johnson, Thomas H., ed. *The Letters of Emily Dickinson*. Cambridge, MA: Belknap Press of Harvard University Press, 1914.

Jones, Malcolm. "Mr. Wolfe Bites Back." *Newsweek*, January 4, 1999.

Kafka, Franz. *Letter to His Father*, trans. Ernst Kaiser and Eithne Wilkins. New York: Schocken Books, 1953.

Kaplan, Justin. *Walt Whitman: A Life*. New York: Simon & Schuster, 1980.

Klam, Matthew. "Some of My Best Friends Are Rich." *New York Times Magazine*, June 7, 1998.

Konigsberg, Eric. "Making Book." *New York*, February 10, 1997.

Korda, Michael. *Another Life*. New York: Random House, 1999.

———. "The King of the Deal." *New Yorker*, March 29, 1993.

———. "Wasn't She Great?" *New Yorker*, August 14, 1995.

Koteliansky, S. S., and Philip Tomlinson, eds. and trans. *The Life and Letters of Anton Tchekhov*. New York: George H. Doran, n.d. (circa 1923).

Lamott, Anne. *Bird by Bird: Some Instructions on Writing and Life*. New York: Pantheon Books, 1994.

Lillelund, Niels. "Literature Lives: Interview with Gary Fisketjon." *Danish Literary Magazine*, Autumn 1998.

McCullough, David. "Interview." In *The Writing Life: National Book Award Authors*. New York: Random House, 1995.

McEvoy, Dermot, and Michael Coffey. "Bestselling Books 2009 Hardcover Old and New." *Publishers Weekly*, March 23, 2009.

MacFarquhar, Larissa. "The Cult of Joyce Maynard." *New York Times Magazine*, September 6, 1998.

Mailer, Norman. *Advertisements for Myself*. New York: G. P. Putnam's Sons, 1959.

Malcolm, Janet. *The Journalist and the Murderer*. New York: Alfred A. Knopf, 1990.

Mandell, Judy. *Book Editors Talk to Writers*. New York: John Wiley & Sons, 1995.

Manus, Elizabeth. "Dale Peck: Now It's Time to Say Goodbye to Farrar." *New York Observer*, July 13, 1998.

Maryles, Daisy. "The Stakes Rise for Chart Toppers." *Publishers Weekly*, March 22, 2004.

Max, D. T. "The Carver Chronicles." *New York Times Magazine*, August 9, 1998.

———. "The Unfinished." *New Yorker*, March 9, 2009.

Maynard, Joyce. *At Home in the World*. New York: Picador, 1998.

Middlebrook, Diane Wood. *Anne Sexton: A Biography*. Boston: Houghton Mifflin, 1991.

Miller, Alice. *Banished Knowledge: Facing Childhood Injuries*, trans. Leila Vennewitz. New York: Nan A. Talese/Doubleday, 1990.

———. *Prisoners of Childhood*, trans. Ruth Ward. New York: Basic Books, 1981.

Moore, Lorrie. *Self-Help*. New York: Alfred A. Knopf, 1985.

Nabokov, Vladimir. *Strong Opinions*. New York: McGraw-Hill, 1973.

Naylor, Gloria. "The Love of Books." In *The Writing Life: National Book Award Authors*. New York: Random House, 1995.

Neruda, Pablo. *Twenty Love Poems and a Song of Despair*, trans. W. S. Merwin. New York: Penguin, 1969.

Neubauer, Alexander. *Conversations on Writing Fiction.* New York: HarperCollins, 1994.

Orwell, George. *A Collection of Essays.* San Diego: Harcourt Brace, 1981.

Parker, Dorothy. *The Portable Dorothy Parker.* New York: Viking 1944. Reprint, Penguin, 1976.

Patchett, Ann. *Truth and Beauty.* New York: HarperCollins. 2004.

Paumgarten, Nick. "The Baby Binkys." *New York Observer,* April 22, 1996.

Percy, Walker. *The Moviegoer.* New York: Alfred A. Knopf, 1961.

Phillips, Larry W., ed. *Ernest Hemingway on Writing.* New York: Charles Scribner's Sons, 1984.

Plath, Sylvia. *The Collected Poems,* ed. Ted Hughes. New York: Harper & Row, 1960.

Plimpton, George. *Truman Capote.* New York: Nan A. Talese/Doubleday, 1997.

———, ed. *Writers at Work: The Paris Review Interviews,* 2nd series. New York: Viking Press, 1963.

———, ed. *Writers at Work: The Paris Review Interviews,* 5th series. New York: Viking Press, 1981.

Poynter, Dan. "Book Industry Statistics." BookStatistics.com (accessed October 10, 2009).

Proulx, E. Annie. "The Book Tour." In *The Writing Life: National Book Award Authors.* New York: Random House, 1995.

Radosh, Daniel. "A Book In You." *New Yorker,* May 31, 2004.

Reginato, James. "Nobel House." *New Yorker,* November 9, 1987.

Rhodes, Richard. *How to Write.* New York: William Morrow, 1995.

Rilke, Rainer Maria. *Letters on Cézanne,* trans. Joel Agee. New York: Fromm International, 1985.

———. *Letters to a Young Poet,* trans. M. D. Herter Norton. New York: W. W. Norton, 1934.

Roorbach, Bill. "Ping-Pong: The Secret to Getting Published, Long Withheld, Is Revealed." *Poets & Writers,* September/October 1998.

Roskill, Mark, ed. *The Letters of Vincent van Gogh.* New York: Atheneum, 1986.

Roth, Philip. *The Facts: A Novelist's Autobiography.* New York: Farrar, Straus & Giroux, 1988.

———. *Goodbye, Columbus.* Boston: Houghton Mifflin, 1959.

Ruas, Charles. *Conversations with American Writers.* New York: McGraw-Hill, 1984.

Rush, Norman. "Healthy Subversions." In *The Writing Life: National Book Award Authors.* New York: Random House, 1995.

Safire, William, and Leonard Safir. *Good Advice on Writing.* New York: Simon & Schuster, 1992.

Salkin, Allen. "Why Blog? Reason No. 92: Book Deal." *New York Times,* March 30, 2008.

Schiff, Stephen. "Big Poetry." *New Yorker,* July 14, 1997.

Scribner, Charles, Jr. *In the Company of Writers.* New York: Charles Scribner's Sons, 1990.

Sewall, Richard. *The Life of Emily Dickinson.* New York: Farrar, Straus & Giroux, 1974.

Sexton, Anne. *The Complete Poems.* Boston: Houghton Mifflin, 1981.

Sexton, Linda Gray. *Searching for Mercy Street: My Journey Back to My Mother, Anne Sexton.* Boston: Little, Brown, 1994.

Sexton, Linda Gray, and Lois Ames. *Anne Sexton: A Self-Portrait in Letters.* Boston: Houghton Mifflin, 1977.

Shengold, Leonard. *Soul Murder: The Effects of Childhood Abuse and Deprivation.* New Haven: Yale University Press, 1989.

Shnayerson, Michael. "How Wily Is Andrew Wylie?" *Vanity Fair,* January 1988.

Smith, Dinitia. "A Book Award Dark Horse." *New York Times,* November 24, 1998.

Solotaroff, Ted. "Writing in the Cold." In *A Few Good Voices in My Head: Occasional Pieces on Writing, Editing, and Reading My Contemporaries.* New York: Harper & Row, 1987.

Stevens, Wallace. *The Necessary Angel.* New York: Vintage Books, 1942.

Streitfeld, David. "Betrayal Between the Covers." *Washington Post,* October 27, 1998.

Strunk, William, Jr., and E. B. White. *The Elements of Style,* 2nd ed. New York: Macmillan, 1972.

Styron, William. *Darkness Visible: A Memoir of Madness.* New York: Random House, 1990.

Theroux, Paul. "Memory and Invention." *New York Times Book Review,* November 1,1998.

———. *Sir Vidia's Shadow: A Friendship Across Five Continents.* Boston: Houghton Mifflin, 1998.

Trollope, Anthony. *An Autobiography.* Edinburgh: William Blackwood and Sons, 1883. Reprint, Berkeley: University of California Press, 1978.

Turnbull, Andrew, ed. *The Letters of F. Scott Fitzgerald*. New York: Charles Scribner's Sons, 1963.

Twain, Mark. *On Writing and Publishing*. New York: Book-of-the-Month Club, 1994.

Updike, John. "At War with My Skin." *New Yorker*, September 2, 1985.

——. "Interview." *The Writing Life: National Book Award Authors*. New York: Random House, 1995.

——. *Of Prizes and Print*. New York: Alfred A. Knopf, 1998.

——. "On One's Own Oeuvre." In *Hugging the Shore*. New York: Alfred A. Knopf, 1983.

——. *Picked-Up Pieces*. New York: Alfred A. Knopf, 1966.

——. *Self-Consciousness*. New York: Alfred A. Knopf, 1989.

Waldron, Ann. *Eudora: A Writer's Life*. New York: Doubleday, 1998.

Weber, Bruce. "David Foster Wallace, Influential Writer, Dies at 46." *New York Times*, September 14, 2008.

——. "Sam Cohn, Powerful Talent Broker, Dies at 79." *New York Times*, May 6, 2009.

Weinraub, Bernard. "Separating Fact, Fiction and Film." *New York Times*, January 2, 1998.

Welty, Eudora. *The Eye of the Story: Selected Essays and Reviews*. New York: Random House, 1978.

——. *One Writer's Beginnings*. Cambridge, MA: Harvard University Press, 1984.

Wernecke, Ellen. "Why Buy the Cow? 27 Popular Websites That Became Books." The A.V. Club, September 7, 2009, www.avclub.com/articles/why-buy-the-cow-27-popular-websites-that-became-bo,2535.

Wharton, Edith. *A Backward Glance*. New York: Curtis Publishing, 1933. Reprint, Touchstone, 1998.

Whitman, Walt. *Complete Poetry and Collected Prose*. New York: Library of America, 1982.

Woodhouse, Barbara. *No Bad Dogs*. New York: Fireside, 1978.

Woolf, Virginia. *A Room of One's Own*. New York: Harcourt Brace, 1929.

ABOUT THE AUTHOR

Betsy Lerner received an MFA from Columbia University. She was a coeditor of Columbia's literary magazine and a cofounder of the now defunct underground magazine *Big Wednesday*. She has won a Thomas Wolfe Poetry Prize and an Academy of American Poets Poetry Prize and was named by American PEN as one of three emerging writers in 1987. She has also received a Simon & Schuster Fellowship and the Tony Godwin Fellowship for Editors. She worked in the editorial departments at four New York trade publishers, finally as executive editor at Doubleday, before becoming an agent. She is a partner in the Dunow, Carlson, and Lerner Literary Agency in New York City. She is also the author of a memoir, *Food and Loathing*, and blogs regularly about writing and publishing on her website, www.betsylerner.com.